)RI"NTAI AN`)

OF ORIENTAL AND AFRI(

University of London

er than the last (
~d for late ret
· b

We extend our thanks to Louise Tait
for her patience and help.

A Major Crisis?

The Politics of Economic Policy in Britain
in the 1990s

WERNER BONEFELD
University of Edinburgh

ALICE BROWN
University of Edinburgh

PETER BURNHAM
University of Warwick

Dartmouth

Aldershot • Brookfield USA • Singapore • Sydney

Published by
Dartmouth Publishing Company Limited
Gower House
Croft Road
Aldershot
Hants GU11 3HR
England

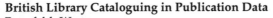

Dartmouth Publishing Company
Old Post Road
Brookfield
Vermont 05036
USA

British Library Cataloguing in Publication Data
Bonefeld, Werner
  Major Crisis?:Politics of Economic Policy in Britian
  in the 1990s
  I. Title
  330.9410859

Library of Congress Cataloging-in-Publication Data
Bonefeld, Werner, 1960-
    A Major crisis? : the politics of economic policy in Britain in
  the 1990s / Werner Bonefeld, Alice Brown, Peter Burnham.
      p.   cm.
    Includes bibliographical references and index.
    ISBN 1-85521-544-6. – ISBN 1-85521-550-0 (pbk.)
    1. Great Britian–Economic policy–1945- 2. Major, John Roy,
  1943-   . I. Brown, Alice, 1946-   . II. Burnham, Peter, 1959-   .
  III. Title.
  HC256.6.B6   1995
  338.941'09'049–dc20   95-19398
                                                               CIP

ISBN 1 85521 544 6 (hbk)
ISBN 1 85521 550 0 (pbk)

Printed in Great Britain at the University Press, Cambridge

Contents

1 A Major Crisis: The Politics of Economic Policy in Britain in the 1990s

Introduction

This book assesses the politics of economic policy under the Major governments between 1990-1994. In contrast to the plethora of publications analysing the Thatcher governments and the so-called phenomenon of Thatcherism, very little attention has been given to the administrations of John Major, and this despite the fact that he is one of the longest serving premiers in Britain this century. It is not our main purpose to explore the politics of economic policy in terms of the well-worn theme of 'continuity or change' by directly comparing the administrations of Margaret Thatcher and John Major. Rather our purpose is to analyse economic policy in the 1990s by focusing on the position of Britain in the global political economy.

This approach distinguishes our treatment from the few existing attempts to understand the Major governments. Most existing studies assess the Major governments against the background of the Thatcher governments (Kavanagh and Seldon, 1994; Savage et al., 1994; Hall, 1993). Although it is clearly impossible and would be unwarranted, to treat the Major governments in isolation from the Thatcher legacy, a focus simply on this legacy yields very limited results. This is because concentration on the issue of continuity versus discontinuity tends to lead to the not too surprising conclusion that forces for continuity are powerful.

Our aim is to locate the Major governments in the context of the relationship between the international political economy and the national state. We conceptualise this relationship in chapter 2 and provide an analysis of its development over the last three decades in chapter 3. Firstly, we will show that the national state has only limited control over economic relations and that these relations are best analysed at the global level. Economic relations exist in a global form and are processed through national states. In other words, the 'domestic economy' represents the national form of global relations and the national state represents the political processing of these relations within the confines of a territorially defined legal and monetary framework.

The view that the national state is a node within the global economy highlights the circumstance that national governments are subject to constraints and forces outside their political control. These constraints constitute, at the same time, the condition through which the national state exists. This does not mean that governments' role and function is only of minor significance or that it can be dismissed easily. Global economic relations have not led to the transcendence of the national state. Whilst exploitation conditions are standardised nationally, individual states, via the exchange rate mechanism, are interlocked internationally into a hierarchy of price systems. The implication of this is two-fold. Firstly, the national state provides the domestic political underpinning for the stability of global capitalist relations. Secondly, in order to maintain their position in the global hierarchy of prices, national states are under constant pressure to make more efficient use of available resources, particularly labour power. The position of a national state's integration into the world market depends, therefore, upon competitive unit labour costs, that is, productivity growth. Failure to achieve this will result in a loss of reserves, precipitated by balance of payments difficulties, and inflationary pressure, provoking global exchange instability and financial crisis.

Our second focus thus concerns working class resistance to the improvement of labour productivity. To put the same point more broadly, the national state's management, through law,

2

money and force, of exploitative conditions is not only constrained financially through the balance of payments, exchange rate fluctuations and inflationary pressure but also, and importantly, by working class resistance to improved productivity performance. The attempt to secure a favourable position in the global economy depends on the creation of conditions conducive to higher labour productivity. These conditions involve not just low wage costs but also the efficient use of resources. The achievement of a low wage economy is, by itself, not necessarily a competitive advantage. A low wage economy does not automatically mean a high productivity economy. On the contrary, as the example of Britain in the 1970s shows, comparatively low wages and comparatively low productivity might well coincide. In order to increase productivity, labour has to be intensified and available resources have to be used efficiently. The improvement of exploitative conditions means that the working class has to be confronted in the production process, its resistance to the reduction of unit labour costs overcome and its consumer power contained.

The third focus of our book is on the interrelation between economic crisis and political crisis. It is tempting, for instance, to see the issue of inflation as simply a technical economic matter. However, it is important to be aware, as Goldthorpe argues, that it is ultimately a political problem. Like other policies, a monetarist anti-inflationary stance carries implications for the structure of class relations. In particular, prioritising anti-inflationary policies amounts to an 'underwriting of market forces as the key determinant of inequality' (Goldthorpe, 1978, p. 209). Anti-inflationary policies carry the threat of heightening the social conflict which stems from the unmediated character of market criteria. In this way such policies are likely to increase class conflict and ultimately risk the serious danger that a crisis in the sphere of distribution will become a crisis of political authority itself. To prevent the realisation of this scenario, governments are well served by an 'automatic pilot' which takes responsibility for imposing financial discipline on the working class. As Clarke (1990, p. 27) argues, the driving force behind the state's attempt to restructure social relations is not so much the attempt to provide a resolution of 'economic crisis', as the attempt to resolve the 'political crisis' of the state by trying to disengage the state politically from the economy so as to depoliticise economic policy formation.

Our guiding thesis is that economic policy making is concerned with the creation of conditions which are conducive to the achievement of both domestic political stability and a more favourable integration into the world market. Depoliticisation enhances the ability of governments to deliver on both fronts. We address these topics in theoretical and practical terms.

Chapter outline

The next chapter conceptualises our understanding of the interrelationship between the national state and the global economy. Our argument develops through a critique of other approaches, particularly realist 'domestic polity' approaches and interdependency theory. Attention is paid to the politics of economic policy assessing the issue of depoliticisation and the part played by government in resolving economic crisis. Chapter 3 charts the global development of monetary accumulation and productive accumulation from the early 1970s until the early 1990s. Particular attention focuses on the liberation of credit creation from the regime of fixed exchange rates associated with the Bretton Woods system. The impact of this liberation on national states is shown and assessed in terms of a crisis of both Keynesianism and monetarism. Chapter 4 analyses the political economy of the recession 1990-94 focusing on the Major government's economic policy. We look especially at the politics of the European Exchange Rate Mechanism (ERM) and the significance of the pound's forced exit from the ERM in 1992. The Major governments' attempt to lower unit labour costs is analysed and the politics of fiscal tightness assessed. Chapter 5 charts the Major governments' record in a number of policy areas which are examined in three substantive subsections. We look at the Major governments' labour market policies, emphasising in particular the effect of labour legislation and debates on education and training. Furthermore, we examine the development of the welfare state under Major and the relationship between central and local government. Chapter 6 supplies a conclusion. We place the Major governments in the context of British governments since 1945. We argue that all postwar governments have faced similar problems to those encountered by Major and that each government has struggled with the problems presented by global finance, the working class and Britain's position in the world market. In the final section of our conclusion we look in broad terms at the issues raised in the previous section and argue that economic policy formation is dependent on the development of the global political economy rather than party-political preferences. The Labour Party's economic policy proposals are briefly examined and we conclude that party competition is, to a great extent, a ritual conflict, disguising fundamental agreement over economic policy.

2 National States and the Global Economy: The Politics of Economic Policy

The plain fact is that the economic cycle is endemic - which means, incidentally, that all the current talk of no return to "boom and bust" is somewhat premature to say the least. As experience throughout the world makes clear, abolition of the economic cycle is simply not within the power of any government to deliver.

Nigel Lawson, lecture organised by the Social Market Foundation and the London School of Economics (20th June 1994)

In the best traditions of adversary politics both parties blamed the performance of the economy on the world recession when they were in government and on the government when they were in opposition.

Andrew Gamble and Stuart Walkland, *The British Party System and Economic Policy 1945-1983* (1984, p. 21)

The language of globalisation increasingly dominates the

discourse of politicians across Europe. The quote from Nigel Lawson's lecture illustrates the implications which the global economy has for national states and their governments. The globalisation of culture (Americanisation), food (McDonaldisation), working practices (Japanisation), war (armchair generals with smart weaponry), and of course, the global information superhighway are now seen to complement the more familiar economic and environmental claims that we live in a multicultural, multinational, borderless world. Most politicians are of course adept at using the latest populist slogans to bolster their own national image and deflect criticism of their policies. In Britain, after a decade in which the Conservatives claimed credit for single-handedly delivering economic success, John Major cast around for a new explanation of recession and found it in globalisation. As with most successful ideologies that contain a rational kernel (but which nevertheless represent sectional interests as universal) the language of globalisation does reflect significant changes which have occurred in the global political economy since the 1970s. However, these changes are by no means as socially transformative or as geographically even as most techno-enthusiasts and economic liberals would have us believe.

The attempt to chart the changing contours of the global political economy, and in particular the changes in state-form which accompany globalism, is of fundamental importance in the study of contemporary politics. Although this type of analysis has long been the focus of the sub-discipline of international political economy (IPE), there are relatively few studies of 'British politics' which recognise the importance of conceptualising the global system.[1] The fundamental analytical premise of this book is that traditional political science approaches to economic policy which treat as unproblematic the category of the 'nation state' are no longer adequate in explaining the development of contemporary capitalism. Whilst the dominant orthodox IPE approach, that of the 'interdependence school,' represents a distinct advance over national accounts of crisis, this chapter will indicate why we consider that it is limited in its conceptualisation of global capitalism. The alternative approach developed in this chapter draws directly upon Marx and upon some of the traditions of 'Open Marxism' (Bonefeld et al., 1992; 1995) to conceive of bourgeois social relations as global class relations. These global relations are nationally processed, hence the necessity for

7

detailed empirical study of individual governments. However, our premise is that each state exists only as a political node in the global flow of capital. The world market constitutes the global mode of existence of the contradictions of the social reproduction of capital. Hence, 'each national economy can only be conceptualised adequately as a specific international and, at the same time, integral part of the world market. The nation state can only be seen in this dimension' (von Braunmühl, 1976, p. 276; and 1978). As a precursor to introducing our distinctive approach we will assess both 'nation state' and 'interdependency' approaches to the problem of economic policy making in a globalised economy. Although these approaches differ in emphasis they both owe a significant debt to Max Weber's view of the relationship between economics and politics and therefore to his conceptualisation of economic policy. It is appropriate, therefore, that we should begin this chapter by outlining how our view of economic policy differs from dominant Weberian inspired approaches.

Economics, politics and economic policy

Orthodox political science has been slow to acknowledge its debt to Max Weber. However, almost all contemporary non-Marxian methodologies build upon Weber's view of the relationship between the economy, the polity and society. In this sense, however much they later diverge, liberal pluralist writers and 'statist' theorists, including structuralist neorealists such as Waltz (1979), share a common methodology built on the supposed analytic autonomy of the political realm. This methodological premise, which has crucial implications for the study of economic policy, has its modern day roots in Weber and Morgenthau but stretches back to the nineteenth century marginalist revolution in economics(2)

The basis of Weber's approach to social science is his typology of social action, built to complement the marginalist conception of the economy. The forerunners of the marginalist revolution, William Jevons, Carl Menger and Leon Walras, displaced the binding explanatory principles of classical political economy (class, capital, and the labour theory of value) with abstract assumptions of individual rationality grounded in a subjective preference theory based on the concept of utility. Economics could henceforth be restricted to an analysis of individual rational choice occurring in a spontaneously given 'market', which established prices exogenously by supply and demand responding to conditions of consumer taste and resource scarcity. Politics, history, and sociology were now deemed irrelevant. As Perlman (1973) perceptively notes, the 'replacement' of political economy by positive economics, actually constituted an omission of a field of knowledge - a headlong dash from reality - in effect a 'great evasion'. Space was now created for the fragmentation of social science into 'disciplines' each established in relation to a specific irreducible type of action. This task fell to Max Weber. Weber's schema classifies actions not only with regard to their value orientations but also according to the types of means and ends to which they are directed. Variables which comprise a social order, such as the economy, the polity, and civil society, are given no overall structure in Weber's assessment, but rather each is presumed to have a real autonomy which enables any 'factor' to act as a 'determinant'. The autonomy of the economy from the polity and civil society, finds expression in Weber's statement that political action is directed to the achievement of political power for its own sake. Political actions, therefore, although they may have economic implications, are deemed to be not directly oriented to economic gain and as such they must be analysed independently of economic factors since their orientation is to a distinctive form of action.

Postwar political realism, which provides the foundations for most modern 'nation state' approaches, fully accepts that politics is to be studied as an autonomous domain. Morgenthau (1978) provides the clearest example. Political actions, he argues, are to be judged according to political criteria. The economist, the lawyer, and the realist ask different questions, with the prerogative of the latter being the power politics of the nation. The dominant perspective in international relations, that of neorealism, also reproduces this fragmented, ahistorical methodology. Kenneth Waltz (1979), for example, constructs his theory self-consciously on the model of neoclassical microeconomics (although he claims a link with Adam Smith, his interpretation of the latter is decidedly neoclassical). The market, he argues, is 'individualist in origin, spontaneously generated, and unintended' (Waltz, 1979, p. 91). In the manner of standard textbook positive economics, Waltz maintains that 'the market' created by self-directed interacting economic units, selects and rewards behaviours according to their consequences.

In so doing, 'microeconomic theory explains how an economy operates and why certain effects are to be expected' (ibid., p. 90). This methodology is directly transposed to the political level (to a study of political action), to provide Waltz's theory of international politics.[3]

This conception of the relationship between politics and economics is often championed by neo-Weberians as offering a methodology which has no pre-conceived image of society or its patternings and is thus seen as replacing theoreticism and determinism with pure empirical assessment. However, the true consequence of Weber's position is that an analysis concerned simply with the construction of a typology of motivational characteristics is only able to study the given institutions and organisations of society resting on the abstraction of the individual from the historical social relations within which he/she exists in a contradictory manner. Such a move severely restricts social science to a form of pluralist empiricism which lacks explanatory power since the mere elaboration of a typology of hypothetical social action can explain neither the systematic connections between values, social relations, and institutions nor ironically provide an adequate interpretation of the historical specificity of the development of the global capitalist economy. In relation to economic policy, the Weberian view accepts a clear cut distinction between disciplines however much it may argue for the centrality of economics in the political process and vice versa. In a recent review of the politics of economic policy, Grant (1993, p. 2) provides a classic example of the Weberian position arguing that, 'economic policy has distinctive characteristics which can be identified and analysed by political scientists to complement the insights provided by economists ... it is not suggested that the reasoning of political science should displace that of economics'.

Our approach rejects the fragmentation of social science into separate disciplines and builds on Marx's critique of classical political economy. One of the shortcomings of classical political economy is that it simply brings outward appearances into an external relationship with one another, 'the crudity and lack of comprehension lies precisely in that organically coherent factors are brought into a haphazard relation with one another, i.e. into a purely speculative connection' (Marx, 1986, p. 26). This necessarily fails to grasp the inner connection of social relations and precludes an understanding of their totality. The point here is that non-dialectical research begins with an isolated unit and attempts to reconstruct the whole by establishing 'external' connections. Dialectical research, on the other hand, starts with the whole and then searches for the 'substantive abstraction' which constitutes social phenomena as interconnected, complex forms different from, but united in, each other (Bonefeld, 1993, p. 21; Ollman, 1993, pp. 12-17). Notions of externality and structure are replaced by the dialectical categories of process and contradictory internal relationship. Whilst non-dialectical methodologies segment the social world and analyse the contingent relations of external phenomena, Marx focuses on how social relations take different forms, such as the economic and the political, creating a differentiated, contradictory unity. This conceptualisation understands the apparently isolated features of life as comprising a mode of existence of social relations. Hence diverse phenomena such as the state and the economy do not exist as externally related entities but as moments of the class relation from which they are constituted. As Simon Clarke (1978, p. 42) clarifies, it is the concept of the class relation as being prior to the political, economic and ideological forms taken by those relations (even though class relations have no existence independently of those forms) that makes it possible for a Marxist analysis to conceptualise the complexity of the relation between the economic and the political, and their interconnections as complementary forms of the fundamental class relation, without abandoning the theory for a pragmatic pluralism. In other words, we view the 'economic' and the 'political' as different forms - constituted by the social relations of capitalist production. This enables us to develop a distinctive view of economic policy.

Unlike many Weberian inspired accounts which see state intervention as arising from 'market failure', we see state management of labour power and state management of money as inseparable from capitalist production and circulation in general. Although the state has, of course, a direct presence in numerous areas of social life we view the state's management of the particular commodity labour power (inseparable from a regular supply of cheap labour) and the state's management of money (which is linked to the accumulation of money capital) as the principle axes of state 'intervention' (de Brunhoff, 1978). Economic policy both modifies and encompasses the state's management of labour power and money, but these two key areas of state economic action are of determining importance when, in capitalism, the working class becomes an active subject in the circuit of flows representing the formation and allocation of monetary revenues.

The following study therefore focuses on three central aspects of economic policy under Major. Firstly, the state's management of labour power. The institutions concerned with this management vary enormously in space and time from systems of poor relief to welfare and social insurance (see ibid., p. 19). Accordingly, these systems are a permanent site of class conflict. Reforms in the area of social policy, industrial relations legislation, law and order, and labour market policy all fall within this category. They represent the political attempt to achieve work discipline through insecurity of employment and the inducement of work incentives. As we will show the Major government pursued these policies in an attempt to increase labour productivity.

Secondly, we focus on the state's management of money. As de Brunhoff again makes clear, 'any social formation in which a general equivalent exists has certain institutions and social characteristics adapted to this purpose' (ibid., p. 39). The creation of a monetary system depends on state regulation of the national currency with reference to an agreed international monetary standard. The development of a national monetary space - the site on which different levels are articulated in relation to one another (private bank money, central bank money and international money) - is therefore inseparable from the formation of national capitalist markets within the international money market (see ibid., p. 54). The state's management of money in these conditions becomes monetary policy. Moreover since the banking system is the strategic sector of the credit system, a centralised banking system regulated by the state assumes importance as the site 'upon which the formation and regulation of credit is located, it [therefore] lies at the junction of the relationships between capitalists and wage earners and between capitalists themselves' (ibid., p. 56). The capitalist state is thus directly integrated into monetary and financial flows and indeed the social presence of the state can be accounted for through the budget and it's share of the national currency (see ibid., p. 103). As we indicate below, as a temporary solution to the deepening fiscal crisis of the state Major pinned his hopes on depoliticising the state's management of money by securing membership of the ERM. When this strategy collapsed Major shifted greater attention to the public management of labour power whilst rejigging the relationship between the institutions designated to manage monetary policy.

Finally, we develop a focus on inter-state relations, specifically looking at the British state's articulation with the European Union (EU). The attempt to centralise some aspects of economic policy making in the EU has significant implications for all signatories to the Maastricht Treaty. However the view that we are witnessing a simple transfer of authority from the national to the regional is based on flawed assumptions. Although the privatisation of state institutions, the 'internationalisation' of capital and the creation of the EU pose a problem for state 'intervention' formulated on the basis of Keynesian economic policy, these developments do not alter the indispensability of a state apparatus in the management of labour power and money. Changes in both economic policy and the form of the state are therefore envisaged but not the abolition of the national state itself. At present it seems likely that a more complex pattern will emerge whereby some national state capacities are transferred to pan-regional or international bodies, others devolved to local levels within the national state, and yet others are usurped by emerging horizontal networks (local and regional) which by-pass central states and connect localities and regions in several nations (Jessop, 1992; Rosewarne, 1993). The management of monetary relations looks set to follow a similar line as evidenced in the changing role of the International Monetary Fund (IMF).[4] To claim that current developments represent a decline in the independence of monetary policy is also naive since, 'posed in this way, the question assumes that national currencies were actually controlled by the states which managed them before the development of large multinational enterprises' (de Brunhoff, 1978, p. 139). To anyone familiar with the conduct of British economic policy since 1945 de Brunhoff's comments ring especially true: every nation is obliged to manage its own currency with reference to its value in international transactions - only the conditions and forms of this management have changed. The fundamental political preconditions of capitalist reproduction are never secured once and for all and to talk of state management of economic policy is not to imply that the state controls the economy: 'it is not necessary to confuse the ideology of economic policy with its actual practice as a capitalist strategy, even if the practice requires such an ideology' (ibid., p. 64). Having clarified our view of economic policy we are now in a position to review both 'nation state' and interdependence approaches to the study of politics in a globalised economy.

The problem with nation-state and interdependence approaches to contemporary political economy

Before analysing how most commentators have understood the crisis facing John Major, it is worth reflecting on one noticeable aspect of the theories developed within mainstream political science to explain 'Thatcherism' during the 1980s. Almost without exception, orthodox commentaries on Thatcherism failed to consider the global dimension of the crisis of Keynesianism, and later monetarism, experienced during the 1970s and 1980s. As Andrew Gamble has noted, 'Thatcherism' came to stand for the distinctive ideology, political style and programme of the British Conservative Party after Margaret Thatcher was elected leader in 1975' (Gamble, 1994, p. 1). Accounts focus on Thatcher as a personality and leader (Abse, 1989; Hall, 1988; Harris, 1988; Webster, 1990; Young, 1989); assessments of policies pursued by the Thatcher governments (Hirst, 1989; Holmes, 1985 and 1989; Kavanagh and Seldon, 1989; Marsh and Rhodes, 1992; Riddell, 1985 and 1989; Jessop et al., 1988; Savage and Robins, 1990); texts which assess the performance of the economy under Thatcher (Keegan, 1984 and 1989; Maynard, 1988; Michie (ed.), 1992; Thompson, 1986; Smith, 1993); others which place Thatcher in the context of postwar British politics (Gamble, 1994; Kavanagh, 1990; Bulpitt, 1986; Letwin, 1992); and a few feminist analyses (Brunt, 1987; Campbell, 1991; Lovenduski and Randall, 1993; Ten Tuscher, 1986; Wilson, 1987). Outside of some Marxist literature (Clarke, 1988; Bonefeld, 1993), little attempt has been made to theorise the phenomenon known as Thatcherism as a response to global crisis. This is a defect characteristic of most studies in British political science.

Most of the literature on 'domestic politics' in British political science starts from the nation state as an unproblematic category. This is true also of many approaches which conceptualised the development of the British state during the 1980s in terms of 'Thatcherism'. The use of the term 'Thatcherism' implies that there was something special about the development of the British state and that there was and still is a 'British economic recession'. For example, Smith (1993) and Stewart (1993) argue that the recession of the 1990s was a 'home grown recession'. It is alleged that the Major government simply applied inappropriate policies. There are two principal difficulties with this approach. Firstly, there is an assumption that a national government can 'get it right' and that it has certain means at its disposal which, if used properly, can avoid recession and steer the 'national economy' on to a path of growth and full employment. There is thus an implicit assumption that the crisis of Keynesian policies in the 1960s and 1970s was not really a crisis of Keynesianism per se but a result of government failure to use Keynesian instruments properly. The same argument can be heard from proponents of monetarist policies. For them, the crisis of the 1990s is the result of an imperfect implementation of monetarist theory. The defence of Keynesian and monetarist theory is thus based on the assumption that past governments have failed to apply theoretical knowledge in an adequate way. This position can be criticised on a number of counts. Firstly, it assumes that there is close correlation between economic theory and economic practice. As we will argue below the fit between economic theory and economic policy making is always more rhetorical than real (Tomlinson, 1981; Bulpitt, 1986). Secondly, it imputes a degree of rationality to the state which is far from uncontentious. Finally, and perhaps most importantly, it carries the assumption that a capitalist state can directly control 'its economy'. This not only glosses over the burgeoning literature which indicates that globalisation in its many forms has restricted the menu of foreign and domestic policies from which state authorities can choose (McGrew, 1992, p. 321), but it also gives methodological primacy to the state as the principal and autonomous actor in the global system. However, even if one were to put aside these criticisms and accept this view, it would still be difficult to understand why Keynesian policies in the 1970s and monetarist policies in the 1980s failed on a global scale. This leads to the second difficulty with the domestic politics 'nation state' approach.

All western capitalist countries experienced a recession in the late 1980s and early 1990s. Were one to assume that the British recession is 'home grown,' it would follow that the recessions in Germany, France, Japan, the US, etc., are equally domestic affairs. We would thus be confronted with a number of 'home grown' recessions which just happened to coincide in the late

1980s. Although it is possible, and indeed necessary, to emphasise the specific character of each of these 'recessions', a comparison of the peculiar character of, for example, the 'home grown' recession in Germany and the 'home grown' recession in Britain, would not really help us to understand the causes of the recessions and why they appeared at almost the same time. Furthermore, even were one to accept that recessions are 'home grown' the response to a recession in one country would have an effect on the recession in another. For example, in the early 1990s, the German Bundesbank responded to the increase in the money supply by raising interest rates. This response had an immediate effect on economic policy making in Britain as interest rates were raised in order to maintain an adequate inflow of international finance to Britain and to defend the pound against speculative pressure. In other words, the supposedly 'home grown' character of the recession was, even on the most minimalist reading, dependent upon the recession in other countries.

It is at this point that the dichotomies of traditional political science, especially that of domestic versus foreign policy, inhibit our understanding and where the insights of the subdiscipline of international political economy come into their own. By far the most common framework of analysis adopted by liberal institutionalists and neorealists alike is that which goes under the broad heading of the 'interdependence' approach developed in particular by Keohane and Nye (1977).

The notion of interdependence should not be confused with simple interconnectedness. As formulated by Keohane and Nye, interdependence means mutual dependence (1977, p. 8). Thus an increase in 'dynamic density' that is, international transactions and flows which do not have significant costly effects (primarily for states), simply reflects interconnectedness. However, relationships characterised by reciprocal effects of costs and benefits between countries, and actors in different countries, constitute interdependent relationships. Furthermore it is possible to distinguish between sensitivity and vulnerability interdependence. Sensitivity refers to degrees of responsiveness within a policy framework, 'how quickly do changes in one country bring costly changes in another, and how great are the costly effects?' (ibid., p. 12). Vulnerability, by contrast, refers to the relative availability and costliness of the alternatives that various actors face. Thus, 'sensitivity means liability to costly effects imposed from outside before policies are altered to try to change the situation. Vulnerability can be defined by an actor's liability to suffer costs imposed by external events even after policies have been altered' (ibid., p. 13).

In their attempt to portray the contemporary global political system, Keohane and Nye conclude by constructing an ideal type which they term, complex interdependence. There are three main facets of complex interdependence. Firstly, they argue that multiple channels now connect societies, principally through interstate, transgovernmental and transnational relations. Secondly, the agenda of interstate relationships is no longer dominated by issues of military security, in particular the distinction between domestic and foreign issues has now become blurred. Finally, they note that military force is no longer used by governments towards other governments within a region where complex interdependence prevails. This last point has recently been refashioned as the 'absence of war among liberal democracies thesis' which is said to vindicate Kant's writings on international relations and constitutes liberalism's most compelling empirical claim (Krasner, 1994, p. 17).

Each empirical claim made by the interdependence school has been the subject of controversy (Waltz, 1979; Garrett and Lange, 1991). Nevertheless, methodologically the term interdependence is helpful in so far as it indicates that governments are not totally in control of their economies and that economic policy making by one government depends very much on the economic policies pursued by other states (and of course in the interdependence tradition, by other non-state actors). Thus, the notion of interdependence casts doubt on the view that recessions can be adequately theorised as 'home grown' phenomena and that governments possess the capacity to steer 'their economy' independently. However, the concept of interdependence is itself problematic. Whilst Keohane and Nye attempt to break free from the flawed assumptions of classical realism, they nevertheless remain tied to its methodology claiming that 'in international political systems the most important units are states ... and their power resources' (Keohane and Nye, 1977, p. 20). No attempt is made to conceptualise the state or the limits of state action. We therefore return to the fetishised image of the all-powerful state constrained only by other state (and non-state) actors understood as impinging on economic policy making from outside. In other words, for interdependence writers, each state experiences the other as an *external* constraint on its own policy making. Thus, the notion of interdependence leads to a very complicated and complex system in so far as each national state faces a multitude of external constraints because there are so many different national states, each constraining the other. Moreover, although Keohane and Nye emphasise the importance of non-state actors, it is far from clear how such actors articulate with states and how we should judge their relative importance. States are envisaged as separate yet dependent, and their dependency derives solely from their 'external' relations. In a theoretical sense taken to its logical conclusion the interdependence school reestablishes the distinction between domestic and external affairs.

Against this background, the notion of 'externality' becomes problematic. This is because international relations among states cannot be seen simply in terms of 'each' against the others. Such of view is essentially state-based and treats international relations in terms of inter-state relations. At base the question of the international political economy is not adequately conceptualised. The limits of national sovereignty do not arise because one state is constrained by the actions of other states. Rather, the limits arise because the 'national economy' is fundamentally an international economy: capital transcends national boundaries and local markets only exist as nodes within the global movement of capital. Thus, as Picciotto (1991a, p. 47) indicates, the national state was 'born within an international framework. Although it was primarily national socio-economic forces that defined its socio-geographic boundaries, its form and functions developed internationally'. In other words, individual states exist not only in competition with each other, as each tries to divert the flow of capital to its particular territory; they also exist as particular nodes of the regulation in the global flow of capital, so that the failure of one state may create problems for the global circuit of capital and thus for all other states.

By challenging, however incompletely, the dominance of the traditional realist approach to international relations (and the 'nation state' approach to domestic politics), the interdependence school opened the door for more recent fruitful work in the IPE tradition. Whilst most 'nation state' approaches berate the failure of politicians, recent IPE theorists, particularly those focusing on the 'financialisation' of capital, tend to emphasise two rather different points.[5] First, such approaches stress the watershed character of the breakdown of the Bretton Woods system. Following the move towards an open, liberal financial order the policy 'autonomy' of the state is said to have been compromised in a number of ways. Independent macroeconomic policy is adjudged to have been rendered very difficult by the move to a flexible exchange rate system combined with the erosion of capital controls. Large movements of funds and capital flight act in a disciplinary manner on all governments, especially those wishing to pursue a truncated form of social democracy (Helleiner, 1993; 1994). Independent tax policy is also seen as a casualty, whilst the rapidly escalating volume of speculative international financial movements sends shudders through the international trading system. The second feature of the current global political economy emphasised by the new generation of IPE writers, and by far the most significant, is the transnationalisation of finance - the global integration of financial markets to which, a number of theorists argue, nation states are now subordinated. A flavour of this approach is provided by Phil Cerny (1993) who argues, somewhat pessimistically, that as currency and securities are more and more traded internationally, as multinational firms seek increasingly to speculate and hedge their financial resources, as foreign direct investment continues to expand, and as banks diversify and compete on a global basis, then the cycle of deregulation will continue to widen. The result is that

> governments, international regimes and regulatory authorities within governments will increasingly come to be "whipsawed" between different sectors and firms in the financial services industry seeking the most amenable regulators and the most permissive rules - what is called "regulatory arbitrage" or "competition in laxity" (Cerny, 1993, p. 15).

The upshot for many in this IPE tradition is that states will become increasingly fragmented and constrained by the imperatives of global financial competition. Whilst it may be argued that this approach has overstated the significance of the breakdown of the Bretton Woods system and the novelty of the 'financialisation' of capital (Arrighi, 1994), it nonetheless brings into sharp focus the changing relationship between global capital and the national state which, as we shall show in chapter 3, is indispensable to understanding the crisis of Keynesian orthodoxy on a global scale.

Capital, class and the international state system

As indicated above in our discussion of economic policy, our approach derives from Marx and those currents of critical or 'open Marxism' developed most recently by contributors to debates on value and the state in the Conference of Socialist Economists (see for instance Clarke, 1991; Bonefeld et al., 1992 and 1995; Burnham, 1994). This debate rejects all forms of determinism, and emphasises instead the centrality of class struggle. Class is not perceived in sociological fashion as a static, descriptive term applied to groups of individuals sharing common experiences or life-chances or consumption patterns. Rather the existence of private property means we are born into a society where social relations exist as relations between things, such as profit and interest. However the personification of things, and conversely the objectification of the social individual, rests on the shifting sands of the contradictory labour/capital relationship. The 'profit principle' depends upon the productive imposition of work, that is, the efficient use of labour power in production. Struggle is therefore endemic as capital must attempt to yoke the working class daily in the production process. Class struggle is not therefore the spasmodic or intermittent outburst, not the class-conscious demonstration of political awareness but the daily resistance of the labouring class to the imposition of work - a permanent feature of human society above primitive levels (de Ste. Croix, 1983). If the world is understood in terms of class struggle then determinism of all kinds must vanish. Whilst class struggle is at the heart of capitalist production, it is unpredictable and outcomes are open. In essence this version of Marxism puts a premium on the power of labour thereby, unlike objectivist theories, pointing to the fragility of capitalism as a global system of class domination. As we shall indicate in our discussion of the political economy of the recession, the resistance of the working class to the restructuring and intensification of work placed a considerable constraint on the attempt to raise productivity and thereby shaped the trajectory of the Major government.

Our focus is on the changing nature of state-form as the mode of existence of class relations. As indicated above we see state management of labour power and money as inseparable from

20

capitalist production and exchange in general. If the form of state 'intervention' changes it is still necessary for one form or another to have some effect in these areas. Suzanne de Brunhoff (1978, p. 94) puts the point succinctly when she states that

> economic policy proceeds by an alternation between a loosening of market-based constraints ("pseudo-validation" of state currencies in irredeemable currency systems or of "de-monetised" labour-power) and a preservation of these constraints in a form mediated by state intervention (in terms of ratio-systems, percentage systems, financial or cash limits requiring authorisation if they are exceeded). This is the way it operates whatever the specific field of application (whether fiscal, monetary, wage-regulatory, etc.).

The privatisation of the public sector and the globalisation (and financialisation) of capital have been accompanied by changes in the form of the state, which have also, as we shall chart, given rise to changes in economic policy.

The notion that class relations is central is in direct contrast to the deterministic base/superstructure image of Marxism. In this 'hard structural determinist' reading, exemplified by one-dimensional Soviet Marxism-Leninism, the economic base determines the political superstructure thus rendering a serious analysis of politics redundant. Although Engels later tried to soften this view by introducing the notion of 'determinant in the last instance', this has done little to dissuade structuralist Marxists (and technological determinists) that the economy should be awarded primacy when studying social formations. The state in this model is seen as epiphenomenal, its existence reducible to the economic base and changes in state policy are understood as merely reflecting changing economic relations. The notion of 'relative autonomy' has done little to correct this 'reductionist' and 'monistic' emphasis on the economic side of historical development. Our reading realises that the metaphor is all but useless as theory and refutes the idea that Marx would have accepted its hard structuralist reading. Monocausal economism is thereby replaced with the dialectical notion that social relations of production only exist in the form of economic, legal and political relations. It is not simply that each of these relations exercise reciprocal and causative influence, but, much more fundamentally, that antagonistic class relations are always manifest in social, political and cultural forms. In

21

this way 'economics' rests as firmly on 'politics' and 'law' as vice versa. The error of the determinist school is that they understand 'economics' in a technicist, apolitical, marginalist sense and do not give sufficient attention to Marx's critique of political economy which emphasises the *social relations* of production.

Understanding capitalist development in terms of the movement of struggle (the attempt by capital to contain and harness the power of labour) rejects the notion of the unfolding of successive stages or of historical necessity, as unwarranted determinism. Class struggle is not to be added as another factor equally as important as the state, money or the market. Rather these latter categories themselves are seen as the form taken by class struggle in historically specific societies. They are the rigidified thing-like manifestation of definite relations of struggle between classes - the forms through which labour resists in-and-against capital. Holloway (1995, p. 119) perfectly articulates how open Marxism defetishises the notion of the state, 'to dissolve the state as a category means to understand the state not as a thing in itself, but as a social form, a form of social relations'. In short, to think scientifically is to criticise academic disciplines which take rigidified forms as their starting point. The objectivist reading of Marx couched in terms of forces and relations of production, impending cataclysmic crisis and growing class consciousness, is supplanted by a reading which sees the development of capitalism as essentially open, with no predetermined lines of direction.

Our first premise in exploring the relationship between national states and the global economy is that this relationship can only be understood on the basis of an account of the historical development of the rise of capitalist social relations. Although this may seem to be an unnecessary historical detour, we believe that without such an account it is impossible to grasp the specificity of the capital relation or the way in which the state is subsumed in a set of relations characterised by exploitation. Neither the concept of the state nor that of the market give up their secrets easily. They cannot be grasped adequately in terms of relatively or wholly 'autonomous spheres' or levels of an unspecified social structure. Rather the starting point is to pose the question: why do definite social relations between people assume in capitalism the fantastic form of relations between things? It is in this sense that we should see the perspicacity of Holloway and Picciotto's (1991, p. 112) statement that, a materialist theory of the state begins not by asking in what way the 'economic base' determines the 'political superstructure', but by asking what it is about the social relations of production under capitalism that leads to creation of *apparently separate economic and political forms.* Similarly in relation to the market our starting point is why do goods and services take the form of commodities? Why do the products of labour confront each other as commodities? In each phase of history, human life has rested on social production, 'whose relations are precisely what we call economic relations' (Marx, 1986, p. 413). However whilst all production is appropriation of nature by the individual within and by means of a definite form of society, and thereby property is a condition of production, it is 'ridiculous to make a leap from this to a definite form of property, private property' (ibid., p. 25). By briefly contrasting class domination in feudalism with that which exists today we can trace the inner connection between the apparently differentiated spheres of national states and the global economy.

The development of the capitalist form of the state

Our starting point is Marx's famous claim that 'the abstraction of the state as such belongs only to modern times. The abstraction of the political state is a modern product' (1975, p. 32). For Marx, the character of old civil (feudal) society was directly political. The elements of civil life - property, the family, the mode of labour - were raised to the elements of political life in the form of seigniory, estates and corporations. In this sense, an individual's position within an estate determined his/her political relation, that is, his/her separation and exclusion from other components of society. As he later clarified in *Capital* (1976, p. 170), 'here, instead of the independent man, we find everyone dependent - serfs and lords, vassals and suzerains, laymen and clerics. Personal dependence characterises the social relations of material production as much as it does the other spheres of life based on that production'. Hence, in the Middle Ages we find serfs, feudal estates, merchant and trade guilds, and corporations of scholars, with each sphere (property, trade, society, man) directly political - 'every private sphere has a political character or is a political sphere; that is, politics is a characteristic of the private spheres too' (Marx, 1975, p. 32).

Marx characterises the Middle Ages as the 'democracy of unfreedom', since in a context where trade and landed property are not free and have not yet become independent, the 'political' also did not yet exist as separate from the 'economic'. This discussion of the identity of civil and political society in feudalism has important ramifications for theorising the emergence of the capitalist state form. Marx saw the identity of the civil and political *estates* as the expression of the identity of civil and political *society*. Within each individual principality, the princedom (the sovereignty), was a particular estate - 'their estate was their state' (ibid., p. 72) - which had certain privileges but which was correspondingly restricted by the privileges of the other estates. Their activity as a legislative power was simply a complement to their sovereign and governing (executive) power, directed largely to civil affairs. As Marx summarises, 'they did not become *political* estates because they participated in legislation; on the contrary, they participated in legislation because they were *political* estates' (ibid., p. 73).

The emergence of the capitalist state form was neither an automatic response to the development of world trade, nor simply a matter of the transfer of power from one class to another. The historic change in the form of the state occurred gradually as political revolutions overthrew sovereign power (which constituted the political state as a matter of general concern), and fundamental social struggles, which were both prompted by and were expressions of, changing social relations of production, 'necessarily smashed all estates, corporations, guilds, and privileges, since they were all manifestations of the separation of the people from the community' (ibid., 1975, p. 166). These struggles simultaneously abolished the direct political character of civil society whilst creating the modern state. Marx is emphatic, 'the establishment of the political state and the dissolution of civil society into independent individuals - whose relations with one another depend on law, just as the relations of men in the system of estates and guilds depended on privilege - is accomplished by one and the same act' (ibid., p. 167).

Social struggle is therefore at the heart of the rise of the modern state. The unity of the feudal 'state' rested on the political unity of estates comprising the principality. The social struggles which dissolved the personal and corporate foundations of this power effected the separation of state from

24

civil society - which paradoxically underscores the dependence of the contemporary state on the reproduction of capitalist social relations. As Clarke (1988, pp. 127-8) makes clear, the formal separation of the capitalist state from civil society sets limits to its powers. The state 'has to confine itself to a formal and negative activity, for where civil life and its labour begin, there the power of the administration ends' (Marx, 1975a, p. 198). The formal and regulatory activity par excellence of the state is to uphold the new social relations which comprise civil society.

Thus the state is 'based on the contradiction between public and private life, on the contradiction between general interests and private interests' (Marx and Engels, 1975, p. 46). By upholding the rule of law and money, the state maintains the formal discipline of the market, and thereby mediates the contradiction between the expression of general and particular interests. This discipline must necessarily be imposed in an 'independent form' which is divorced from private interests. 'Just because individuals seek only their particular interest, which for them does not co-incide with their common interest, the latter is asserted as an interest "alien" to them, and "independent" of them ... in the form of the state' (ibid., pp. 46-7).

From the foregoing discussion it is clear that the class character of the capitalist state is not determined by the dominance of capitalists or the 'primacy of the economy'. Rather it is the separation of the state from civil society and thus the political regulation of class antagonism upon which the class character of the state rests. Within feudal social relations, although the Holy Roman Emperor and the Pope stood at the apex, the structure was not a continuous hierarchy but rather sovereignty was 'parcellised' and acts of force were not centrally orchestrated or rooted in a general system of right (see Kay and Mott, 1982, pp. 80-4). In the feudal corvée, force was directly applied to the serf as producer compelling him/her to produce rent for the lord. This force was particular, applied to each serf separately, in contrast to the compulsion to work in capitalism which operates through an impersonal labour market. Relations therefore were not mediated through a central authority, but were made directly at all points. Feudal relations of production were immediately relations of power. By contrast capitalist relations take place through the apparent exchange of equivalents. Labour and capital meet in the 'exclusive realm of Freedom, Equality, Property and Bentham' (Marx, 1976, p.

280), brought together by a contract whose very nature expels all immediate political content. As Kay and Mott (1982, p. 83) make clear, a crucial presupposition of modern contract is that both parties are deprived of the right to act violently in defence of their own interests, with the consequence that, 'in a society of equivalents relating to each other through contract, politics is abstracted out of the relations of production, and order becomes the task of a specialised body - the state'. In this way, the state as the particularised embodiment of rule, and the replacement of privilege by equivalence, are part of the same process, since 'citizens' only face each other through the medium of the state which is 'equidistant' from them.

The specificity of the modern state therefore lies in the historical form of the separation of state from civil society achieved gradually with the dissolution of feudal social relations. The enforced separation of state and civil society is, of course, an institutionalised illusion.[6] The institutional existence of the state as a 'political' sphere presupposes the 'depoliticising' of civil society. The act of 'depoliticising' is itself political and this is the reality which the institutional state obscures, a reality founded on the basis of private property. An important conclusion of understanding the development of the capitalist state form in this manner is that it reveals the notion of the 'autonomy' of the state to be pure sophistry. The power of the state in its liberal capitalist form is embodied in the rule of law and money which are, at the same time, its own presupposition (see Clarke, 1988, p. 127). The political monopolies and privileges of feudalism are replaced by the 'divine power of money', whilst man as a 'juridical person' is not freed from property or the egoism of business but receives freedom to own property and to engage in business.[7] The institutional separation of the state represents the historically specific form of political domination - the political moment - characteristic of capitalist social relations. Marx's dialectical approach reveals this separation to be illusory and opens up space to theorise the state-civil society nexus in terms of *differentiated forms of global capitalist power*.

National states and the global economy

One of the major difficulties which has been encountered in developing a Marxist theory of the relationship between national states and the global economy has turned on reconciling a view of the state primarily defined relative to a domestic class structure, with the fact that the state subsists through global capital relations.[8] As Picciotto (1991, p. 217) has pointed out, the Marxist emphasis on the class nature of the state has made it necessary to discuss the state in relation to society, and it has become convenient to assume a correlation between the society and the classes within it and the state within that society.

We have argued above, that the capitalist state form is not derived from a 'domestic' analysis, to which 'external' determinants are then appended *a posteriori* (the method ironically chosen by interdependence approaches). The state form is a product of the struggles which eventually secured the dominance of capitalist social relations. When turning to analyse contemporary global relations it is fundamental to switch our focus from 'the state' (capitalist state form) to particular national states such as the Swedish or Mexican state.[9] In so doing we are confronted with the following paradox. Whilst from its earliest stages accumulation has proceeded on a global level, capitalist states have developed on the basis of the principle of territoriality of jurisdiction. The fragmentation of the 'political' into national states, which from their very inception comprise an international system, has developed in an uneven fashion alongside the internationalisation of capital. Furthermore, as Picciotto (1991, p. 217) clarifies, the transition from the personal sovereign to an abstract sovereignty of public authorities over a defined territory was a key element in the development of the capitalist international system, since it provided a multifarious framework which permitted and facilitated the global circulation of commodities and capital. However the neorealist image of independent and equal sovereign national states is a fetishised account, since the global system does not comprise an aggregation of compartmentalised units, but is rather a single relationship in which state power is allocated between territorial entities. This is significant since exclusive jurisdiction is impossible to define, so in practice there is a network of overlapping and interlocking jurisdictions.

Whilst therefore the class character of the capitalist form of the state is globally defined, the political stability of individual states has been largely achieved on a national basis - although alliance and treaty have tended to broaden the management of stability. The question of why the 'political' fragmented into national states has to be answered through detailed historical analysis. However, for our purposes, this question is less important than the implications which this fragmentation has for national states today. One of the most important features therefore of global capitalist relations - a feature which itself is a historical product of the class struggles which overturned feudal social relations - is the *national political constitution of states and the global character of accumulation.* Although exploitation conditions are standardised nationally, sovereign states via the exchange rate mechanism, are interlocked internationally, into a hierarchy of price systems (Burnham, 1990). In the same way that jurisdictions transcend national legal systems, world money transcends national currencies. National states therefore founded on the rule of money and law are at the same time confined within limits imposed by the accumulation of capital on a world scale - the most obvious and important manifestation of which is their subordination to world money (Marazzi, 1995).

National states in addition to upholding the authority of the market, through forms of regulation of law and money, respond in policy terms to the crises which result from the contradictory basis of their social form. 'Politics' is not therefore to be read off from 'economics'. Rather, the political and the economic are both to be seen as forms of social relations, whose differentiation enables the everyday conduct of government and yet whose contradictory unity circumscribes the volition of states. Governments thereby respond (and take pre-emptive action in relation) to the power of labour at home and are forced to deal with the consequences of labour-capital struggles on a global level. The contradictory basis of capitalist accumulation is expressed in class terms as capital's ability to impose work (abstract labour) through the commodity form (exchange value). The fallout from these endemic class struggles confront national states in terms of declining national productivity and financial crises.[10] Whilst the national state cannot resolve the crisis ridden development of capital on a global scale, it may be able to mobilise resources and refashion international political and economic relations, to gain a more favourable temporary position in the global hierarchy of prices.[11]

National states provide both the domestic political underpinning for the mobility of capital and offer rudimentary institutional schemes aimed at securing international property rights as a basis for the continued expansion of capital. However far from accommodation and even development being the norm, interstate relations are instead characterised by conflict and collaboration, as national states seek to mediate the consequences of the national/global tension. Whilst each national state strives to regulate the terms of class conflict within its jurisdiction, the overall interests of national states are not directly opposed, and relations of antagonism and collaboration are thereby reproduced at the interstate level.

The national/global tension confronts individual national states with the following principal dilemma. The world economy is driven by the creed, 'Accumulate, accumulate! This is Moses and the prophets' (Marx, 1976, p. 724). In response to the vulgar economists who claimed that capitalist overproduction was impossible, Marx (1978, p. 156) clearly outlines that the volume of the mass of commodities brought into being by capitalist production is determined by the scale of this production and its needs for constant expansion, and not by a predestined ambit of supply and demand, of needs to be satisfied. The continued extension of the market has thus accompanied increases in both the production and realisation of surplus value which has depended not only on the globalisation of trade but also of production, capital export, the purchase of labour power and the globalisation of capital ownership. National states derive their revenue from the capital outlay and the working class subsequently employed within the bounds of their jurisdiction. To increase the chances of attracting and retaining capital within their boundaries (Holloway, 1995) national states pursue a plethora of policies as well as offering inducements and incentives for investment. However the 'success' of these 'national' policies depends upon reestablishing conditions for the expanded accumulation of capital on a world scale. The dilemma facing national states is that, whilst participation in multilateral trade rounds and financial summits is necessary to enhance the accumulation of capital on the global level, such participation is also a potential source of disadvantage which can seriously undermine a particular national states' economic strategy. The history of the postwar international system is the history of the playing out of this contradiction. In other words, the crisis of the capital relation is thus at the same time a crisis of the international state system. Crisis, is therefore not the result of domestic policy failures, as proposed for instance by Smith (1993) when analysing the recession under Major, rather crisis is an endemic feature of the capital relation manifest in the overaccumulation of capital (Clarke, 1991b). The effects of overaccumulation are worked out differentially across the globe. It is at this point, on the basis of this prior analysis of crisis, that a focus on 'domestic policy' is justified and where governments economic policy making can be assessed.

Summary

The present study views capitalism as a single global relationship of class antagonism in which state power is allocated between territorial entities. Class relations do not impinge on the state, they do not exist in 'domestic' society and make their presence felt by influencing the state which operates in the international realm. Rather the state itself is a form of the class relation which constitutes global capitalist relations. These relations appear, for example, as British relations on the world market. Yet as Marx clarifies in *The Civil War in France*, struggles between states are to be understood, at a more abstract level, as struggles between capital and labour which assume more and more the character of the national power of capital over labour. The most important tension of contemporary capitalism, is the national political constitution of states and the global character of accumulation. Although exploitative relations are global, exploitation conditions are standardised nationally and sovereign states are integrated into the global political economy through the price mechanism. The notion of 'integration' does not imply that a state could choose not to be integrated. A political strategy of 'national economic autonomy' is impossible. Policy is not made in the absence of the global economy. It is made within an international context as each state is a participant in the global economy. Such a perspective does not mean that national policies are of secondary importance. Rather, it locates them within a context in which these policies exist and through which they develop. National states subsist through the global accumulation of capital which sets limits to the way in which political authorities contain social conflict. As indicated, capitalist crisis confronts the national state in term of declining national productivity and financial crisis. The state cannot resolve the global crisis of capital. It can, however, gain a more favourable foothold in the hierarchy of the price system by increasing the efficiency of capitalist exploitation operating within its boundaries as well as by adopting a restrictive monetary policy which maintains a strong link between consumption and productive activity.

Rather than focus on realist debates couched in terms of the loss of state sovereignty or those perspectives which view global capital as external to the state, we understand 'international relations' as the national processing of global class relations - and the study of forms of resistance to that processing (Burnham, 1993; 1994). A conceptualisation of capital in terms of its national organisation makes it impossible to understand the monetary constraints on national states. Unless one conceptualises the global mode of existence of the labour/capital relation, then balance of payments problems, pressure on currency, exchange rate fluctuations, and problems of public debt can only be understood as impinging on individual states through external forces (Bonefeld, 1993). In our view, the contradictory character of capitalist social relations means that crisis is endemic, producing constant change on a global scale. National states are not simply affected by 'economic trends' or 'globalisation', rather they are part of this crisis of the social whole.

In response to the latest and deepest crisis of postwar global capitalism we have not yet witnessed the extinction of the national state but the concerted and paradoxical attempt to retain a restructured national form of the political, through schemes aimed at the regionalisation of the world market. The experience of the EU points, in many ways, to the reformulation of aspects of national state policy towards an inchoate system of regional political coordination. The recasting of class relations which has occurred since the crisis of Keynesianism in Western Europe in the mid 1970s, has reached a new level of intensity and instability with the refashioning of the global political economy which maintains the 'real freemasonry' of the capitalist class vis a vis the working class as a whole. In short we are witnessing the recomposition of labour/capital relations expressed as the restructuring of relations of conflict and collaboration between national states. The moves to regionalism evident across the globe (EU, NAFTA, APEC)[12] represent an attenuation of the tension between national states and the global economy because the crisis of the class relation is simultaneously expressed as a crisis of the international state system.

Seen in this light it is no wonder that the Major government has experienced a prolonged process of crisis which has taken economic, political and social forms. The political ruptures evident in the Conservative Party over strengthening and deepening ties with the EU reflect the difficulty of reorienting the relationship between the British state and the global economy. Similarly, Major faced acts of collective and individual working class resistance to the attempt to restructure social relations in Britain. As we will indicate below one of Major's most significant and successful 'tactics' in this regard was his endeavour to 'depoliticise' economic policy making through membership of the ERM. By prioritising the government's commitment to 'solving' the problem of inflation Major risked heightening the threat of the social conflict which stems from the imposition of unmediated market criteria. The ERM provided the perfect 'automatic pilot' to impose financial discipline on social relations in general, resolving the 'political' crisis of the state by 'depoliticising' the process of economic policy making.

The processes of restructuring which have characterised the life of the Major administration are seen not only in Britain but across the globe. From Gingrich's 'Contract with America' to public sector reforms in Berlusconi's Italy and across central and eastern Europe, the form of the national state is undergoing dramatic change. Accordingly, the relationship between national states and global capital is one of continuous realignment. In many ways this realignment is well captured in the notion of the 'competition state'. In Cerny's version this refers to the state using new forms of economic intervention intended to 'marketise' the state itself as well as to promote the competitive advantage of national industrial and financial activities within a relatively open world economy (Cerny, 1990, p. 241). Whilst we do not agree with the view that the 'competition state' is a fractured, internally fragmented state of government with different state actors pitted against each other as members of different 'transnational networks' (Cerny, 1993, p.15), the restructuring of relations which has occurred since the demise of Keynesian economic policy is a global phenomena aptly conveyed by this shorthand. The following chapter takes this argument further and locates the Major government in the context of the crisis of Keynesianism and monetarism as experienced in Britain from the early 1970s.

---

[1]   The need to conceptualise the global system in this manner has been recognised by Clarke (1988); Picciotto (1991); Radice (1984); and, of

course, in work carried out by the present authors, Bonefeld (1993); Bonefeld and Holloway (eds.) (1995); and Burnham (1990).

2 Space does not allow a detailed discussion here, but see S. Clarke (1982); Cole, Cameron, and Edwards (1991); Menger (1963); Walker (1988); and Weber (1949 and 1968).

3 For further details and a class based critique, see Burnham (1993).

4 There has not been a single western borrower from the IMF since 1979, reflecting the enhanced role of the European Monetary Committee/European Commission.

5 The 'new generation' of IPE theorists to which we refer build directly on the work of Susan Strange (1986; 1994). For an overview of a more 'heterodox' approach see RIPE Editorial Board (1994).

6 This is emphasised by Murray (1988, p. 32).

7 Marx (1975b, p. 325) and (1975c, p. 167).

8 See the debate between Chris Harman, Alex Callinicos and Nigel Harris, summarised in Callinicos (1992).

9 A point well made by John Holloway (1995).

10 Since our particular focus is on economic policy we have not sought to develop an analysis of the security implications of the fragmentation of the 'political' into national states. For a useful introduction to this issue, see Buzan (1991).

11 See Hall (1986) for a useful analysis of the institutional structures which affect 'competitiveness', namely, the organisation of labour; the organisation of capital; the institutional organisation of the state; the position of the state within the international economy; and the organisation of its political system.

12 North American Free Trade Agreement (NAFTA); Asia-Pacific Economic Co-operation (APEC).

3 The Politics of Monetarism and the Crisis of Keynesianism

This chapter surveys the development of the global economy since the breakdown in the early 1970s of the international monetary system associated with the Bretton Woods Agreement. The focus will be on the changing relationship between the national state and global financial markets. The shift from Keynesian to monetarist policies in the mid 1970s and the crisis of monetarism which became apparent by the late 1980s, will be situated within this context. It will be argued that financial crisis and speculative runs on currencies were a consequence of a widening gap between productive accumulation (the so-called real economy), and monetary accumulation. In this way it can be argued that the integration of national states into the global economy has changed significantly since the breakdown of Bretton Woods. This change is analysed in terms of the crisis of Keynesianism. We use this term in a broad sense. Keynesianism sought to bring 'economic' forces under control in order to contain social conflict through demand management.[1] It supposes that the state should assume responsibility for the economy, intervening where the market fails, to stimulate economic growth and maintain full employment. In times of recession, the state should stimulate demand through deficit financing, i.e., state expenditure based on credit. The state was thus charged with creating demand through an increase in the money supply. Neither the use of credit nor the creation of budget deficits were new. Keynesianism, however, raised these means to a principle of capitalist reproduction. In order to contain the inflationary consequences of demand management, trade unions were made responsible for the avoidance of wage inflation. In other words, inflationary growth in the money supply was to be balanced by wage restraint. Further, demand management was seen to support industrial investment, creating conditions conducive to the achievement of full employment. Trade union wage restraint was thus compensated by a political commitment to full employment.

By the mid 1970s, Keynesian policies were in crisis. Public deficits and rising unemployment, and high rates of inflation and a stagnant economy appeared simultaneously, casting doubt on the capacity of the state to manage the economy. The legitimacy of Keynesian solutions was questioned as policy makers addressed the problems facing the economy. Monetarism appeared to provide an answer to the crisis of Keynesianism by offering a cure to inflation which would in turn have a positive effect on employment growth and government spending. The new orthodoxy claimed that the economy was not in crisis, but government intervention kept an otherwise healthy economy from self-stabilisation. Thus, Keynesian interventionism was criticised for fuelling the flames of inflation and undermining market self-regulation through the politicisation of economic processes. Proponents of monetarism argued that government should 'get off the backs' of the people and allow greater market freedom to improve economic performance. Monetarism endorses the notion of market self-regulation and calls upon the population to adapt their aspirations to the operation of the free market, so absolving the state from economic responsibilities. However, as this chapter demonstrates, monetarism did not overcome the crisis of Keynesianism. Furthermore, within the context of a finance-driven and dominated global economy, the role of the state was not diminished. Rather, it changed its form. The monetarism of the New Right expresses this change in form: the endorsement of market self-regulation amounts to an acknowledgment that global financial liberalisation has undermined national systems of financial regulation, forcing the state to distance itself from the economic processes which Keynesianism had set out to

control. At the same time, however, global financial liberalisation emphasised the role of the state as lender of last resort. The stability of the international financial order depends upon the lender-of-last-resort activities of the national state. During the 1980s, this role proved to be both vital in preventing a major global financial crisis and insignificant for the creation of financial stability. The 'monetarist' attempt at depoliticising economic policy making - the market knows best - was always spurious. Its apparent success was the boom of the 1980s. The recession of the 1990s presents a crisis of the monetarist notion of market self-regulation. The aim of this chapter is to establish the groundwork for a more detailed analysis of the crisis facing the Major government in the 1990s.

The crisis of Keynesianism

During the 1970s, not only in Britain but on a global scale, governments abandoned Keynesian expansionary policies and adopted deflationary policies associated with monetarism. The ascendancy of monetarist policies can be interpreted as a response to the failure of Keynesian policies to secure economic growth. The shift from Keynesianism to monetarism was very clearly expressed by the British Prime Minister, James Callaghan, in his oft-quoted speech to the Labour Party conference in 1976:

> We used to think you could spend your way out of a recession, and increase employment by cutting taxes and boosting government spending. I tell you in all candour that that option no longer exists, and that in so far as it ever did exist, it only worked on each occasion since the war by injecting a bigger dose of inflation into the economy, followed by a higher level of unemployment at the next step. Higher inflation followed by higher unemployment. That is the history of the last twenty years (The Labour Party, 1976, p. 188).

Callaghan's assessment of the economic consequences of Keynesian policies is revealing. A Keynesian policy of full employment was rejected because of its inflationary consequences and the control of inflation became of paramount importance. Thus a policy of full employment was seen as incompatible with the control of inflation. Callaghan argued that government has to make a trade off between tackling inflation or unemployment but that priority must be given to combating inflation.

Callaghan's speech of 1976 was, however, a belated articulation of his government's abandonment of a policy of full employment and its replacement by a policy of deflation. The Labour government had repudiated expansionary policies before Callaghan's speech and before it sought IMF assistance to combat pressure on the pound in December 1976 (Ludlam, 1992). The IMF loan provided financial assistance to halt the slide of the pound which had come under speculative pressure and was depreciating rapidly in 1976.[2] However, it also supplied a seal of approval for Labour's deflationary policies supporting the government in its attempt to distance itself from the political responsibility for a policy of austerity. The IMF loan has, as indicated by Clarke (1988, p. 314), 'entered the mythology of the Labour Party as the crucial turning point in the strategy of the Labour government as it capitulated to the demands of foreign bankers'. In fact, the IMF loan helped the Labour government in its attempt to disengage itself politically from the consequences of 'unpalatable deflationary policies' (cf. Coates and Topham, 1986). It insulated the Labour government from criticism because it appeared to be responding to the demands of the IMF for the shift in policy which had, in fact, occurred long before the IMF was called upon.

The postwar period in general is often characterised as one in which governments maintained a commitment to a policy of full employment growth. The achievement of full employment after the second world war has become part of the mythology of the so-called postwar consensus. According to this view Keynesian techniques were used to guarantee full employment and economic growth which became the essential foundation for the establishment and growth of the welfare state. However, detailed analysis fails to support this generalisation.[3] As we argue in the conclusion, the priority of avoiding inflation was a major one throughout the postwar era. National governments did not implement Keynesian techniques systematically to guarantee full employment. 'Full employment was maintained in the 1950s and 1960s not because of Keynesian policies but because of the buoyancy of the world boom' (Gamble, 1984, p. 84). As Tomlinson (1990 p. 274) puts it, 'the maintenance of full employment was for most of this time unproblematic because it involved few costs'. When the postwar boom began to deteriorate in the late 1960s, 'the post-war ethos dependent on full employment started to evaporate' (ibid.). Governments which had proclaimed in favour of a policy of full employment started to distance themselves from this policy objective as soon as the economy failed to deliver sustained growth.

Global demand management and the crisis of Bretton Woods

The replacement of Keynesianism by monetarism in the mid 1970s, as the political and intellectual framework of governments' economic policy, has to be seen in the context of the end of the postwar boom in the late 1960s. At the global level, the end of the boom was expressed in the collapse of the system of fixed exchange rates associated with the Bretton Woods Agreement of 1944. The system established at Bretton Woods was charged with regulating global currency exchange relations with the dollar as the dominant currency. Other currencies were fixed to the dollar and the dollar was readily convertible into gold at a fixed price.[4] However, the Bretton Woods system was not in full operation until the end of 1958 with the general convertibility of western European currencies (Tomlinson, 1990, p. 239). Thus, it could be argued that as a system governing the rules of currency exchange relations, 'Bretton Woods only really worked for one short decade, from the end of 1958 to March 1968' (Strange, 1994, p. 105).[5] The importance of the Bretton Woods system was its regulative control of global credit relations. Postwar economic recovery was aided by the creation of global credit, most importantly the Marshall Plan.[6] The international deficit financing of demand was regulated on the basis of a supply of dollars to the rest of the world. Bretton Woods institutionalised the competition between, and mutual dependence of, nation states on the basis of global demand management built around the recognition of the dollar as the key international currency. The immense transfer of dollars into Europe provided the financial foundation for postwar recovery. The central feature of Bretton Woods was the definition of the dollar in parity to gold. In other words, global credit relations were based not only on the dollar but also, and importantly, on the convertibility of the dollar into gold at a fixed price of $35 per ounce. The dollar performed the function of global credit which was supplied to European countries, guaranteed by gold and repatriated to the US through the

38

purchase of US-produced commodities.

By the mid 1960s, the expansion of international liquidity developed a market in dollars outside the regulation and control characteristic of the postwar Bretton Woods order. This market is usually referred to as the Eurodollar or Eurocurrency market.[7] We will refer to these markets as Eurodollar markets because of the dominant role of the dollar.[8] The Eurodollar market is a market in international debt (Strange, 1994). The development of the Eurodollar market coincided with the recovery of capitalist economies after the war putting growing pressure on the US economy (Mandel, 1970). The shortage of international liquidity after the war gradually changed into dollar saturation which began towards the end of the 1950s. Dollars previously spent to purchase commodities exported from the US, were increasingly kept in European based banks. These dollars were thus no longer repatriated to the US and existed outside the control of US regulation.[9]

The conditions that had prevented the occurrence of capitalist overaccumulation were exhausted by the end of the 1960s. Rates of profit dropped and rates of investment started to decline (documented by Mandel, 1975; Glyn and Sutcliffe, 1972; Armstrong et al., 1984). Further, the exploitation of labour grew more and more expensive because of higher wage demands and, most fundamentally, because of a rise in the investment required to set labour in motion. The difficulties of capitalist reproduction led, between 1968 and 1973, to the slowing of the rate of productivity growth in all major economies (Armstrong et al., 1984, p. 249). As profits fell and the costs of appropriating labour's productive power increased, two things happened: on the one hand capital borrowed more money to make up for falling profits to overcome difficulties for expanded accumulation. On the other hand, earned profits were increasingly placed on money markets. This situation arose because of the risks of productive investment, because earned profits were not big enough for instant reconversion into productive accumulation and because financial investment yielded higher returns than productive investment.

From the late 1960s depressed rates of accumulation and depressed rates of profit coincided with rapid monetary expansion. There has been a persistent growth in the imbalance between the expansion of money and the creation of assets against which to charge the expansion of money. The expansion of credit meant that there was a growing claim on future profits in that a claim is made on the future income of the debtor. In order to reduce the burden of debt, wages have to be reduced and work has to be intensified. In other words, the link between money and exploitation has to be strengthened. The ratio of debt to profits will become intolerable the less the burden of debt is guaranteed by the exploitation of labour. Equally, financial markets will supply credit for as long as credit investment yields profitable returns. However, investment in company debt will slow and creditors will demand payment or sell on the stock market as soon as profits start to dip. While the indebted producers will require additional credit to overcome difficulties, the deflation of credit will fuel capital liquidation. However, the bankruptcy of producers will feed back to the lender through the default of credit. In this case both financial institutions and producers face bankruptcy. Therefore, the avoidance of bankruptcy depends on an effective exploitation of labour. The exploitation of labour has to generate profits large enough to pay the interest on accumulated borrowing and to withstand competitive pressure. In the absence of effective exploitation of labour, the ratio of debt to surplus value will continue to increase, undermining profitability and future accumulation of capital, and so creating bad debt, bankruptcy and financial crisis.

Governments responded to the tremendous industrial conflict of the late 1960s and early 1970s pragmatically through expansionary policies (cf. Clarke, 1988). However, such a response threatened the Keynesian agenda in its entirety. The postwar international monetary order depended 'on the ability of the Keynesian nation state to so manipulate internal money flows as to be able to achieve any required adjustments in international accounts' (Cleaver, 1995, p. 152). The stability of the Bretton Woods system of fixed exchange rates rested on the ability of national states to handle problems of adjustments internally. The maintenance of a stable exchange rate and high industrial investment depended upon the national state to achieve a balanced budget as well as a balance in payments. The stability of the system of fixed exchange rates, and therewith of the relationship between 'national' Keynesianism and global financial relations, depended upon the use of money for expansive industrial investment and the management of sound finance within nation states based upon the acceptance of wage restraint by trade unions. However, the industrial militancy of the late 1960s undermined wage restraint (as documented, for

40

example, by Panitch, 1976). While inflation eroded real wages, expansionary policies were no longer conducive to maintaining levels of economic growth. Rather, the recession 'freed' money from industrial engagement and led to a development where monetary expansion became more and more dissociated from industrial accumulation, and instead financed public and private credit requirements.

The dollar saturation and the spillover of earned profits into interest-bearing investment led to a growth in the Eurodollar market which 'grew from $3 billion in 1960 to $75 billion in 1970' (Strange, 1994, p. 107). This market was not only an 'engine of credit creation' (cf. ibid., p. 106). It also undermined the pillars of the Bretton Woods' system of fixed exchange rates. The expansion of credit on Eurodollar markets coincided with declining rates of accumulation, falling rates of profit and industrial unrest against the intensification of work and pressure on wages. In this way, the growth of the Eurocurrency markets was not matched by a corresponding expansion of productive investment. While 'the Eurodollar loan became a new unregulated growth point in the international financial system' (ibid.), the inflationary growth of credit was still officially regulated within the Bretton Woods system, so permitting a growing conflict between official and private liquidity. In the face of the growing competitive strength of the main allies of the US and a growing competitive erosion of the US economy, Strange (1986) argues that the deterioration of the US balance of trade expressed itself in a growing overliquidity of money in the form of Eurodollars and that the inflationary supply of dollars far exceeded the gold kept in Fort Knox. The deterioration of the US balance of trade coupled with the increasing foreign expenditure necessary to suppress the rising tide of unrest throughout the world (especially, of course, the Vietnam war) involved a crisis of the global system of currency exchange relations. This crisis showed the loosening of the bond between money and exploitation, just as it expressed the slackening of the link between state revenue and expenditure. There was a pyramiding of potentially worthless dollars. The dollar's parity to gold, at a fixed price of $35 per ounce, became increasingly difficult to maintain. As money holders rejected the issue of the 'phantom dollar' (Mattick, 1980) and demanded real payment (gold), the economic crisis turned into a severe monetary crisis. The breakdown of Bretton Woods was officially acknowledged when the Nixon administration announced the freeing of the dollar from gold parity in 1971, ended fixed exchange rates of other currencies to the dollar in 1973, enabling the devaluation of the dollar in the same year.

The growth of unregulated global credit markets destabilised the way in which national states were integrated into the global economic during the postwar period. Bretton Woods had left adjustment in the hands of national states. But their ability to cope with currency speculation and industrial militancy was undermined the more their ability to achieve sound finance was disrupted. As indicated by Walter (1993, pp. 189-90), 'the breakdown of a system of fixed exchange rates reflected the tension between growing international financial integration and the continued primacy of the national interventionist state'. Cleaver (1989, p. 22) makes a similar point when he argues that the abandonment of the Bretton Woods system of fixed exchange rates 'constituted the *de facto* admission on the part of national governments that they had no longer the power to manage accumulation internally in ways compatible with global accumulation'. Further, the expansionary response of governments did not secure a growth in productive capital formation nor did it maintain full employment. Instead it produced inflation and growing financial uncertainty at the same as which the economy stagnated. Although the expansionary response led to a temporary boom between 1970 and 1972, this boom was based on an overextension of credit without a corresponding improvement in capital profitability. Following the quadrupling of oil prices at the end of 1973, which coincided with a downturn in capital accumulation, output stagnated or fell in most industrial countries. By 1974, the recession hit all advanced capitalist countries. The chain of bankruptcies and defaults was not confined to productive capital, but included the banking system. When the crisis struck, the banking system was overextended. The most serious international aspect of the crisis was in the unregulated Eurodollar markets where some banks failed and where many banks came within a whisker of default.[10] From the mid 1970s onwards unemployment increased to levels unknown since the second world war. The avoidance of unemployment was replaced by the priority of controlling inflation and rising unemployment was seen as a means of bringing down inflation (Ludlam, 1992, p. 742).

The Eurodollar market took over aspects of a developed domestic credit system operating globally and independently from central banks. Speculative capital assumed the function of national and international institutions, financing budget and balance of payment deficits. On Eurodollar markets there is no regulation, no control, and no central bank as lender of last resort (Strange, 1986). However, Eurodollars are not stateless. Money on unregulated financial markets exists as a claim on central bank money in national states. All unregulated Eurocurrencies, be they dollars or pounds, are readily convertible into 'native' dollars or pounds, since they are all promises to pay dollars in New York or pounds in London (Tew, 1982). Although national governments exercise only indirect control over much of the expansion of credit, as most of the credit market is outside their control, the stability of the unregulated credit system depends on the ability of the state to guarantee all money as a claim on the reserves.[11]

The global limits of a domestic policy of credit expansion impose themselves upon the state through speculative pressure. Eurodollars move around the world in an instant, targeting weak currencies and forcing national states whose currency is under attack to change their policy direction in order to adjust. Floating exchange rates established multi-currency standards with flexible rates between them. Floating established a market for currency speculation. If any one country is having difficulties in adjusting the ratio of its debt to Gross Domestic Product (GDP) through restrictive policy, speculative pressure on currency leads to an outflow of capital. The integration of the multiplicity of states on the basis of floating rates imposed monetary discipline over the national organisation of money through the destabilising movements of speculative money capital against national currency. In the case of economic decline, accumulation of public debt, balance of payment problems, high inflation and global loss of confidence in the monetary management of a state, speculative movement against a currency diverts money capital away from national states and threatens their competitive position in the world market. As Cleaver (1995, pp. 155-6) puts it,

> multinational corporations, as well as the banks themselves, could and did with growing ease shift funds from country to country, or from currency to currency

in hedges or speculative betting on future changes in national policies or business conditions ... So, for example, if any given nation was having particular a difficulty in imposing a "cooling off" on its economy (i.e. rising unemployment and slower wage growth), due to working class resistance, massive movements of funds out of that country or out of its currency could provoke crisis or devaluation.

The anti-inflationary police force of currency speculation has grown enormously over the last two decades. For example, Walter estimates that Eurodollar markets grew on average 'about 30 per cent per year since the 1960s' (Walter, 1993, p. 201). Capital flows have also become increasingly separated from trade-related payments. One study conducted in April 1989 'estimated that *daily* turnover in London, New York and Tokyo was $187 billion, $129 billion and $115 billion respectively. By April 1992, the equivalent figures had grown to £300 billion, £129 billion and £128 billion, while daily world foreign exchange turnover averaged about $1 trillion. The great majority of these transactions, perhaps 90 per cent or more, are unrelated to current account flows' (ibid., 1993, p. 197). This represents a vast amount of speculative capital ready to use its force whenever a country shows a slack response to the control of its working class through a policy of austerity.

 Some commentators have analysed the crisis of the postwar order in terms of a fiscal crisis of the state.[12] This argument states that, because of stagnant economic growth, the expansionary response to industrial militancy and rising unemployment meant that the tax base of the state was eroded. Expansionary policies and existing commitments to welfare and social services increased budget deficits which were no longer balanced by fiscal income. In the face of rising unemployment, the continuing expansion of welfare spending meant not only growing inflationary pressure but also an accumulation of public debt. Budget deficits mean that the burden of debt on future state revenue also increases. This increase weakens the strength of the link between consumption and economic growth, leading to a growth in the ratio of debt to GDP. The thesis of the 'fiscal crisis of the state' shows that the level of spending was not balanced by fiscal income and thus the continuing expansion of the welfare state was placed in jeopardy. However the notion of a 'fiscal crisis' does not go deep enough. The problem of the Keynesian welfare state was not simply that of an imbalance between fiscal income and public expenditure. Rather, the problem was the undermining of the global monetary framework of the Bretton Woods system. Since the collapse of Bretton Woods in the early 1970s, the stability of global finance is no longer based on the convertibility of world money - the dollar - into gold. Instead, states and their central banks took over the function of gold 'by acting as guarantor of the credit system' (Innes, 1981, p. 9). Deflationary policies, associated with monetarism, became 'essentially a means of establishing internal financial discipline in a world of floating exchange rates' (cf. Gamble, 1984, p. 85).

The guarantee of global credit depends upon the capacity of Adjustment the state to adjust the ratio of debt to GDP. 'Adjustment' is much more than just a technical term which describes the control of public debt. It means a policy of tight money and thus the replacement of an expansionary policy by a policy of state austerity which accepts unemployment as a means of containing inflation. Further, adjustment means the eradication of balance of payments deficits through improved export earnings. Thus, 'adjustment' amounts to an attempt at replacing deficits by a policy of sound finance and containing inflation by closing the gap between the expansion of the money supply and productive activity. A growth in deficits which is not matched by capital growth sooner or later becomes unsustainable. Interest charges will absorb a growing proportion of the national product. In order to reduce the ratio of debt to GDP, 'we have to live on less than that what we produce and earn' (Friedman, 1989, p. 31). However, the 'incomes from which we will have to pay interest on this debt will already be diminished as a result of inadequate capital formation and sluggish productivity growth' (ibid.). In order to repay and service interest on credit, standards of living will have to deteriorate and the efficiency of the use of resources, including the efficient use of labour power in production, will have to improve. In other words, the guarantee of global credit goes forward through a policy of austerity which aims at making people pay the price for the repayment of credit through wage restraint and intensification of work. To adjust the ratio of debt to GDP, the economy has to generate large surpluses so that a net transfer of resources pays the interest on accumulated borrowing. Failure to achieve real savings in state expenditure through, for example, the dismantling of the welfare state, and sluggish productive performance will only exacerbate the burden of debt and growing inflationary pressure will lead to increasing speculative pressure on currency, making it harder to attract the money required to finance deficits.

Expansionary policies involve an inflationary gamble unless the expansion of the money supply induces a decisive breakthrough in productive investment, productivity growth, and efficient utilisation of resources, especially social labour power. Unless this were the case, the ratio of debt to future national income would increase and so mortgage the future. The gamble with the future is 'policed' by the movement of speculative capital. The movement of this capital imposes global monetary tightness upon expansionary solutions to the containment of social conflict through inflationary demand management. Credit sustained financing of deficits means that the state draws means of payment from unregulated Eurodollar markets. However, the validity of this credit is backed by the state as lender of last resort. Since the late 1960s, international borrowing has not been matched by a corresponding accumulation of real capital. The principle borrowers have frequently been governments and/or central banks, including not only the governments and central banks of so-called debtor countries but also those of the western industrialised countries, especially the US during the 1980s. At the same time as the deficits of national states are sustained by credit, the validity of the credit depends on the capacity of the state to guarantee the convertibility of credit into central bank money. Failure to impose austerity and to improve economic performance by increasing labour productivity will result in speculative pressure, leading to a depreciation of the currency and increasing inflationary pressure which, itself, will fuel further speculation. This will undermine not only the competitive position of a state but result in a disruption of global exchange relations. Speculative pressure on currency prompts not only a diversion of the global flow of money, threatening to undermine the level of integration of the national state into the global hierarchy of prices. It also involves a destabilisation of international credit relations as creditors demand cash payment at the same time as the ability to service credit is disrupted. [13]

The growth of globally unregulated financial markets has had major implications for the national organisation of money. Since the breakdown of Bretton Woods in the early 1970s, capital movements within the international economy began to dominate balance of payment and exchange rate considerations. 'With conditions of high inflation and little economic growth the spectrum of economic activity about which decisions have to be made shifts to a much quicker and unstable regime, led by the exchange rates' (Thompson, 1986, p. 48). Global monetary pressure on national currency put constraints on budget-deficit financing as international capital movements undermined domestic attempts to contain labour by stimulating productive activity through deficit spending. Pressure to deflate the money supply and to reduce public deficits impressed itself upon the state in the form of a destabilising movement against the exchange rate by private capital. The ultimate sanction for a domestically engineered management of accumulation (expansive policy) that is 'incompatible' with global accumulation, is speculative pressure on its national currency. 'This meant that national authorities needed larger, not smaller, reserves to defend floating currencies, while the latitude to pursue domestic policies independently of external considerations was reduced, not increased' (Clarke, 1988, p. 344). The barrier to sustained economic reproduction appears in the form of a limited supply of official reserves with which to support the domestic currency in the face of speculative movements of private capital. The deregulation of global credit relations replaced the formalised structures of currency adjustment between states with an imposition of money upon states. The implication of unregulated global credit relations is that states are transformed not only from redistributors of wealth in the last instance to lenders of last resort but also to distributors of cuts (see Marazzi, 1995).

The attempt to reduce the ratio of debt to GDP entails the abandonment of deficit demand management. Regaining control over the money supply involves a deflationary attack on social relations through the intensification of work and a reduction in public spending that put money into the hands of workers. Further, the attempt to oppose speculative pressure demands the creation of conditions conducive to the intensification of work by, for example, undermining trade unions and making it easier for employers to confront their labour force through deregulation of wage protection and, indeed, unemployment. From the mid 1970s onwards, restrictive policies were called upon to secure the stability of international exchange and the global flow of capital. The significance of monetarism did not arise from its coherence as an economic doctrine. Rather its importance lay in the opportunity it offered policy makers to depoliticise economic policy making. While the policies of deregulation came to be identified in particular with the administrations of Reagan in the US and Thatcher in Britain, the fundamental shift to which their policies responded was the disruption of the relationship between the national state and global monetary relations and their integration on the basis of unregulated international money.

Summary

The defence of floating exchange rates means that an attempt is made to strengthen the link between consumption and productive activity and to create conditions conducive to a closer link between money and exploitation. Speculative attacks on currency emphasise the urgent need to improve labour productivity by lowering unit labour costs through wage restraint and intensification of work. Further, the defence of floating exchange rates means that the state needs to maximise accumulation within its own boundaries to create sufficient reserves to fend off speculative pressure. Domestic attempts at containing social conflict through an inflationary expansion of the money supply were thus undermined. Governments are now more directly answerable to the police force of global financial markets. The punishment for a slack policy of austerity is severe as shown by the example of debtor countries. A policy of state austerity involves two things. First, any attachment to values other than those of material gain is ruthlessly penalised. Secondly, for those who already possess it, money is the means of freedom and prosperity. For those who do not have money their lack of money defines their poverty and also their existence as a labouring commodity.

Relative high inflation in one country leads to outward flows of capital and downward pressure on currency. However, in order to finance balance of payments deficits and budget deficits, political authorities need to attract money. The principal means is to raise interest rates. However, higher interest rates increase the cost of credit, which makes it harder for companies to avoid bankruptcy. On the other hand, a devaluation of the national currency will result in 'inflationary pressure, which would fuel further speculation and a further depreciation in a downward spiral, which could only be checked by the adoption of restrictive policies' (Clarke, 1988, p. 344). The containment of inflation involves a policy of state austerity which aims at adjusting levels of spending to levels of income.

Thus spending and taxes have to be brought into line sufficiently for the ratio of debt to income to decline. Adjustment means an attempt to strengthen the link between consumption and the efficient use of labour power in production.

James Callaghan's proclamation to the Labour Party conference in 1976, of the inflationary consequences of demand management, reflected the changed relationship between the national state and the global economy through unregulated credit markets. The divorce of these markets from national systems of credit regulation and the tremendous expansion of these markets relative to industrial activity meant that national states had to adjust their monetary and fiscal policy in order to avoid financial crisis. Movements in 'confidence' tend to appear in the market in government debt and foreign exchanges. These movements have always existed. However, since the end of the postwar boom, the integration of the world economy subsists through floating exchange rates. Governments have become vulnerable to changes in financial market sentiment. The breakdown of the Bretton Woods system in the early 1970s meant that they were no longer insulated from speculative attacks through regulative exchange rate policies associated with the Bretton Woods Agreement. Public deficits, balance of payments deficits and slack monetary policies undermine the confidence of global credit markets in the convertibility of credit into means of payment. The Eurodollar markets revolutionised the credit creating process and constrained the ability of states to manage monetary relations. Global credit markets operate outside the regulative control of national states and are at the same time backed by the states as lender of last resort. States will secure the confidence of global money through the imposition of austerity measures. The containment of social conflict through economic growth, full employment and welfare was thus undermined. During the 1970s, the incorporation of the trade union movement could no longer be legitimated on the grounds of full employment and price stability. Wage restraint and public expenditure cuts had 'to be legitimated on the grounds that wage restraint would *restore* full employment and price stability, or, even more difficult, on the grounds that it would prevent the situation from getting worse' (Panitch, 1986, p. 202). The politics of incorporation meant that austerity had to be endorsed by the trade unions. The incorporation of the trade unions amounted to an attempt at depoliticising the state from the social consequences of austerity. However, the legitimation of austerity through the incorporation of trade unions was precarious. Although incorporation helped to arrest the industrial militancy of the early 1970s, and although trade unions exercised wage restraint (cf. Panitch, 1986), it prevented a sustained deflationary response to inflationary pressure and fiscal crisis, and politicised wage bargaining, industrial restructuring and economic development.

Further, the integration of national states with floating exchange rates undermined the so-called steering capacity of the state. This capacity has always been precarious but became more so with the floating rate. Within the context of fiscal crisis and mass unemployment, the incorporation of the trade unions politicised themes such as welfare cuts and distributive conflicts. This gave rise to the notion of a legitimacy crisis of the state (Offe, 1984, Habermas, 1976) and to the thesis of overload.[14] This thesis was presented by proponents of Conservative and liberal market persuasion. It was claimed that the 'economic consequences of democracy' (cf. Brittan, 1977) resulted in inflationary pressure, reinforced by a political demand inflation for welfare which not only exacerbated the fiscal crisis of the state but also prevented people from being enterprising. The thesis of overload and the solutions proposed by the monetarist New Right overlapped. Both advocated that social and economic claims had to be redirected towards monetary exchange relations, that is the market. It was argued that this would insulate the state from excessive welfare claims and so depoliticise conflicts over distribution and economic well-being. The Keynesian view that the state should intervene where the market fails was rejected and replaced by the notion that the state should keep out of the market and merely ensure the condition of its operation. Thus while Keynesianism espoused the idea of political responsibility for market relations, the monetarism of the New Right advocated a clear separation between the political and the economic. Keynesian demand management was rejected because it politicised economic relations and conflicts. The monetarism of the New Right sought to depoliticise these forces and conflicts by endorsing values such as self-restraint, market discipline, responsibility and market freedom.[15] It thus responded to the crisis of Keynesian policies by criticising welfare claims as constraining economic progress and freedom. The proposal that the state should 'exit' from market relations meant in practice that the welfare state should be restructured, that the political position of trade unions should be undermined and that public services should be deregulated, national corporations be privatised and protectionist labour market policies demolished in order to open the labour market to competitive pressures. Unemployment was no longer seen as a problem of political regulation but, rather, as a form of market self-regulation. The attempt to free the state from political responsibility for the decline in employment and to depoliticise the issue of unemployment was based on the monetarist notion of unemployment as a natural phenomenon.

During the 1970s, the legitimation of a policy of state austerity was achieved not only on the basis of trade union cooption but also, and importantly, by the claim that government's hand was forced by international bankers and, in particular, the IMF. The role of the IMF has changed considerably since the breakdown of the regime of fixed exchange rates. Before this breakdown, the IMF in theory financed short term balance of payment deficits and supervised exchange rate adjustments which were possible only in the case of a fundamental dealignment. However, within the international system the IMF remained a 'relatively marginal' player (Walter, 1993, p. 174). The integration of national states on the basis of unregulated credit markets led governments to give greatly expanded power to the IMF. This is not surprising given that governments used the IMF to deflect criticism over deflationary policies and governments found it easier to have an unpopular policy imposed upon them from the 'outside'. The IMF had at last found a role in the global economy, 'exercising "surveillance" over exchange rate practices' (Cleaver, 1995, p. 158). This was coupled with an enhanced enforcement role. Preconditions for official and commercial borrowing are spelled out by the IMF in terms of exchange rate policy, credit control mechanisms, and budgetary measures. In this way, as Cleaver indicates, 'national governments sought to insulate themselves from domestic class conflict over economic policy by shifting to international adjustment mechanisms'. Thus deflation could be justified in terms of an obligation to adhere to international commitments.

51

Monetarism and debt

Introduction

The significance of monetarist policies since the mid 1970s has been the rejection of a political commitment to full employment in favour of the subordination of social relations to so-called market freedom. The concerted attempt by monetarism to bring back the ideology of the market to the centre of the political stage involved, fundamentally, the imposition of tight money upon social relations, seeking to adjust global monetary constraint with a policy of state austerity. In order to adjust the ratio of debt to GDP, public expenditure was to decrease relative to GDP and incomes were to be held back relative to profitability. To reduce the inflationary growth of the money supply, public and private consumption had to be capped and borrowing, on the expectation of future income, to be curtailed. Rather than mortgaging the future through inflationary demand management, deficits had to be cut. There was thus a shift in emphasis from the accommodation of wage increases and the encouragement of investment by low interest rates to the limitation of the growth of the money supply to contain inflation. Monetarism replaced Keynesianism by offering a cure to inflation. Since the late 1970s, the attempt to cut back on credit has meant an attack on the whole way in which social relations had been constituted since the war: pushing the trade unions out of the political arena, imposing severe cuts in social welfare expenditure, deregulating wage protection and restricting the ability of the unemployed to qualify for benefits, and making the whole state more repressive through bureaucratic forms of control to enforce the imposition of tight money upon social relations. The control of public expenditure helps to sustain the exchange rate because the reduction of the ratio of debt to government expenditure suggests financial discipline and so guarantees credit as a claim on taxation.

In the beginning, monetarism promised a policy of sound finance: 'you cannot spend what you have not earned'. However, when, in 1982, Mexico threatened to default, monetarist orthodoxy was abandoned. During the 1980s, rather than cutting back on credit, it was expanded to a degree unprecedented in modern history. However, monetarist policies were retained in so far as social relations were held to be responsible for the increase in debt. While the governments of the New Right privatised public corporations in order to balance their books, debt was socialised through fiscal reforms, rescue of banks, the use of public expenditure as a means of imposing the discipline of poverty, and the encouragement of credit based private consumption. The disciplining impact of personal debt cannot be overestimated. Should debtors fail to respond adequately to market forces or should they be in disagreement with 'management's right to manage', loss of employment, loss of wages, or even a reduction in overtime, all carry the threat that contractual agreements on interest payments might be disrupted. The incentive not to risk essentials, such as housing, education, health, clothing, and heating, helps to undermine solidarity and makes social relations exploitable for a policy of state austerity.[16]

The increase in personal debt belies the monetarist rhetoric as spending on what had not been earned increased during the 1980s. Throughout the 1980s, there was an unholy alliance between mass unemployment and sluggish productive investment, on the one hand, and growing public and private indebtedness, on the other. This alliance did not last. The crash of 1987 indicated that the neo-liberal policy of market freedom had entered crisis. While the monetarism of the New Right had claimed that Keynesian policies had overloaded the state with inflationary welfare demands, the politics of the New Right succeeded in overloading the population as well as companies with inextricable debt problems. Monetarist regimes also presided over a dramatic divorce of monetary accumulation from productive accumulation, overloading central banks with growing claims on reserve money (Walter, 1993).

Debt, boom, crash

The 1980s witnessed three major economic events. There was the global debtor crisis, a long economic boom and finally the financial crash of 1987 which was followed by the long recession of the 1990s.

The crash of 1987 was intrinsically connected with the eruption of the global debt crisis in 1982. The debt crisis was a response to the tightening of monetary policy particularly under Presidents Carter and Reagan in the US and in Britain under the chancellorship of Healey and the premiership of Thatcher.[17] The attempt at deflating the money supply sent real interest rates to record heights. The burden of interest payments rapidly became intolerable for many companies which had used credit to finance new investments or to overcome financial difficulties at the start and during the recession of the early 1980s. It became intolerable also for many so-called Third World and developed country debtors. The debt burden was 'exacerbated by the collapse of commodity prices, comparable in real terms to those that occurred in the Great Depression' (Walter, 1993, p. 218). The result was growing social conflict in debtor countries (Cleaver, 1989), a severe drop in export earnings (Walter, 1993), and a severe financial crisis for Western banks who were confronted with a huge bad debt burden. The 'debtor crisis' disrupted the global financial system as (the threat of) default fed through global credit markets with lightening pace. At the same time, deflationary policies reinforced mass insolvency and liquidation of industrial capital as well as mass unemployment in 'metropolitan' countries. Further, by clamping down on credit the anticipated profitability of new investment programmes fell below the rate of interest, so permitting a continued transfer of earned profits into money markets. Although high interest rates prevented banks from defaulting in the early 1980s, the restoring the confidence of money capital through a policy of tight money did not deliver financial stability.

Against the background of the debtor crisis, the economic recession involved a crisis of credit which threatened the stability of banks because of the overextension of credit. Further, the rapid deterioration and devaluation of capital left gaping holes in the dividends of shareholders. At the same time as industrial capitals went into receivership, slashed investment, laid off workers and reduced productive capacity, the money supply, far from contracting, exploded as companies borrowed heavily from global credit markets to maintain solvency and cash flow. Further, the fiscal crisis of the state intensified. The unprecedented increase in unemployment led to an increase in the volume of welfare spending despite reductions in individual benefit rates. Expenditure on law and order increased, especially military expenditure. The recession saw an increase in public expenditure (Mullard, 1987; Friedman, 1989; Malabre, 1988). At the same time as public expenditure grew, high interest rates made government borrowing more expensive.

The western world responded to the debtor crisis with expansionary policies. The driving force of 'expansion' was the US. In the autumn of 1982, the head of the Federal Reserve, Paul Volcker, eased monetary policy and lowered interest rates.

The US supported the world boom of the 1980s through two spectacular deficits: the budget deficit and the trade deficit. Demand management particularly in the area of military expenditure paved the way. As Mandel (1988) put it, the most committed Conservatives became the most ardent Keynesians. Their monetarist rhetoric notwithstanding, they supported the boom with huge deficits. This support was not dissimilar to Keynesian 'deficit spending', i.e. the creation of debt, the inflation of the money supply, and the spending of money for which there was no corresponding expansion of assets. The expansion of money did not launch the economy into sustained recovery as the real economy lagged far behind monetary expansion. Also the boom of the 1980s was not investment led. Rather, money accumulated independently and separately from trade and industrial investment. Speculation and investment in government debt, as well as in the developing security market, fed into itself. All this investment, however, represented an unprecedented mortgage on the future. Money expanded without having been earned and without being checked by the generation of industrial profits. In other words, the expansion of money 'pre-validated' the exploitation of labour to an extent which far outstripped anything which had gone before during the Keynesian era.[18]

The budget deficit of the US grew enormously. During the 1980s, 'interest on the debt and the cost of defence accounted for nearly 40 per cent of all federal expenditures' (Malabre, 1988, p. 110). The average budget deficit for 'the six years 1982-87 was $184 billion' (Friedman, 1989, p. 19). By 1986 the US had accumulated over $250 billion foreign debt. 'This $250 billion is only the foreign debt: as of 1986, the US government owed an additional $1,750 billion to American purchasers of government securities, so its total public debt was actually $2 trillion' (George, 1988, p. 25).[19] The financing of the US trade and budget deficits through capital imports transformed the US from the 'world's largest net creditor to its largest net debtor in book-value and current cost terms' (Walter, 1993, p. 231). The dollar was sustained by an inflow of speculative capital. Banks 'disengaged' from risky 'Third World' lending and global money flew to the US attracted by high interest rates and also a lack of attractive investment opportunities elsewhere. Further, there was a huge transfer of capital from debtor countries to the US. Debt bondage had been imposed upon debtor countries. 'It's clear that the Third World can't pay - and yet it does! For

Latin America alone, new capital inflow (both aid and investment) came to under $38 billion between 1982 and 1985, while it paid back $144 billion in debt service. Net transfer from the poor to rich: $106 billion' (George, 1988, p. 63). Reagan's attempt to make the US politically and economically strong again by 'living beyond its means' turned the supply side policy into a policy of importing speculative capital.

Despite the lowering of interest rates in 1982, interest rates remained higher than the rate of inflation during the 1980s. In other words, real interest rates remained high. However, high real interest rates did not prove an effective brake on the inflationary expansion of credit. Creditors were shielded from the full burden of outstanding debt (George, 1992), while debtors were shielded from the debt burden through fiscal relief. Embarrassed creditors, like the big banks, received tax relief on 'bad debt' and sold 'bad debt' on secondary markets. While indebted countries were, during the 1980s, not allowed to grow out of debt, the banks were able to socialise their debt problems. As George (1992, p. 106) puts it, 'during the 1980s, the only thing that was socialised rather than privatised was debt itself'. Not only in the US but on a global scale, tax cuts laid the basis for the fiscal absorption of high interest rates. Further, public credits were given, for example through the IMF, to debtor countries helping them to pay interest on accrued debt to private banks. This did not let debtors off the hook. Their payment of interest charges to banks increased their debt exposure. The recycling of the debt crisis helped banks to maintain solvency at the same time as public finances were used to bail them out. Banks were also allowed to treat 'Third World Debt as "losses" for tax purposes' (ibid., p. 65). This became common practice from 1987 onwards following Citicorp's decision to set up a loan loss reserve. Banks started to make provisions against possible losses on their loans. These provisions are tax deductible. Thus, national authorities supported banks by exempting their bad debt provisions from tax duty. Although the creditors had not lost any money because of debt default they were 'refinanced' on their exposure. Further, the IMF was given considerable responsibility over financing and enforcing economic adjustment in the 'developing' world. IMF agreements were associated with economic reforms which involved the 'imposition of austerity measures' (Lehman, 1993, p. 208). These included not only budgetary measures but also the privatisation of nationalised industries. The driving force behind privatisation in debtor countries was the desire to reduce public debt. In other words, banks were not only receiving tax exemption on bad debt provisions and receiving interest payment from debtor countries, they were also given the opportunity to engage in the dislocation of the public sector.

The politics of deregulation and privatisation were also pursued vigorously in so-called metropolitan countries. Not only in Britain, but on a global scale, financial markets were offered the opportunity to engage in the privatisation programme. Governments sought to balance public expenditure finances through the privatisation of national corporations and the restructuring of formal collective bargaining arrangements. Financial markets were offered new profitable outlets for their money. However, as Rowthorn (1992, p. 266) indicates in connection with the UK, the attempt to 'reduce the need for overt borrowing by selling assets does not represent a genuine improvement in public sector finances, since it is merely operating on one side of the balance sheet instead of another, swapping assets for liabilities.' Although privatisation offered some windfall profits for subscribers, it failed, as will be shown below, to redress the balance between monetary expansion, on the one side, and slack industrial performance, on the other. Privatisation underpinned the merger boom of the 1980s and fed the stock market boom of the 1980s. Governments sold their assets in an attempt to fend off speculative pressure deriving from budget deficits. However, they acquired liabilities because state deficits were no longer backed by the ownership of national corporations making a future defence of floating rates through further privatisation difficult.

Boom, debt and productive activity

The worst of the recession had passed on a global scale by 1983 'as the world economy was moving into a recovery phase of the cycle, under the impact of expansionary policies in the US' (Clarke, 1988, p. 336). The boom vindicated the market based attack on Keynesian collective bargaining and wage protection and the acceptance of unemployment as 'natural' and thus a consequence of market self-regulation. However, the boom of the 1980s was a boom in money. Despite downward pressures on wages and mass unemployment, and in spite of the introduction of new working practices, ongoing resistance to industrial restructuring prevented either a sufficient rise in profit

57

rates on productive investment or the generation of state surpluses to induce or finance a new cycle of investment. Capital opted for monetary over productive investment, fuelling property bubbles, takeover mania and the esoteric art of speculation. However, all these investments represent a considerable avoidance of productive investment. The expansionary response to the failure of monetarist policies during the recession of the early 1980s had tried to induce, but failed to achieve, economic growth. As Friedman (1989, p. 198) put it, in the US there was 'not more capital formation but less.'

After the recession of the early 1980s, productivity increased in most Western countries. However, this was partly due to the shake-out of the early 1980s and the heavy cuts in the labour force. The increase in productivity arose also from changes in working practices and the pace of work. For example, in the UK, the recession of the early 1980s supported managers in their attempt to impose new working practices and, generally, to intensify work. Productivity was restored at the cost of mass unemployment, and the liquidation of capital. 'Rising productivity, soaring profits and a healthy stock market enabled the government to argue that British industry was "leaner and fitter" as a result of its experience, while the determination of the government and employers had checked the powers of trade unions' (Clarke, 1988, p. 336). However, while profits rose, investment in manufacturing industry did not. Expansion in productive accumulation was sluggish. 'The most fundamental point is that the more than 50% rise in manufacturing productivity took the form mainly of reduced employment (down 26%), whilst output increased only by 12.2%' (Glyn, 1992, p. 79). The striking productivity gains were the result of a marked decrease in the number of workers. Not only in the UK, but on a global scale, unemployment remained high during the 1980s. There was thus an inadequate 'utilisation' of the available labour force or, to put it differently, the size of the population was too large in relation to productivity growth. The notion 'you cannot spend what you have not earned' entails that the unemployed through their reliance on welfare benefits were 'eating' resources which were not generated by productive performance, so widening the gap between expenditure and incomes, on the one side, and capital formation, on the other. For example, in the US, consumption per worker in the 1980s rose by $3100 over the current decade. However, 'only $950 of this extra annual consumption has been paid for by the growth in what each of us produces; the other $2150 has been funded by cuts in domestic investment and by a widening river of foreign debt' (Peterson, quoted in Wilber and Jameson, 1990, p. 107). These cuts involved not only savings in expenditure to maintain the public infrastructure of motorways, sewers, bridges, subways, and so on, but also decreasing federal support for local infrastructure investment, leading to a visible decay of many inner cities. These savings were compounded by social security cuts targeting 'aid to the poor' (Wilber and Jameson, 1990, p. 100). Between 1982 and 1985, cuts from the Food Stamp Programme totalled $6.8 billion; $5 billion was cut from four child nutrition programmes; and 419,300 disabled persons were dropped from the rolls of the Social Security administration, of whom 200,000 were reinstated, and the actions were found to be illegal. Unemployment benefit programmes were cut back. By 1988 'less than 33 percent were covered' compared with 50 per cent in 1980 (ibid.). The attempt at reconciling debt with a policy of austerity meant that those whose labour power was surplus to demand were held responsible for containing the increase in public debt. They did not contribute 'national wealth' through work and their mere existence meant that they spent 'what the nation had not earned'.

During the 1980s, many companies which found themselves with considerable liquidity and declining investment opportunities diversified their operations, to include financial operations where securities or currency speculation yielded returns which were not matched by profit rates. At the same time, companies borrowed heavily to finance new investment, takeovers and mergers. The financialisation of capital as well as the increasing indebtedness of companies grew unchecked, driven forward by the deregulation of credit markets, aided by new technology and sustained by tremendous profits which the investment in future earnings provided. There was no investment breakthrough in industry. This was the case particularly in the US and in Britain where the boom in financial investment coincided with 'stagnant manufacturing investment' (Glyn, 1992). There was a sustained increase in service investment which Glyn (1989) argues represents a considerable avoidance of real investment. For example, in the UK, between 1979 and 1989, the level of investment carried out in the 'real economy' rose by 10.3 per cent. 'Over the same period, investment in the service sectors ... rose by 108.3%.' Further, 'manufacturing investment … was 12.8% higher in 1989 than 1979, whereas investment by financial and business service sector … rose by 320.3%' (Glyn, 1992, p. 84). The boom was financed from borrowing, from dividends and interest income, and from a steady growth in real wages. There was investment in sectors, like credit markets, which service consumption and which provide financial resources for producers. Between 1981 and 1984, bank lending to the private sector increased by 50 per cent 'and by almost 200% from 1984-1988. In addition, the various forms of credit used to finance consumer expenditure increased two and a half times between 1981 and 1988' (Michie and Wilkinson, 1992, p. 197). Increased consumer spending was driven forward by the effects of fiscal redistribution, a growth in consumer credit (Ford, 1988) and a fall in personal savings as well as wage increases (Keegan, 1989; Glyn, 1989; Michie and Wilkinson, 1992). Deregulated financial markets offered new and competitive credit facilities, sustaining consumption with borrowing and making it easier for enterprise to sustain production through easy access to credit. Corporate debt increased as companies borrowed to finance acquisitions, investments and takeovers. Between the years 1982 and 1990, 'the net borrowing of industrial and commercial companies increased almost four-fold' (Coakley and Harris, 1992, p. 52). In other words, the exploitation of labour did not deliver the resources with which to check the debt burden. The result was indebtedness and bad debt as well as bankruptcies and insolvencies. Company failures remained high compared with the 1970s and increased sharply in the 1990s.

In sum, during the 1980s, the dissociation of money from production continued unabated. The expansionary response to the 'crisis of 1982' was not checked by the creation of assets against which to balance the debt. The market, helped by the deregulation of credit controls, took the opportunity to liberate money from labour. Monetarist regimes indulged in an expansion of credit *during* the boom. This expansion was not without problems. During the boom there was a record number of bank failures. In scale these failures far exceeded the 1930s (cf. Mandel, 1987, p. 300). Many of the surviving banks were themselves for a time 'technically bankrupt' particularly by the late 1980s (cf. Keegan, 1993, p. 185). When the shock arrived in the early 1990s there was a widespread fear of a credit crunch. The recession of the 1990s showed that the economic miracle of the 1980s was, in fact, a delusion.

Despite the proliferation of debt during the 1980s, it would be wrong however to see monetarism as a contradictory doctrine. It did not preach monetary tightness only to practice profligacy in debt. Monetarism was, in the 1970s at least, an ideology of hope in increased productivity, promising a stronger link between money and exploitation. During the 1980s monetarism retained its reputation as a tough opponent of a policy of incorporation and formalised systems of collective bargaining. The Keynesianism of the New Right was peculiar: expansionary credit policies and fiscal policy were used pro-cyclically rather than anti-cyclically. Since the late 1970s governments, on a global scale, used restrictive policies during recession and expansionary policies during boom. The Keynesian notion that government should expand demand through credit creation during a recession and deflate the economy during a boom was thus turned upside down. Further, the Keynesianism of the New Right remained anti-Keynesian insofar as policies of incorporation and political responsibility for economic development were rejected. Expansionary policies and a policy of state austerity were pursued simultaneously. Against the background of the failure to squeeze the money supply in the early 1980s, the attempt to control the money supply was abandoned and government started, instead, to support 'market self-regulation' through the privatisation of national corporations and the deregulation of financial markets. This support amounted to an acknowledgment on the part of government that global unregulated credit-markets undermined 'domestic' attempts to regulate financial activities. The abolition of regulative restrictions and controls on credit growth was declared a requirement for setting the economy free and so vindicating governments' overall approach. While attempts at applying the brakes to credit growth were avoided, governments sought to impose financial discipline upon those whose labouring existence generates the assets through which money subsists. Economic adjustment no longer focused on the control of the money supply. Rather,

> inflation and unemployment were now both the result of the excessive power of the trade unions, reinforced by the indiscriminate generosity of the benefit system that subsidised strikers, reduced competition for jobs, and allowed three million people to choose unemployment rather than engaging in productive work (Clarke, 1988, p. 334).

The deflation of the money supply was to go forward by undermining the institutions associated with Keynesian policies of incorporation, such as the welfare state, wage council protection, and other forms of collective provision and protection.

The other side of global deficit demand management was a dramatic decrease in the savings ratio, compounded by an equally dramatic increase in private borrowing (Keegan, 1989; Friedman, 1989, Malabre, 1988). From 1983, consumer credit grew unchecked. In the US, savings fell dramatically from about 6 per cent of personal income in the 1970s to 2.9 per cent in 1985 (Guttmann, 1989, p. 42; for UK: Keegan, 1989). The unregulated and uncontrolled banking system made it possible for a great number of people to maintain, in the face of a policy of state austerity, living standards through access to private credit. Monetarist policies developed, after 1982, in two ways: credit-sustained accumulation and the unrestricted and unregulated expansion of credit on the one hand, and the integration of private debt with a policy of austerity, on the other. The ballooning of consumer debt was not without problems. In the US, for instance, by 1985 consumer debt losses posed a serious problem to the Savings and Loans sector. 'In all, nearly $50 billion of some $2.6 trillion of consumer debt was past due in 1985' (Malabre, 1988, p. 122). These losses strained the financial system with some Savings and Loans companies coming 'within a whisker of having to close down' were it not for the intervention of the Federal Reserve nationalising the debt. However, it was not only the increase in consumer debt which strained the financial system. During the 1980s there was also a dramatic increase in company debt. For example, in the UK, 'financial liabilities of industry rose from 45 per cent of pre-tax incomes at the beginning of the Eighties to 81.3 per cent at the end of 1987' (Keegan, 1989, p. 209). By 1986, in the US, 'business corporations needed 56 per cent of available earnings to pay interest' (Friedman, 1989, p. 100). While tax relief shielded debtors from the effects generated from high interest rates, the ratio of debt to profits rather than being arrested continued to increase. Tax cuts fed directly into consumption at the expense of investment. In other words, capitalist accumulation was sustained by a relaxation of credit constraints, a massive redistribution of wealth through fiscal policies, and a resource transfer from debtors to creditors.

Throughout the 1980s new working practices were

introduced, the strongest sections of the working class, like the miners in the UK and the air controllers in the US, were undermined, and welfare reforms were introduced 'designed to cut the floor out from under the wage hierarchy' (Cleaver, 1995, p. 163). However, the attempt to remove restrictions from the operation of the labour market and undermine the organisational strength of the trade unions was unsuccessful in transforming the working class into a profitable labour force. Capital took the opportunity to liberate itself from labour rather than financing a decisive breakthrough in labour productivity. The increase in global finance was not matched by a corresponding increase in labour productivity. Monetary accumulation was feeding itself and the increase in productivity looked less and less likely to guarantee the convertibility of money into means of payment. In other words, 'phantom credits' accumulated.

Competitive deregulation and regulative cooperation

The credit sustained boom of the 1980s was always weak. High US interest rates stabilised the world boom but had a detrimental effect on the US balance of trade as high interest rates pushed up the dollar and made it harder for the US export sector to retain markets. At the same time, the high dollar put pressure on other currencies. The US was faced with a detrimental combination of balance of payments problems, high budget deficits and high interest rates which supported the inflow of capital required to finance its deficits. Further, the integration of national states on the basis of globally unregulated credit markets prompted competitive deregulation of national credit controls. As Helleiner (1994, p. 160) indicates, 'the deregulation and liberalization of the U.S. financial system in the 1970s and 1980s greatly increased this competitive pressure [not to lose financial business and to attract global financial by improving efficiency of financial services] because they enhanced the attractiveness of U.S. financial markets and firms vis-à-vis their West European counterparts'. Competition among states over the diversion of money to their territories led to a progressive deregulation of credit controls, culminating in the Big Bang in Britain in 1986 (Coakley and Harris, 1992). Competitive deregulation of credit control removed a central element of 'national Keynesianism and corporatist planning strategies throughout Western Europe' (Helleiner, 1994, p. 161). These controls were now 'viewed as a component of outdated economic policies, constraining individual freedom, and in particular, inhibiting the efficiency of the financial intermediation process both domestically and internationally' (ibid.). Competition between states to attract global money led to competitive deregulation of existing regulative controls. As Walter (1993, p. 209) states, the 'effect of one country adopting onerous regulations has usually been to push financial business to other centres'. National states responded to global capital markets undermining the effectiveness of their regulative controls by declaring the deregulation of these controls as a means of achieving economic freedom. While states deregulated their credit controls in order to improve their competitive position for attracting money capital and sustaining their financial centres, they depended upon regulative cooperation to prevent financial crisis. For example, the UK and the US cooperated in early 1987 by requiring banks to set minimum capital adequacy ratios. This culminated in 1988 in the Basle Capital Adequacy Accord which established 'a goal of capital requirement for all banks of 8 per cent of "risk adjusted assets"' (Walter, 1993, p. 209; see also pp. 228-9). Before 1987, regulative cooperation and agreement was reached in response to major upsets like the 1974 bank crisis, the 1982 debt crisis and, in particular, the crash in 1987 (see Helleiner, 1994). Attempts at regulative cooperation also concerned matters of taxation (Picciotto, 1992), regional cooperation on coordinated exchange rate policy, such as the ERM, the liberalisation of global trade such as the Uruguay Round of GATT, and the creation of common markets such as the EU and the North American Free Trade Area.

Cooperation also included the regulation of 'confidence'. The sterling crisis of early 1985 was the first indicator that financial markets were losing confidence in the sustainability of the boom. However, the main focus of deteriorating confidence was the dollar. Following on from the sterling crisis, concern grew about the sustainability of the large US budget and balance of payments deficits. In the US, between January 1985 and May 1985, 43 banks failed and 7 of these on a single day. The total number of bank failures in 1985 was 120, compared with 73 in 1982 and 83 in 1983 (Malabre, 1988, p. 129). In 1985, the US responded to increasing speculative pressure on the dollar that threatened to halt the US boom by devaluing the dollar in an attempt to 'reduce its need for foreign finance not by curtailing domestic accumulation, but by devaluation so as to make exports more attractive' (Evans, 1988, p. 13). This devaluation drove the dollar into an uncontrollable slide threatening to destabilise the international monetary system which was working with an overextended volume and turnover of money capital that, itself, was spreading into more and more speculative channels. This led to the Plaza Agreement of September 1985, in which the major industrial countries 'agreed to try to reduce the U.S. current account deficit by encouraging the dollar to fall' (Helleiner, 1994, p. 1983). The aim was to 'encourage a depreciation of the dollar to levels compatible with long-term balance' (Walter, 1993, p. 222). The Plaza Agreement attempted to restore confidence on financial markets on the basis of a controlled devaluation of the US external deficit. The dollar's devaluation increased inflationary pressure in other western countries and made it harder for them to sustain export rates. However, against the background of increasing credit-requirements by the US and a global financial market which grew dramatically in scope, scale and volume, the attempt at rectifying the global balance of payments imbalance through concerted exchange rate policy 'on the cheap' (ibid.) did not soften the danger of currency turmoil and a financial crash. In 1986, a further 150 banks failed in the US (Malabre, 1988, p. 129). There was a renewed round of competition for financial capital and real investment between the United States on the one hand and Germany and Japan on the other (Walter, 1993). The US depended upon large capital inflows in order to finance its deficits. Although the Plaza Agreement helped to ease the concerns of financial markets, it failed to square the circle. Deficits continued to grow and the real economy showed no signs of providing the assets against which to balance debt. The expansionary response to the crisis of 1982 led to a development in which more and more credit was required in an attempt not only to underpin existing credit requirements but also to service the increasing ratio of debt to GDP on a global scale. Although the policy of state austerity was geared around the incentive effect of poverty, the gap between consumption and productive growth increased. At the same time governments tried to appear credible by creating a harsh economic climate which trapped people in poverty and forced them to fight their way out of deprivation only to be thrown back into poverty. Governments' attempt to restore financial confidence trapped people in debt. People were forced to pay for the increase in credit through worsening conditions, intensification of work, downward pressure on wages as well as an increasing ratio of debt, particular mortgage debt, on wage income.

Financial crash and industrial recession

During the 1980s growing indebtedness was not matched by the expanded exploitation of labour. Indeed, during the boom investment in money was not matched by investment in industrial activity. The result was the accumulation of increasingly irredeemable debt. No wonder, the *Economist* reported in May of 1987, that American economists were asking themselves 'what lies ahead this year, continued growth or slump?' The Keynesianism of the New Right was a desperate measure of crisis management. Rather than tightening the relation between money and exploitation, the gap between the two widened.

Throughout 1987, financial markets became increasingly reluctant to support the dollar. There was growing concern that the ratio of debt to GDP was becoming intolerable. The investment in debt no longer yielded returns big enough to support the continuing supply of credit. There was a fear of an uncontrollable collapse of the dollar, threatening the world boom. In February 1987, the US agreed, in the Louvre Accord, to 'defend the dollar jointly with foreign central banks and to reduce its deficit' (Helleiner, 1994, p. 184). This regulative cooperation did little to restore confidence in spite of massive intervention by central banks to support the dollar (see Walter, 1993). There was a sharp reduction in investments in US debt. Monetary policies were tightened and interest rates raised. The rate of return on US bonds increased from 8 per cent in January 1987 to just over 10 per cent at the beginning of October. However, while the stock market boom continued to attract capital, the price of shares had risen, by the end of August, 'to a level that yielded a return of only 5 per cent' (Evans, 1988, p. 14). In the face of an enormous accumulation of debt, the combination of overliquidity of money capital, declining rates of return and loss of confidence in the dollar, gave momentum to increased speculation that collapsed in 1987.

The crash of 1987 indicated the precarious foundations of the boom.[20] However, the crash did not result in a meltdown of the stock market. This was prevented by a huge reflation package which included the lowering of interest rates, the relaxation of controls on the money supply, and financial support for banks and other financial institutions. The reflation package helped to sustain the credit based boom. Samuel Brittan's advice was well observed: 'When a slump is threatening, we need helicopters dropping currency notes from the sky. This means easier bank lending policies and, if that is not enough, some mixture of lower taxes and higher government spending' (quoted in Harman, 1993, p. 15). The impact of the crash was controlled through the easing of credit policies in the US and other countries who intervened on the foreign exchanges in an attempt to protect the dollar from a major depreciation as interest rates came down. This rescue operation reinforced credit expansion, so sustaining the boom against the background of the so-called economic miracle. The only miracle of the 1980s was that of credit expansion; the 'miracle' in manufacturing was a delusion (see Nolan, 1989).

Before the crash, the leading Western states had failed to square the circle of simultaneously balancing foreign trade and domestic budgets, stable interest and exchange rates and economic growth without triggering inflation or recession. The room for manoeuvre was even more restricted for national states after the crash. The boom was sustained by reconciling global credit expansion with controlled devaluation of money capital. A series of partial defaults were 'juggled skillfully by the bureaucrats and money mandarins of the international financial system (primarily the US Federal Reserve, International Monetary Fund, Bank for International Settlements), and backed by easy government 'lender of last resort' liquidity for highly exposed and especially vulnerable financial institutions' (Bond, 1990, p. 173). The skillful control of partial default coincided with a further increase in global debt (George, 1992; Walker, 1993). The refinancing of global money markets through financial support for banks and the lowering of interest rates amounted to a major reflation of the global economy. Private borrowing reached record levels in the US, Britain and Japan (Harman, 1993). In Britain, the ratio of household debt to disposal income 'which remained steady at 40-50 per cent in the 1970s and early 1980s, rose from about 45 per cent in 1982, to just over 50 per cent in 1984, and then to *over* 90 per cent in 1990' (Dunn and Smith, 1994, p. 84). Property speculation rose to new heights. After the crash, most company borrowing was no longer by means of stock market issues. The lion's share of company borrowing was from banks. For example, in the UK, 'in 1988 and 1989 together, companies borrowed £113 bn, an average of 74 per cent of income', of which £65 billion was from banks (Smith, 1993, p. 192). 'By the end of the 1980s bank loans in the US had more than doubled and in Japan they were three times their level at the beginning of the decade' (Harman, 1993, p. 15). The expansionary response to the crash of 1987 fuelled inflationary pressure on a global scale and intensified speculative betting on the future direction of policy. Interest rates were raised soon after the crash. By 1988, monetary policies tightened because of a number of fears which included the danger of fierce speculation on the future direction of policy, the liquidity crisis of national states, and a sharp increase in speculative runs on currency as debt increased and profitability declined.

The boom was shortlived. Bad debt problems mounted. Depressed rates of profit failed to guarantee credit-worthiness; the number of company insolvencies increased and unemployment rose while brokers focused their attention on companies' ability to generate cash so as to guarantee dividends. Banks were faced with huge bad debt exposure and companies were faced with insolvency. In the US, 180 banks failed in 1987 and a 'record 220 in 1988, putting severe pressure on the insurance pools whose role is to avoid financial panic' (Wilber and Jameson, 1990, p. 102). The recession brought to the fore the fact that the expansion of credit during the 1980s was not checked by a sufficient growth rate of productive accumulation. The crash of 1987 was followed by the deep and prolonged recession of the 1990s.

The expansionary response to the crash led to a development in which the composition of social capital looked more than ever like an upside-down pyramid. 'Phantom credits' accumulated at the same time as the ratio of debt to surplus value meant that the exploitation of labour looked less likely to support shareholders' dividends. By the late 1980s, there was growing concern that the increase in profitability during the 1980s was no longer sufficient to maintain expanding investment. The fall in profits triggered a vicious circle as companies were forced to borrow in an attempt to overcome difficulties. High interest rates cut into profits at the same time as the life-blood of the boom, i.e. credit, changed, by the early 1990s, into the forcible collection of unpaid debt. Big firms such as Pan Am and Maxwell Communications were forced out of business. Everywhere profits dived. Against this background it became not only increasingly 'unprofitable' to make money out of the growing ratio of debt to surplus value, it also became more dangerous. In the US, the Savings & Loans sector collapsed followed by the collapse of the junk-bond market. The Savings & Loans sector was bailed out to the tune of $130 billion (Wilber and Jameson, 1990, p. 3). Investors were confronted with a huge amount of non-recoverable debt and the rapid increase in bankruptcies meant that banks ended up with bad debt problems. The precarious financial situation of producers intensified at the same time as credit based consumer spending came to a halt. By the early 1990s, there was growing concern that a global credit crunch was imminent. Many companies had been overburdened with debt and more than a few of these companies lacked the means with which to pay off their debt. Banks could not get the money they lent and their balance sheets suffered. Just as speculation had fed into itself for years, so too did the new scepticism. Not only in the UK, but on a global scale, company liquidations increased, unemployment soared and private debtors were faced with consumer credit and mortgage default.

As we have argued in the previous chapter, national states are not insulated from the rest of the world but integrated through the exchange rate mechanism and their capacity of imposing austerity upon the working class is 'policed' through speculative capital movements. While governments might have been tempted to inflate the debt away and thereby to reduce the burden of debt on many firms as well as devaluing real wages and eroding standards of living, speculative runs on currency would have resulted in a liquidity crisis, reinforcing the fiscal crisis of the state and making it difficult to finance balance of payment deficits.

In response to the breakdown in consumer spending, retailers were hit by debt deflation on a global scale. There was a dramatic increase in redundant retail capacity and office space, causing the property market, against the background of mortgage default and closure of offices, to bubble and then to burst. The housing market transformed from a state of excitement into desperation, leaving many with inextricable mortgage debt. Indeed, the so-called property owning democracy (cf. Brittan, 1984) transformed into a republic of debt. The crisis in the property market fed back into the financial system reinforcing debt default at the same time as bad debt problems caused by company failure mounted. Profits did not withstand high interest rates and so started to dip seriously. The weight of corporate failures and personal bankruptcies brought many banks to the brink of collapse. Banks supported their accounts by higher bad debt provisions and sought to socialise their debt problems through redundancies, higher fees, and wider interest rate margins on loans. Credit became more expensive and more difficult to obtain and financial markets concentrated more and more on currency speculation. As the *Financial Times* (9.9.93) pointed out: 'Governments know that if policy ceases to be credible, international markets will simply switch off the financial tap'.

By the mid 1990s, the volume of speculative capital had grown to such an extent that it easily dominated the official sector, reducing the ability of central banks to act as lender of last resort and to stabilise exchange rates. Indeed, 'central bank reserves are less than the equivalent of *two days'* turnover in the world's foreign exchange markets. which indicates that one central bank or even a number of central banks intervening together in exchange markets cannot hope to oppose a concerted onslaught on a particular currency or currencies by the exchange markets' (Walter, 1993, p. 199). Without a dramatic reduction in unit labour costs and a decisive policy of state austerity, capitalist development will remain a speculative gamble. At the same time, however, the attempt to lower unit labour costs and implement a decisive policy of state austerity will make it very hard for government to insulate itself from and contain social conflict. Little wonder the IMF began privately to fear that the debt threat was moving north. 'These days it is the build-up of first world debt, not Africa's lingering crisis, that haunts the sleep of the IMF officials' (E. Balls, *Financial Times*, 27.9.93). The collapse of the ERM in 1992 bore witness to the inability of central banks to prevent a concerted speculative run on a currency.

It was in the context of the collapse of Keynesianism and the crisis of monetarism that Major took over as Chancellor in October 1989 and as Prime Minister in 1990. The next chapter analyses the Major government's economic policy from 1989 to 1994. Particular attention focuses on the role, function and politics of the ERM between 1990 and 1992, and on the way in which the Major government sought to depoliticise economic policy making.

70

1   The view that postwar capitalism had been pushed into reforming itself because of the threat posed by the Eastern bloc is shared by authors as diverse as Burnham (1990); Holloway (1995a); Keegan (1993); Marquand (1993); Negri (1988).

2   The sterling crisis was only one amongst several currency crises in the 1970s. The dollar crisis of 1977 and the crisis of the Italian lira in 1976 led to growing fears about a severe financial crisis. These fears were fed also by the bank crashes of 1974 and uncertainty about the security of loans to countries such as Argentina, Turkey, Peru and Indonesia, all of whom had asked for the postponement of payments (see Mandel, 1987).

3   See Bulpitt (1986); Land et. al. (1992); and Matthews (1968).

4   Space forbids a detailed analysis of the Bretton Woods system and its operation. Wachtel (1990) offers a conventional and accessible account and Pilbeam (1992) supplies a good introduction to the technicalities of the system. For an analysis of the politics of the Bretton Woods system and its breakdown see Bordo and Eichengreen (eds.) (1993); Brett (1983); Burnham (1990); and URPE (1978). The contributions to Bonefeld and Holloway (eds.) (1995) offer a class based analysis of the world after Bretton Woods.

5   In March 1968 a two-tier gold price was introduced, weakening the pillar of the Bretton Woods dollar-gold standard, see Strange (1994).

6   On Britain's position within the global framework of credit creation see Burnham (1990).

7   Some commentators refer to the Eurodollar also as the Petrodollar. This is because the market in unregulated credit expanded rapidly after the increase in the price of oil in 1974. However, by then unregulated credit markets had already replaced the regulated exchange system of Bretton Woods. Further, the main creditors to these markets are productive capitals. This was because profits were not big enough for instant reconversion into productive activity, and the recession from the late 1960s onwards made suspension of money capital into interest bearing capital, as well as speculative capital, a worthwhile investment despite the dangers of financial crisis.

8   The dominant currency on these markets is the dollar although its importance declined from 77 per cent in 1982 to 53 per cent at the end of 1989 (Walter, 1993, p. 201).

9 On the technicalities of Eurodollar offshore banking see Strange (1994).

10 See, for example, Mandel (1987); Sampson (1983); and URPE (1978).

11 Thus, the characterisation of the global economy after the collapse of Bretton Woods in terms of a 'deregulated' financial system is at first sight misleading. The state is and has remained the main regulator of global finance, mainly through its role as lender of last resort. Since the early 1970s domestic credit controls have been undermined by national states competing for international finance (see below). However, deregulation has always meant an 'attempt by the state to impose upon market forces - and upon itself - *new market-oriented rules*' (Cerny, 1993, p. 52). This attempt amounts to the introduction of new regulative mechanisms. As Helleiner (1994) has shown, the last two decades have been characterised not so much by 'deregulation' but rather by 'reregulation'. We will use the term 'deregulation' to mean the competitive deregulation of regulative rules and their replacement by new regulative arrangements.

12 See Gough (1975); O'Connor (1973); for critique of the 'fiscal crisis of the state': Clarke (1991; 1992); and London (1980).

13 The US represents, in part, an exception. The dual function of the dollar as national and world currency means that the main source of global liquidity is a constant US balance of payments deficit. The global role of the dollar makes it possible for the US to meet monetary constraint on its trade balance by expanding the supply of dollars. This helps the US to insulate itself from inflationary pressure. Instead, strains are transmitted abroad.

14 See, for example, Brittan (1976, 1977); Hirschman (1970); Huntington (1975) and King (1976).

15 That poor people go hungry is, in this view, not a consequence of welfare policies, debt, poverty, or unemployment. Rather, they simply go hungry because they 'buy the wrong food' (A. Widdecombe, Junior Social Security Minister, *Guardian*, 4.6.91).

16 On this see the contributions to Bonefeld and Holloway (eds.) (1995).

17 Despite the popular image, the move towards a policy of sound money took place under the last Labour government in the 1970s, long before the election of the first Thatcher government in 1979. As

Gamble has argued, 'the impact of the Conservatives' embrace of monetarism after 1975 was limited by the adoption of practical monetarism by the Labour government' (1984, p. 43). On this issue also see Rose (1984).

18 On the term 'pre-validation' see de Brunhoff (1978). The term refers to the circumstance where money has been committed without a corresponding increase in the exploitation of labour through lower unit labour costs, especially through a breakthrough in productivity. All committed money is seen as a claim on future exploitation which is already anticipated by the existing supply of money.

19 On the debt in other western capitalist countries see Mandel (1987), Mandel and Wolf (1988). In the UK budget deficits and the trade deficit improved during the 1980s due to revenue from North Sea Oil (Keegan, 1984; 1989), privatisation (Gamble 1994); a higher tax burden (Rowthorn, 1992), and a credit based consumer boom which increased receipts from VAT. See also the contributions to Michie (ed.) (1992).

20 On the crash see the contributions to *Capital & Class*, no. 34; Harman (1993); Mandel and Wolf (1988).

4 The Political Economy of Recession 1990–1994

By the close of 1993, 17.9 million people were registered at unemployment offices throughout the twelve member states of the EU. The official unemployment rate in Britain topped 10 per cent and despite a 13 per cent depreciation of sterling since 1991, Britain's competitive position (in terms of relative export prices) continued to fall.[1] Gross government debt had risen to a level of 46.5 per cent of GDP and Britain's trade balance had deteriorated - to record a deficit to the tune of £20.5 billion in 1993 (OECD, 1994, pp. 32-45).

The severity of Major's recession prompted many commentators to make comparisons with the Great Depression of the 1930s.[2] However, despite some striking similarities there is no simple way in which the recession of the early 1990s replayed the debacle of the 1930s. History is not hermetically sealed nor is it appropriate to conceive social development as a pendulum that swings to and fro between progress and reaction. The everyday confrontations and struggles which reproduce global capitalist social relations result in constant change and each moment of class relations has therefore a contemporary character which can be elucidated only through close empirical study.

This chapter charts the form of the crisis of the early 1990s by analysing the changing patterns of rule and the forms of conflict that were generated out of the attempt by capital and the state to reorganise social relations. As we have indicated in chapter 2, 'crisis' is not to be perceived in purely 'economic' terms, but rather as a crisis of the entire social structure. The temporary resolution of crisis, therefore, involves not only increasing the rate of exploitation in the workplace, but also transforming other aspects of social relations such as welfare services, family relations and law and order campaigns. Moreover, since national states exist only as part of a global system, the resolution of crisis involves the attempt by states to gain a more favourable foothold in the hierarchy of the price system by ensuring conditions for productivity growth and refashioning international trade and monetary arrangements. To understand the present phase of crisis it is, therefore, necessary to analyse the class conflict in the context of the reorganisation of the state itself and the position of the state in the global economy. It will become clear from the following account that, although, the state continually attempted to use the power of money and law to restructure class relations in Britain, the limits to the success of Major's strategy were set fundamentally by the organisation of labour, capital and the institutional arrangement of the state itself in Britain, in addition to the constraints constituted both by the domestic political system and the global economy.[3] Whilst it is clear, that Major was hampered by the power that deregulated global financial markets brought to bear on exchange rate stability and the ability of other national states to achieve a more 'efficient' restructuring of capital and the working class, it may seem contentious to highlight the organisation of labour in a period which saw the lowest level of official disputes for decades. However resistance to the restructuring/intensification of work takes a variety of forms ranging from unofficial workplace disputes to official industrial stoppages, such as the Timex and the RMT dispute; from community action to one-day demonstrations; and from simple lack of cooperation at work to absenteeism, illness and sabotage. In short, these factors help paint a 'much more complex picture of the industrial scene than the one with which we are usually presented' (German, 1993, p. 30). In particular, the impact of such action on capital's attempt to raise productivity represented a significant, though often unacknowledged, barrier to the government.

In this light the familiar question of whether Major continued Thatcher's 'monetarist' revolution becomes almost irrelevant.

The fit between economic theory and economic policy making is always more rhetorical than real. As Tomlinson (1990, p. 313) points out when discussing the Conservative's economic strategy between 1979 and 1988, like that of previous governments, it was much more qualified, ad hoc and incoherent than its ideologies suggested.[4] The attempt to bring down the level of inflation via tight control of the money supply can only be depicted as allegiance to monetarism in the most simplistic terms since governments around the world, irrespective of their political ideologies, have sought to impose sound financial policies in the 1980s as a means of halting speculative pressure on currencies. Since the 1970s when the balance of influence in international capital markets began to shift significantly from public bodies to private operators (Strange, 1986; Helleiner, 1994), it has become clear that the characterisation of governments as either Keynesian or monetarist is an increasingly redundant polarity. As chapter 2 pointed out, what is more significant is the extent to which national states can become more successful 'competition states' thereby enhancing the accumulation of capital within their territorial boundaries. This chapter presents a chronology of selected aspects of economic policy under Major. It focuses on the state's management of labour power and money tracing the latter in particular detail, given the importance Major attached to the ERM.

Major's chancellorship: 26th October 1989 to the 27th November 1990

The fight against inflation

In retrospect most commentators argue that Nigel Lawson's first budget after the 1987 Conservative election victory, with its cuts in income tax rates to 25 per cent and 40 per cent and his later base rate cuts to 7.5 per cent in 1988, tipped an already overheated economy into an inflationary upsurge.[5] Lawson's easing of monetary and fiscal policy enabled Margaret Thatcher and Alan Walters to strengthen the hand of the Eurosceptics and argue that 'we picked up our inflationary tendency during the time when we were trying to hold our pound level with the Deutschmark'.[6] Similarly, Robin Leigh-Pemberton, Governor of the Bank of England, claimed in his Durham Castle speech that government economic policy making 'went quite badly wrong' under Lawson when 'interest rates were reduced over a period when we now see they clearly should not have been' (*Financial Times*, 6.4.90).

Accordingly, from the Summer of 1988, the central objective of government economic policy was to slow down the rate of domestic demand and thereby combat inflation. In his first speech as chancellor in the House of Commons, John Major vowed to use 'all the practical levers at our disposal to bring inflation down' (*Financial Times*, 1.11.89).[7] This stance was reiterated in his first March budget which highlighted that tackling inflation was the government's most urgent problem.

Behind this commitment to bring down inflation lay stark class politics. From a low point of 3 per cent in January 1988 the retail price index had climbed steadily to reach 9.4 per cent by April 1990 - the highest level of inflation for 8 years in spite of interest rates biting at 15 per cent (CSO, 1994). In assessing the causes of rising inflation Major veered away from a strict monetarist explanation which would prioritise excessive monetary expansion. Although he agreed that the central element in the battle against inflation must be tight monetary policy, he diverged from Friedmanite doctrine by emphasising that the 'outcome is not entirely in the Government's own hands' (*Financial Times*, 2.1.90). In particular Major drew attention to the actions of the organised working class, which threatened to fuel inflation through demands for high pay settlements that had not been 'earned' through increased productivity. As wage costs per unit of production moved ahead of inflation in the latter stages of Lawson's chancellorship, and manufacturing labour productivity in Britain still lagged 20.4 per cent and 17.4 per cent behind German and French levels respectively,[8] Major faced a dilemma familiar to British chancellors since the mid 1960s. Unless demands for higher pay could be resisted, and productivity increased, then rising inflation would scupper the government's entire economic strategy.

In the first half of 1990, the government's anti-inflationary pay stance came under pressure from ambulance workers, workers at Ford who rejected a 10 per cent pay deal and public sector unions representing 750,000 local government white collar staff who submitted a 14 per cent pay claim. In contrast to government rhetoric, Jack Adams the chief union negotiator at Ford, insisted that his members were not the cause of inflation, 'they are the victims of it' (*Financial Times*, 12.1.90). From the Treasury's viewpoint, the UK economy was now in the stop phase of its latest stop-go cycle. The lagged effect of wages on past excess growth in demand was now seen to be clashing with a downturn in economic activity and as the *Financial Times* (12.1.90) stated bluntly, 'the trade unions (always the last to know) cannot see the abyss opening up before them.'

Although the issue of inflation is often seen as a technical economic matter it is important to be aware, as Goldthorpe (1978) argues, that it is ultimately a political problem. Like other policies, a monetarist anti-inflationary stance carries implications for the reproduction of class relations. In particular, as Goldthorpe (ibid., p. 209) points out, prioritising anti-inflationary policies amounts to an 'underwriting of market forces as the key determinant of inequality in the distributional and relational aspects alike' - the major, but not the only, illustration of this being, of course, the requirement for an increase in unemployment, to an unknown level and for an indeterminate period. Anti-inflationary policies carry the threat of heightening the social conflict which stems from the unmediated character of market criteria. In this way, such policies are likely to increase class conflict and ultimately risk the serious danger that a crisis in the sphere of distribution will become a crisis of political authority itself. To prevent the realisation of this scenario it became increasingly clear, even to Thatcher during her leadership, that the government would be well served by an 'automatic pilot' which took responsibility for imposing financial discipline on both capital and the working class. As we indicated in chapter 1, the driving force behind the state's attempt to restructure social relations is not so much the attempt to provide a resolution of 'economic' crisis, as the attempt to resolve the 'political' crisis of the state by trying to disengage the state politically from the economy so as to depoliticise economic policy formation (Clarke, 1990, p. 27). In this way money replaces the state as the agent of restructuring, while the money form is itself imposed on the state, and large sections of the public sector are privatised.[9] By restructuring the activities of the state, capital and the working class, governments operating with anti-inflationary concerns uppermost are well placed to resolve temporarily the political crisis of the state. For Britain in 1990, the ERM (like the gold standard for previous governments) provided, at least in theory, the perfect automatic pilot to impose financial discipline on social relations in general and the working class in particular.

Imposing discipline through the Exchange Rate Mechanism

In May 1990, in the same month that the National Institute of Economic and Social Research reported that inflation was slowing economic activity faster in the UK than in any other leading country (NIESR, 1990), Thatcher publicly dropped her veto to full British membership of the European Monetary System (EMS). Major's view of the benefits of joining the ERM derived in large part from Lawson's analysis of how firm financial discipline could best be imposed on industry and the working class. Throughout his chancellorship, Lawson stressed that the overriding objective of macroeconomic policy must be the suppression of inflation. United in their rejection of formal incomes policies, Lawson and Thatcher agreed that the best strategy should be constructed around the greatest practicable amount of market freedom within an overall framework of firm financial discipline to bear down on inflation. The issue which explosively divided Lawson and Thatcher was precisely *how* that discipline would best be applied (Lawson, 1992, p. 9). In his resignation speech to the House of Commons, Lawson clarified that the exchange rate could not be seen as an aspect of market freedom but on, the contrary, it must be part of the essential financial discipline required to suppress inflation. In Lawson's view entry to the ERM would make the exchange rate floor more credible and thereby underwrite the anti-inflationary resolve of the government. The ERM would provide a new framework for monetary policy in which, 'a fixed exchange rate became the main anti-inflation instrument and domestic interest rates became subordinated to it' (Johnson, quoted in Grant, 1993, p. 57). To complete the picture, Lawson favoured the creation of an independent central bank to 'depoliticise interest rates', and further insulate the government from the full consequences of a tough anti-inflationary stance (Lawson, 1988).

For her part, Thatcher of course derided the view that the government should 'abdicate responsibility' for dealing with inflation by setting up an independent central bank. Thatcher's opposition to the ERM has been depicted by some commentators as simply reflecting her distrust of the European Community (EC) in general. However her position, so often caricatured as 'Little Englandism', embodied a rational alternative route to low inflation. Initially Thatcher employed the familiar 'free-floater' critique of fixed rates, arguing that the UK had low foreign exchange reserves and, in the absence of exchange controls, a fixed rate system would result in massive speculation against the pound, particularly in a run up to a General Election, thereby forcing a politically embarrassing rise in interest rates (Lawson 1992, p. 495). This situation would reduce the government's room for manoeuvre since 'equilibrium' could not be achieved in the ERM by letting the rate take the strain. After the publication of *Britain's Economic Renaissance* by Alan Walters, Thatcher used the so-called 'Walters critique' to bolster her objection to the ERM.[10] Lawson refused to take the 'critique' seriously. His approach centred on deriving as much help as possible, in exerting a low inflation discipline on the British economy, from linking his country's currency to that of another country with a proven track record of reasonable price stability. Walter's however questioned Lawson's logic by applying a variant of the 'interest rate theorem' to suggest that the ERM would drive countries with different inflation rates further apart. In a situation with no currency realignments, foreign exchange markets would favour currencies offering the highest interest rates (typically high inflation economies such as France and Italy) and thus low inflation economies, such as Germany, would paradoxically suffer weak currencies (Smith, 1993, p. 59). France or Italy would thereby be forced to have interest rates that were too low, and Germany interest rates that were too high (Lawson, 1992, p. 505). While this would reinforce the deflationary resolve of the lower inflation country, the high inflation rate partner would be confronted with a further increase in its money supply.

At base, despite the technicalities of the debate, Thatcher and Lawson offered two distinct strategies designed to reduce inflation. Thatcher's position focused primarily on the 'domestic' conditions of inflation, with government regulating wage increases and enabling capital to expand accumulation. It was for government to supply the right monetary policies, break the institutionalised power of the working class expressed in trade union organisation and force the unemployed to work for very low wages. Woolley (1992, p. 164) summarises Thatcher's position as follows:

> Depreciation would bring in train an increase in the price of imports and a relative shift in consumption to domestic goods. This would improve the trade balance,

but it would also produce a fall in the domestic standard of living. Sluggishness in adjusting to higher import prices may mean that over some period both inflation and the trade balance may deteriorate.

At the same time, government would have the ability to bail out manufacturing by letting the pound fall. Any external constraint on the exchange rate was viewed as an obstacle to this strategy, unnecessarily limiting the government's room for manoeuvre by reducing the ability of the national state to conduct economic policy. However by prioritising the issue of national sovereignty, Thatcher failed to grasp the subtleties of Lawson's approach to managing class conflict. For its advocates, the ERM imposed a constraint on the exchange rate which implied an indiscriminate confrontation with the working class through downward pressure on wages and intensification of work. By taking the alternative route of depolicitising this act of economic policy making, the government would increase its chances both of attaining low inflation and re-election since class politics would be disguised in the language of globalisation. Ultimately Thatcher had neither the foresight nor the Tory radicalism of Lawson and for that lack of vision she paid the ultimate political price.

After he took over as chancellor, Major often reiterated Thatcher's line that membership of the ERM would be useful only as a supplement to, not a substitute for, sound financial policy. However, it gradually became clear that he sided with Lawson on how best to apply financial discipline. In June 1990, Major announced Treasury proposals for moving beyond stage one of the Delors plan, under which members had agreed to join the ERM. In building on stage one, he proposed the formation of a new institution, the European Monetary Fund to act as a currency board supplying Ecus on demand for Community currencies (*Financial Times*, 21.6.90). In addition, a new 'hard Ecu' would be created which, unlike existing Ecus, would never devalue against other Community currencies. These proposals, to which Major returned in early 1994, were designed to act as a powerful lever against 'lax' monetary policies. Moreover, by advocating these seemingly radical measures, Major put useful political distance between himself and Thatcher. For the new chancellor the 'hard Ecu' was hailed as Europe's future common currency destined ultimately to replace sterling in a Single Financial Area with its exchange value to be guaranteed by a new European Hard Ecu Bank. Whilst this of course was anathema to Thatcher, it was a move welcomed by the Bank of England and many EC central bank ministers. In July, Major's more positive approach to Europe was further strengthened when the Eurosceptic Nicholas Ridley (Trade and Industry Secretary) was forced to quit the Cabinet following his description of the Economic and Monetary Union as 'a German racket designed to take over the whole of Europe' (*Financial Times*, 13.7.90).

In the context of rising inflation and working class pay demands, Major accepted in full the assessment of the Bank of England and the OECD that Britain would reap substantial benefits from joining the ERM. In particular by ruling out periodic exchange rate realignments both sides of industry, in Major's view, would be forced to face the long-standing problem of inflationary wage settlements. Thatcher's remedy for the 1980s, that policy should focus on the control of monetary aggregates, weakened as the government 'found increasing difficulty in controlling the money supply, and as different measures of money contradicted each other' (Emerson and Huhne, quoted in Grant, 1993, p. 56). For a government that would have found it difficult to impose monetary discipline in the run up to a General Election, the ERM offered a golden opportunity to have it 'implemented from without' (Sandholtz, 1993, p. 38). The government could be shielded from the unpalatable consequences of 'economic adjustment' by shifting responsibility on to an international regime and thereby Major hoped the government would evade electoral punishment (see Busch, 1994, p. 84). With the expectation that the Gulf Crisis would exacerbate inflation in 1991, Major finally committed Britain to the ERM on the 8th October 1990. In timing the entry statecraft concerns were obviously uppermost.[11] The cut in base rates from 15 per cent to 14 per cent, which accompanied Major's decision, was presented as contingent on entry thereby enabling the government to ease slightly the pressures on capital and the middle class, whilst signalling to the working class that they now had to reckon with the consequences of 'excessive' pay demands. This is a view which the Governor of the Bank of England and the CBI were happy to confirm. Whilst Thatcher's personal antipathy towards Europe pushed the Conservative government into crisis with the resignation of Geoffrey Howe as Leader of the House on the 1st of November, Major's handling of Britain's entry to the ERM killed the popular image of him as 'Thatcher's poodle' and paved the way for his surprise victory in the second Conservative leadership ballot on the 22nd of November 1990.

The factors precipitating Thatcher's demise were well summarised by a *Financial Times* editorial (23.11.90):

> Mrs Thatcher's political corpse has the words "poll tax", "exchange rate mechanism" and "Europe" engraved upon its heart. The poll tax was her greatest single mistake, the fruit of hubris and her indifference to injustice. The ERM was her nightmare. It divided her government and cost her a chancellor. Europe was the source of her greatest agony. It led to the resignation that brought her down and it may yet shatter her party.

However, above all, it was the resurgence of inflation that made the issue of the ERM so contentious after 1988. In conditions of mounting unemployment, high prices, rising pay claims and the explosion of public sector borrowing it became increasingly clear that the government would preside over a second recession within the life-span of the Conservative administration. If the government were unable to engage the services of an automatic pilot, then the political fall out would be so great it that it could render the Conservatives unelectable for the foreseeable future.

Major's first government: 27th November 1990 to the 9th April 1992

Throughout the period leading up to Major's re-election as Prime Minister in April 1992, the chancellor Norman Lamont and the Governor of the Bank of England repeatedly made bullish noises about the recovery of the UK economy. Growth was deemed 'round the corner', 'faint stirrings' were detected in the housing market and 'green shoots' were seemingly abundant throughout the economy. In reality, Major presided over what Peter Norman dubbed as 'the second worse recession since the Second World War' (*Financial Times*, 16.11.91). Towards the end of 1991, UK unemployment had risen by 700,000, business failures ran at 930 a week, and house repossessions climbed by astronomical proportions. The second quarter of 1992 saw Britain's GDP fall 3.6 per cent from its 1990 level whilst other EC nations experienced a rise of 2.8 per cent on average. Similarly, industrial production fell from an index of 113.6 in 1990 to 108.6 in 1992 and the balance of payments continued to slide recording a current account deficit of £13,680 million in 1992 (CSO, 1994, No. 488).

Before the April 1992 election, Lamont's economic policy represented a difficult balancing act between electoral economics and the financial rectitude imposed by ERM membership. In an effort to distance himself from some aspects of Thatcher's enterprise culture, Lamont, in his first budget, restored the principle of taxing the return from domestic property and phased out some fiscal privileges for home owners through the abolition of mortgage interest relief against the higher tax rates (*Financial Times*, 21.3.91). By raising central government spending programmes which had been increased by £11 billion in his first Autumn statement, and most importantly by abolishing the poll tax, he also marked a clear break with the latter stages of Conservative policy under Thatcher. Against the background of the ERM, Lamont used caution in monetary policy, reducing the base rate over seven stages to 10.5 per cent by September 1991. Whilst this policy stance cut the headline rate of inflation by the second quarter of 1992 from a highpoint of 10.4 per cent in Summer 1990 to 4.1 per cent, it failed to kickstart the economy in the way predicted by government advisers. As the number of property transactions in England and Wales fell by 450,000 over the period 1989-1992, the number of repossessions and the scale of personal and corporate debt increased accordingly. Although less severe than the crisis which hit the American and Japanese banking system, the main British clearing banks found that their aggressive lending to borrowers in real estate and construction in the late 1980s left a disastrous bad debt problem in the early 1990s. When real estate prices around the globe plummeted, bankers to companies such as Olympia and York (the world's largest property developer responsible for the Canary Wharf project in London's docklands) were pushed to the brink of crisis as the gap widened between debt and asset values. Consequently as Olympia and York recorded a debt of approximately £6 billion in March 1992, NatWest suffered the biggest losses ever incurred by a UK bank on its domestic lending and Barclays, Britain's biggest bank, recorded its first ever loss due to bad debt problems in its core UK operations (*Financial Times*, 26.2.92; 21.3.92; 7.8.92; *Wall Street Journal*, 6.11.92). Moreover the world's largest and most experienced financial shock absorber, Lloyds of London, faced imminent collapse as Lloyds' 'Names' accumulated losses totalling £8 billion in the early 1990s (Sinclair, 1994, pp. 241-

2).[12] In essence, while Major saw a reduction in inflation on the domestic front, his economic team was unable to cope with the consequences of global recession. In the run up to the April General Election, it became clear that the price of reducing inflation in Britain would be paid in escalating unemployment and increased central government debt.

The foundations of the budgetary crisis which engulfed the government in the latter stages of 1992 were put in place in March 1991 by Lamont in his budget. In slashing the poll tax and introducing a higher rate of VAT, Lamont fostered the illusion that there would be 'no losers' from the reduction and eventual abolition of the community charge. However, as Samuel Brittan was quick to point out, the consequence of Lamont's move was that local authorities could raise only 11 per cent of their revenue in 1991-92 with the shortfall to come primarily from central government grants. From a financial deficit in 1990 of £2 billion, the government ended 1992 burdened to the tune of £37.5 billion (*Financial Times*, 21.3.91; CSO, 1994, p. T68).

Between 1990 and 1992 the number of people registered as unemployed in Britain increased by 1.1 million. This meant 9.8 per cent of the total workforce was now unemployed. By the end of the second quarter of 1992 high levels of unemployment had hit the traditional Conservative heartlands of the South East and the South West. From levels which stood at 3.6 per cent and 4 per cent in 1990, the South East and the South West now recorded unemployment rates of 9 per cent and 9.1 per cent respectively. Whilst manufacturing industry fell away in the North and the West Midlands, the surge in non-manufacturing investment, which occurred in the 1980s, left a huge surplus of vacant office and retail premises in the South. Falling house prices, along with the spread of the negative equity trap, and the fear of unemployment, thwarted the government's hopes of recovery as early signs of growth gave way to further decline and economists proclaimed that Britain was in the throes of a double dip - W-shaped - recession.

With the life of the Conservative administration ebbing away, Major was forced to call a General Election on the 9th of April. Although the Conservatives were returned to office securing 42 per cent of the vote, their overall majority had been cut to 21 seats. This slender majority constrained the Cabinet's room for manoeuvre and increased the significance of the actions of Tory rebels. Ahead of Major lay the most turbulent 18 months in recent British political history.

A Major crisis: 10th April 1992 to the 1st January 1993

Storm clouds gather over the European Exchange Rate Mechanism

In the first few months following Major's re-election, the headline rate of inflation fell to 3.6 per cent and the Treasury seriously considered committing Britain to the narrow band of the ERM thus exerting even stronger discipline over labour. Within the narrow band, the exchange rate floor for sterling would have been DM2.88 and the ceiling DM3.01. Towards the end of April, sterling surged to DM2.92 and Lamont took the opportunity of emphasising the 'sea-change in attitudes to inflation' that had occurred in Britain since joining the wide band. Entry to the narrow band, the chancellor stressed, would represent a regime change in monetary policy in as much as industry and labour would be taught once and for all that high pay awards 'translate directly into a loss of competitiveness and hence of market share, profits and jobs' (*Financial Times*, 20.5.92).

Since the creation of the ERM the Deutschmark had been its centre of gravity, with the pound kept within limits set by the German mark. This enabled the government to argue that Britain had to adapt to an environment in which inflation performance must match or even undercut that of Germany. By the middle of May, the Bank of England, encouraged by Britain's falling headline rate, began to wonder whether the Bundesbank's stronghold on the ERM could be broken and whether UK interest rates could fall below German levels (see Smith, 1993, p. 235). These fanciful considerations flew in the face of a number of indicators of real economic performance which would later influence dealers on foreign currency markets. Between 1985-92, GDP in Germany grew uninterrupted, with unemployment reaching only 4.6 per cent in 1992 and net output per worker running 25 per cent higher than in Britain. The underlying strength of the German industrial economy underpinned the Deutschmark. The stability of sterling depended upon sustained economic recovery to competitive levels. Failure to achieve this would mean that sterling's credibility in financial markets would plummet.

Towards the end of May 1992, it was becoming clear that a number of unresolved problems in the global political economy were causing extreme uncertainty in foreign exchange markets. As Peter Norman (*Financial Times*, 29.5.92) summarised, the strength of the US economy was unclear, and the long term capacity of the German economy to absorb the new eastern Länder without allowing inflation to run out of control was identified as a possible source of future monetary instability. In addition doubts were voiced over whether the authorities in Tokyo would be able to stave off recession while managing the problem of asset price deflation in Japan. Overshadowing these worries, there remained the unfathomable outlook for the republics of the former Soviet Union as they stumbled along the road to the market economy. Added to this list was the uncertainty presented by the integrationist ideals in Europe, particularly with national referenda approaching, and the real fear that GATT as well as NAFTA would not be concluded. In these circumstances, conditions had been created for financial markets to respond much more decisively to perceptions of underlying economic and political strength than interest rate differentials. For all Lamont's talking up of Major's achievements, the underlying industrial condition of the British economy hardly inspired sustained market confidence. The chancellor's claim that Britain would soon be able to match Japan's inflation performance of 1.7 per cent in 1992, and thereby resume 'first-rank commercial power' status, rang hollow as the government's financial deficit spiralled to £38 billion by the end of the year.[13]

Britain counted out of the European Exchange Rate Mechanism

August 1992 saw Britain's unemployment rate rise above 10 per cent and with interest rates remaining relatively high at 10 per cent, serious concern over the long awaited recovery began to mount. With Britain now inside the ERM and Major committed to a 'vision of Britain having the lowest inflation rate amongst the world's leading industrial powers', the chance of kickstarting the economy into recovery rested either on a revaluation of the Deutschmark or a devaluation of a range of European currencies against the Deutschmark (*Financial Times*, 3.8.92). German reunification had resulted in a mini-boom which threatened to overheat the German economy and increase inflation. To maintain price stability in Germany, the

Bundesbank continued its policy of high interest rates. This situation, as Sinclair (1994, p. 226) clarifies, led 'all ERM currencies to appreciate in terms of others, particularly the US dollar'. This significantly weakened Britain's dollar export trade at a time when the US economy was in the throes of an equally deep recession. Whilst Britain needed to cut interest rates and improve competition to combat recession, German reunification called for high interest rates and a disinflationary stance. The disciplinary straitjacket of the ERM quickly became a noose for British, Italian, Spanish and French chancellors as pressure to devalue mounted. As Peter Jay (1994, p. 183) summarises:

> Since interest rates cannot be substantially different in two economies linked by supposedly immutable exchange rates (even with a 6 per cent band) and capital movements, the EC economies outside the natural greater German economy (Germany, Austria, Holland, Belgium and Luxembourg) faced a choice between devaluing (or floating down) against the German mark and raising their interest rates to compete with German rates, thereby subjecting their already cyclically weak economies to further deflationary pressures.

Whilst Major insisted that ERM membership had banished the term U-turn from the lexicon of economic policy, Labour's Trade and Industry spokesman, Robin Cook, now wryly observed that 'when you are heading for a precipice there is nothing wrong with doing a U-turn' (*Financial Times*, 25.7.92).

Towards the end of August the Deutschmark appreciated sharply against the dollar and the Bank of England lost $1 billion in an attempt to prevent sterling from falling below its ERM floor. As exchange rate volatility increased, it became apparent that Major would now be forced to maintain high interest rates to defend the pound, thereby consigning the UK's manufacturing and construction industries to further decline and job loss. The government's attempt to impose a pay freeze on public sector workers - breaking long-standing agreements with the police, fire-fighters and the majority of civil servants - intensified political pressure on Major weakening the credibility of the government's emergency measures in the eyes of the world's financial markets. Lamont's last throw of the dice occurred on the 3rd of September when he announced a foreign currency borrowing plan designed to strengthen sterling within the ERM - and finally scotch suggestions of devaluation. In a move dubbed by the *Financial Times* (4.9.92) as more 'often associated with the lax finances of banana republics', Lamont borrowed Ecu 10 billion (£7.27 billion), over half in Deutschmarks, as insurance in the event of a French 'No' vote in the September 20th referendum on Maastricht. The weakness of Britain's position was well illustrated by the experience of the Italian government on the 12th of September. As the lira came under intense pressure the Italian government decided on a 7 per cent devaluation of its currency in return for which the Bundesbank agreed to cut interest rates.[14] Lamont's hopes were pinned on a significant German cut. But on the 14th of September the Bundesbank announced a reduction of only 0.25 per cent and the Bundesbank President, Helmut Schlesinger, indicated that in his view a wider realignment was still required. This could only mean one thing to the dealers on the floors of the world's financial markets - that sterling was overvalued. Wednesday the 16th of September saw the Bank of England intervene in foreign currency markets on an unprecedented scale, losing £16 billion in an attempt to maintain sterling at its ERM floor of DM2.77. As sterling continued to collapse - 'it was sold like water running out of a tap' (*Financial Times*, 19.9.92) - Major raised interest rates by 2 per cent. David Smith (1993, p. 243) is surely right to claim that at this point the financial markets knew the game was up. The British economy, now deep in recession, could not withstand a 2 per cent rate rise and dealers realised the measure would have to be temporary. When in the early afternoon Major raised base rates again, this time by 3 per cent, it was clear to all that the centre-piece of the government's economic policy was in tatters. To the great relief of businessmen and mortgage holders, Lamont announced at 5pm that Britain had left the ERM and next morning, base rates had returned to 10 per cent.

It is tempting to interpret these calamitous events as simply confirming the power of financial markets ('states can't buck markets') or as reflecting the short sightedness of British policy makers. However a more sophisticated explanation should be sought at the level of the 'real' economy. Financial markets do not simply sanction good or bad policy. Although speculation is rife, the markets should also be seen as barometers of economic credibility. In terms of manufacturing competitiveness, John Muellbauer (*Financial Times*, 14.9.92) shows that, with the exception of the period 1986-87, British competitiveness since 1979 had been substantially worse than in the previous fifteen years. Similarly, in terms of production capacity, the UK's output rose by only 11 per cent in the period 1979-89 - a disappointing increase in comparison with most EC partners (Italy for instance recorded a rise of 37 per cent). Whilst GDP (at constant market prices) fell in Britain by 0.3 per cent between 1988-92, the EC as a whole recorded a 10 per cent increase, with German GDP increasing by 17.5 per cent (CSO, 1994). Although manufacturing productivity improved, it still lagged behind levels recorded in most other EC nations, and the productivity gains that were made in Britain in the 1980s were, according to Crafts (1994, p. 217), due in large part to a shake out of overmaning and inefficient firms. Deindustrialisation continued apace with the percentage of the workforce employed in industry dropping from 42.6 per cent in 1973 to 25.8 per cent by 1993 (OECD, 1994). Despite weak domestic demand and falling levels of real income and wealth, Britain, throughout Major's chancellorship and early premiership, amassed a visible trade deficit of £80 billion.

The coal crisis: Major's political U-turn

Less than 24 hours after the collapse of sterling in currency markets, Arthur Scargill obtained confidential government documents indicating that British Coal had drawn up plans to close 30 collieries with the direct loss of 25,000 jobs as a precursor to coal privatisation (*Financial Times*, 18.9.92). Within a month Scargill's worst fears were realised. In a move which prompted an immediate public outcry, British Coal announced the imminent closure of 31 of its 50 pits with the loss of 30,000 mining jobs and a possible 50,000 additional jobs to be lost as a result of the pit closures. Coming on the heels of the currency fiasco, the move by the President of the Board of Trade, Michael Heseltine, to decimate Britain's coal communities was seen by many across the political spectrum as a stark and brutal form of class politics. Although Heseltine had earmarked £1 billion for the 'regeneration' of the affected communities, this looked small beer to the £16 billion lost on currency markets by the Treasury in less than 8 hours on Wednesday 16th. The shut down plans also seemed to make little economic sense. Lamont's inability to see that an immediate shut down of the pits would close off any remaining hope of an end to the recession, strengthened the impression that the government's entire economic policy making process was in chaos. Whilst frontal assaults on the working class, and in particular the miners, had on occasions in the past strengthened the hand of the state, this time the government could neither square the economics of the closure nor easily fend off the suggestion that the move was politically motivated to destroy this traditional bastion of working class organisation.

The public cost of the mine closures in terms of unemployment, lost tax revenue, widening balance of payments deficit and state liability for pensions alone indicated that the policy could not easily be justified on purely economic grounds. Whilst the *Financial Times* described Heseltine's move as ushering in 'the most turbulent period in British politics since the winter of discontent in the 1970s', solicitors were engaged to challenge the projected closures, arguing that the speed of the closures was unlawful since it disregarded British Coal's own colliery review procedure and the Employment Protection Act which stipulates a requirement of ninety days notice of closure (*Financial Times*, 17.9.92). Amid mounting pressure from the trade unions, the unorganised working class, the Labour Party and also disaffected Tory backbenchers, Major was forced to offer a temporary reprieve for 21 of the 31 targeted pits whilst the remaining 10 were to close after a 90 day review procedure. To all but the most Tory diehard, the U-turn revealed serious confusion at the very heart of government.

Towards the end of November 1992, John Major had completed two years in Downing Street and presided over an array of political crises built on a deepening economic recession. With a backdrop of falling output, high unemployment, a rising financial deficit and a falling pound, the situation, in early 1993, bore little resemblance to that which prevailed when Britain entered the ERM in October 1990. All talk of sound financial discipline exerted almost magically through an automatic mechanism that would insulate the government from political fall out had now given way to the more familiar Tory policy of direct confrontation with the working class. Whilst some Cabinet ministers were honest enough to admit that this policy marked a severe set back for Major, the general view was much more pragmatic in that, 'if it works who cares' (*Financial Times*, 28.11.92).

Following Britain's exit from the ERM, the government began a search for a 'new framework', or a 'new anchor', in short, for another strategy to depoliticise economic policy. [15] On the 8th of October 1992, in a memo to the House of Commons Treasury and Civil Service Committee, Norman Lamont set out the policy framework which would replace the ERM (see Jay, 1994, p. 187). Depoliticisation would now be effected by restructuring the relationship between the Treasury and the Bank of England. In an effort to bear down on inflation, the government would produce publicly announced long-term inflation targets, a unified budget which examined spending and revenue together, and monthly monetary reports published by the Treasury. A team of independent forecasters was to advise the chancellor whilst the Bank of England was to be responsible for publishing quarterly inflation reports and was to acquire progressively more independence from the Treasury in the execution of monetary policy (ibid., p. 188). The move to publish the minutes of the meetings held between the chancellor and the Governor of the Bank, whilst ostensibly adding to the 'greater transparency' of policy making, was clearly designed to contribute to the government's new attempt to depoliticise its economic policy.

Henceforth government strategy would consist of combining this clearly weaker version of depoliticisation with direct intervention in industrial disputes to hold down inflation. These measures would be buttressed by the attempt to secure an opt-out from the Social Chapter as a way of securing a supposed 'competitive advantage' for Britain in Europe.

Major's route to European Union: 1st January 1993 to the 1st November 1993

Industrial unrest and continued economic stagnation

The first quarter of 1993 saw the total number of registered unemployed rise to 2.96 million - 10.5 per cent of the British workforce (CSO, 1994, p. T30). Regional unemployment rates tipped 11 per cent in the North, the North West, the West Midlands and 14.2 per cent in Northern Ireland. Only a slight fall in female unemployment rates - due to the expansion of low paid part-time work - prevented the first quarter statistics from shooting over the 3 million mark. With manufacturing, construction and transport industries hit the hardest, it came as no surprise that skilled, semi-skilled and unskilled manual workers bore the brunt of the recession. Labour force survey data produced in February 1993 charted a continuing rise in long-term unemployment, with 34 per cent of workers made unemployed in 1991-92 still without a job after 6 months (*Financial Times*, 18.2.93).

The insecurity fostered by these conditions gave employers the green light to try to push through pay freezes and restructure working practices. With official trade unionism in decline across Europe (except in Sweden) and working time lost in official disputes and stoppages at less than half the rate compared with 1990, the government's strategy of holding down inflation through the discipline of high unemployment appeared to be bearing fruit (*Financial Times*, 17.3.93). However, as stressed earlier, without an automatic pilot, this strategy carries a high risk of intensifying class conflict and thereby threatening political authority itself. The re-emergence of industrial unrest in the latter half of 1993 indicated the dangers inherent in Major's economic management. British Coal attempted to secure government approval to repeal the 1908 Coal Mines Regulation Act, which limited underground shifts to seven and a half hours, and Section 46 of the 1946 Coal Industry Nationalisation Act, which established consultation and conciliation procedures. The government's privatisation and restructuring plans provoked a swift response from the five main coal and rail unions who called for one-day strikes. (*Financial Times*, 4.12.92; 21.1.93). The strike call came on the back of RMT's decision to take indefinite strike action on the London Underground in response to a plan, backed by the Transport Secretary, John MacGregor, to shake up pay and conditions, which the union estimated would cut 5,000 of the 21,000 Tube jobs and reduce pay for 30 per cent of remaining staff (*Financial Times*, 18.11.92).

As the government pressed industry to keep pay deals below the rate of inflation - using as an example Lamont's derisory 1.5 per cent ceiling for public sector workers - sporadic unrest broke out at Timex in January, at the Yarrow shipyard in February, and at Ford where manual and white collar workers successfully resisted employers' attempts to impose compulsory redundancies. In spite of relatively passive unionism in the first half of 1993, earnings continued to outstrip inflation as a number of large employers offered bonuses for restructured work practices - such as the 14.5 per cent rise at ICI, 10 per cent at Rover and several deals of 5 per cent plus in the privatised utilities (*Financial Times*, 17.4.93). Although Britain's 5.8 million public sector workers stopped short of widespread industrial action in 1993, employers began, by the end of 1993, to fear a rise in industrial conflict in the coming year - a fear partially confirmed as RMT stepped up industrial action in the form of successfully organised national rail strikes.

Major's political crisis over Europe

The stark realisation that the British economy could not support an exchange rate of DM2.77 left no room for doubt that, unless Britain could forge ahead with the Maastricht Treaty and gain the comparative advantage by opting-out of the Social Chapter, Britain would slip further down the price hierarchy, reinforcing political crises. The opt-out had been secured by Major in 1991, allowing Britain exemptions particularly in the areas of health and safety at work, minimum wage legislation and equality of opportunity between men and women. The clear rationale behind the move was that low non-wage labour costs plus relatively light labour regulation would add up to a distinct competitive advantage for Britain in Europe. According to calculations made by the European Commission in 1993, non-wage labour costs added an average of 30 per cent to employer costs in the EU. These costs amounted to 50 per cent in Germany, France, Italy and Belgium, but only to 13 per cent in Britain, where the main cost is primarily national insurance (*Financial Times*, 16.8.93). Nevertheless, despite support from leading bankers and the CBI, the Social Chapter opt-out presented the government with somewhat of a dilemma. A central economic priority for all national states is to increase productivity, attract foreign investment and compete successfully in global markets. The opt-out clause was seen by Major as Britain's trump card offering a competitive advantage in this respect. However, the opt-out also threatened, by encouraging low levels of skill, inadequate training and lack of investment, to sacrifice medium term growth for the sake of short term economic gain on the basis merely of a low wage economy. Major appeared, in John Smith's memorable phrase, to be increasingly 'inhabiting a "Walter Mitty" world in which he alone suffered from the delusion that getting Britain excluded from a decision-making process of considerable consequence constituted a triumph' (*Financial Times*, 23.7.93).

Yet eighteen months after negotiating the modified Maastricht Treaty, Major's thoughts of placing Britain at the heart of Europe almost came to grief. On the 22nd of July 1993, disaffected Conservative backbenchers showed their anger both with Major's bunker mentality as regards the recession and his determination to ride rough shod over the Eruosceptics even after the near collapse of the ERM. Conservative Eurosceptics sided with the opposition parties in voting against the ratification of the Treaty, despite the Social Chapter opt-out. Building on the blatant anti-Europe rhetoric nurtured by Thatcher, Ridley and other prominent sceptics (and on Rees-Mogg's High Court challenge to the ratification of the European Communities (Amendment) Act), the Labour Party, on the 22nd of July 1993, tabled an amendment obliging the government to abandon the Social Chapter opt-out. Through a combination of 'blatant arm-twisting, backstairs bargaining and passionate pleading' (ibid.), including striking what turned out to be a hollow deal with the Ulster Unionists on 'sustainable democracy' for the North, the government survived Labour's amendment only with the casting vote of the Speaker, Betty Boothroyd (318 for the government, 317 votes against). However, when Major called on the House to approve the government's authority to press ahead with ratification, the government suffered a defeat by 324 votes to 316, with 23 Conservative Eurosceptics lining up with the Labour and Liberal Parties.

Facing calls for his resignation, Major played his only available political card, a confidence motion which read, 'This House has confidence in her Majesty's government on the adoption of the protocol on social policy provisions.' Angered Eurosceptics were now boxed-in with the choice of either ratifying the Treaty or being held responsible for calling a General Election which the Tories looked bound to lose. On the 23rd of July the confidence motion was passed by 40 votes. Nevertheless this pyrrhic victory left an even larger question mark over Major's premiership and the uncertainty continued as the Tories slumped to embarrassing defeats in subsequent by-elections and suffered record losses in local and European elections in 1994.

Salvaging the European Exchange Rate Mechanism: from semi-fixed to dirty floating

As John Major set about resolving the deep political crisis in the House of Commons, Theo Waigel and Edmound Alphandery, the German and French finance ministers, met in secret in

Munich to increase the ceiling of the bilateral 'swap' credit between the Bundesbank and the Bank of France, and to coordinate interest rate policies to help steady the franc (*Financial Times*, 23.12.93). These measures proved grossly inadequate. Two important assumptions underpinning the Maastricht Treaty were that the ERM could evolve smoothly into a monetary union by the late 1990s and that a Franco-German alliance would drive Europe towards full political union (*Financial Times*, 24.12.93). The next two months saw the unravelling of both of these assumptions.

By the 30th of July 1993 the Deutschmark/Franc exchange rate was under such severe pressure that EC finance ministers were forced to dismantle the fourteen year old ERM and institute radically different operating rules in an attempt to salvage the whole future of monetary union. As the French economy failed to pull out of recession in mid 1993 - with the lowest volume of retail sales in Europe, unemployment edging towards 12 per cent and interest rates at 10 per cent - the Bundesbank refused to reduce its key discount rate to assist the franc and the French currency fell to its Deutschmark floor. The 31st of July saw the biggest haemorrhage of monetary reserves in history. At one stage, the Bank of France was selling $100 million a minute in borrowed foreign exchange in an attempt to prevent the franc falling through its FFr 3.4305 floor. By the close of business on that day, France's reserves were wiped out and the Bank of France ended the day with a net deficit of FFr 180 billion. In total the defence of the franc cost central banks £32 billion. The Bundesbank's concern not to weaken its anti-inflationary credibility by making 'political' interest rate cuts, left the Franco-German alliance in tatters (*Economist*, 7.8.93).

The radical restructuring of the ERM agreed on the 2nd of August transformed the semi-fixed system into a 'dirty floating' operation with most currencies being allowed to fluctuate up to 15 per cent (replacing the previous wide band of 6 per cent) before central banks were obliged to intervene.[16] This new degree of flexibility was introduced to allow greater movement of currencies and thereby, it was hoped, make the system less susceptible to speculative attack. It also significantly relieved the pressure on the Bundesbank since the bank, in principle, carried an obligation to buy currencies under speculative attack in order to defend the mechanism.

In Britain both the Eurosceptics and the Euroenthusiasts claimed that the restructuring confirmed their earlier misgivings about the ERM. Sceptics such as Norman Lamont, interpreted the new measures as indicating that 'monetary union is now dead and the monetary part of the Maastricht Treaty has been made redundant' (*Financial Times*, 2.8.93). Major, by contrast, claimed that the restructuring vindicated his decision to suspend sterling's membership of the mechanism in September 1992 (*Financial Times*, 3.8.93). Both interpretations owed more to fairytale than reality. Major's attempt to interpret force majeure as government policy lacked all credibility and subsequent moves to resurrect Economic and Monetary Union proved Lamont's nationalistic assertion to be simplistic. In reality, as Lionel Barber (*Financial Times*, 23.9.93) clarified, the dirty floating operation left European states contemplating four policy scenarios. First, 'purists' such as Belgium and Ireland, looked to the quick reversal of the August restructuring and favoured an early move to stage two of EMU some time in 1994. Second, the 'sceptics', predictably fronted by John Major, whilst remaining committed to the EU, saw the old route to EMU as 'unrealistic' and argued instead for a more flexible multi-speed approach to integration. The third group, led by Spain, offered a more clear cut view arguing for the total abandonment of the ERM and the return to a general floating system, which they sought to combine with the reintroduction of capital controls to guard against speculation. Finally, Germany, the Netherlands, Denmark and Luxembourg argued more pragmatically for a 'wait and see' approach to EMU and for in its existing timetable whenever necessary. With the establishment of the EU on the 1st of November 1993, the claims of the Major government made in 1991, that sterling could replace the Deutschmark as the anchor currency and that a single currency was in sight, looked remarkably naive.

Compounding the crisis: November 1993 - October 1994

Economic recovery, fiscal tightness and industrial unrest

The art of 'talking up' Britain's recovery was ardently pursued by Cabinet ministers in the first few months of 1994. Predictably, however, the indicators chosen to illustrate the new economic miracle convinced neither independent observers nor the wider electorate. Unemployment, the chancellor stated in January, had fallen by a total of 226,000 in the last 12 months

(HM Treasury, February 1994). However, this concealed the fact that most of those leaving the unemployment register had entered either part-time employment or joined government training schemes. By Spring 1994, almost half a million people (460,000) counted by the government as in work were in reality either on government training programmes or existing as unpaid family workers (*Employment Gazette*, October 1994, T7.1). Of the remaining 24.5 million workers in the UK, 18.5 were in full-time employment whilst 6.0 million had part-time work. Despite the increase in employment, the total number of working hours in the UK continued to fall (*Financial Times*, 23.4.94). The Department of Employment recorded in Spring 1994 that redundancies were running at the same rate as in Autumn 1993, with manufacturing employment hit the hardest suffering monthly falls in employment of 6,000 workers in May and 9,000 in June 1994. Even after the government's attempts to redefine, for statistical purposes, the concept of employment, Kenneth Clarke's miracle left the seasonally adjusted rate of claimant unemployment at 9.2 per cent of the workforce in the Summer of 1994.

Whilst government ministers congratulated the chancellor on combining low inflation of between 2 and 3 per cent, relatively low interest rates and rising GDP throughout the first half of 1994, the self-proclaimed 'low tax party' increased the tax burden for the majority of the population beyond the level experienced under the last Labour government in the 1970s.

Since the November 1993 budget, Major's economic policy mix involved a combination of fiscal tightness and monetary 'looseness'. However, despite a fall in interest rates, they remained much higher than the rate of inflation contributing to a continuing transfer of resources from debtor to creditor. In an attempt to reduce the Public Sector Borrowing Requirement (PSBR), the government introduced VAT of 8 per cent on domestic fuel in April 1994 proposing that this should rise to 17.5 per cent in April 1995. The proposal was defeated in December 1994. In addition, the Spring budget of 1994 saw the freezing of personal allowances, a 5 per cent reduction in the married couples allowance, an increase in national insurance contributions, and a cut in mortgage interest relief from 25 per cent to 20 per cent. From October 1994, the government levied a new 3 per cent insurance premium tax, and from November a new air passenger tax. For a single person on average pay, the tax burden - not including the community charge or council tax

- rose from 39 per cent of income in 1992-93 to 41.1 per cent in 1994-95 (*Financial Times*, 24.1.94). Stephen Dorrell, the Treasury financial secretary, in a written answer to Harriet Harman, confirmed figures which indicated that the cost of the combined tax changes from April 1995 would, for a family on average earnings, be as much as £1,250 a year (*Financial Times*, 18.2.94). By April 1994, the average tax burden, in direct and indirect taxes, totalled 35 per cent of earnings. This was set to rise to 36.2 per cent in 1995-96 as compared with a figure of 32.2 per cent in 1978-79 under Labour. In keeping with Tory philosophy the burden of taxation was designed to fall most heavily on those sections of the working class existing on below average earnings. For a married man on three-quarters average earnings the increase was from 27.4 per cent of income in 1978-79 to 31.2 per cent in 1994-95. However a married man with two children on ten times average earnings would see the burden of taxation rise from 37.3 per cent in 1992-93 to just 37.7 per cent in 1994-95 (*Financial Times*, 24.1.94). In a survey of the period from 1979, William Keegan (*Observer*, 16.1.94) indicated that despite the well publicised reduction in the upper marginal rates of tax since 1979, tax increases since 1993 have led to a position where the average family has a greater direct tax burden than in 1979. During the 1980s the increase in VAT and higher National Insurance contributions offset much of the putative benefit from lower direct taxes. At the same time, the direct burden in fact increased - for those earning less than £78,000 a year - because of the erosion of tax allowances.

The political ramifications of the 'tax bombshell' - which prompted 9.3 per cent of electricity customers in the affluent south-west of England to pay in advance to beat the April 1994 VAT imposition - were most obviously felt by the Conservatives in the 1994 local and European elections. Following their disastrous showing in the May 1993 shire elections, which left Major in overall control of just one English county, Conservative expectations in the local elections were not high. Major's worst fears were realised. The disgruntled electorate handed the Conservatives their lowest share of the vote this century. In Scotland, the Conservatives claimed only 14 per cent of the vote behind the SNP on 27 per cent and Labour on 42 per cent. In England, 'middle class disgust in Tunbridge Wells was mirrored by working class anger in Croydon and Basildon' (*Financial Times*, 7.5.94). Fearing an even greater humiliation in the June European elections, Major was relieved to gain 27.8 per cent of the votes for the Strasbourg parliament. Even so, the June result set another new record as the lowest percentage of votes secured this century by the Conservatives in a national poll. Accordingly Major would send only 18 of the 87 British MEPs to Strasbourg (*Financial Times*, 14.6.94). Whilst Labour made inroads in southern England, taking 44.2 per cent of the overall vote, Conservative Central Office engaged in a damage limitation exercise ridiculing the notion that Major now suffered from a democratic deficit.

At the same time, there was a groundswell of popular support for the rail union, the RMT, in its dispute with the government and Railtrack. In a context where the total number of official industrial stoppages in the year to July 1994 was the lowest since 1920 (*Employment Gazette*, 1994), the RMT achieved a remarkable victory over the government whose Transport Secretary, John MacGregor, had intervened in the dispute in order to veto any deal for signal staff which might breach the government's freeze on public sector pay. From March onwards, the Treasury and the Bank of England feared that workers would attempt to claw back the tax inceases through higher pay (HM Treasury, March 1994). Similarly, Howard Davies, the CBI's Director General, pointed to rising unit labour costs in Britain, warning that 'other countries in Europe are now tackling their cost-competitiveness in a determined way' (*Financial Times*, 9.5.94). Pledged to retain the jewel in Kenneth Clarke's crown, low inflation, Major refused to allow Railtrack to settle the signalman's dispute at a 5.7 per cent increase on basic rates. A signalman's basic rate for a 52.4 hour week stood at between £124 and £137 (*Financial Times*, 15.2.94). However, as the cost of the dispute mounted, with national stoppages over the Spring and Summer alone losing Railtrack over £200 million in revenue, and the strike breaking activities of the state failing, the RMT leader Jimmy Knapp achieved a successful settlement in September 1994. Thus, organised labour continued to pose a significant threat to government policy.

The rhetoric of integration: from full-blooded union to loosely knit states

At the Lisbon summit in June 1992, the twelve member states of the Community agreed unanimously the enlargement of the Union offering membership to Austria, Norway, Finland and

Sweden. This was to take precedence over internal reform of the Union's decision-making process. Constitutional reform would in any case be placed on the agenda of the all-important 1996 intergovernmental conference whose remit was to map out the next stage of European integration. The qualified majority voting system in the EU Council enabled a 'blocking minority' to reject policy if the minority could amass 30 per cent of the votes cast. Out of a total of 76 votes amongst the twelve members, 23 votes were needed to achieve a blocking minority. With the enlargement of the Union, a total of 90 votes would exist, raising the blocking minority to 27 votes.

As the deadline for accepting the terms of the enlargement drew near, Major and Douglas Hurd, the Foreign Secretary, threatened deadlock by refusing to accept that minority blocking should still require 30 per cent of the vote. In a move, dubbed by Lord Richard, the Labour leader in the Lords, as 'one of the most crass pieces of British diplomacy I can remember' (*Financial Times*, 29.3.94), Major widened the rift over Europe in the Conservative Party and severely weakened the British government's bargaining position, particularly vis-á-vis Germany, ahead of the 1996 conference. By refusing to accept that minority blocking would now require 27 votes, Major roused Eurosceptic Tory backbenchers, whilst again presenting his Union partners with the image of Britain as a negative, obstructionist force. Major's popularity with the Eurosceptics, however, was shortlived. By threatening to scupper the enlargement process altogether, Major alienated the pro-British free trading Scandinavians - who would certainly be net contributors to the EU budget - and paradoxically played into the hands of the continental Eurofederalists by arguing his case on the basis of the relationship between voting weights and population. The latter issue threatened to undermine the Franco-German partnership in Europe since more votes for the larger population of Germany would end the voting parity between the two states (*Financial Times*, 14.3.94; 24.3.94).

In the face of implacable opposition from all but the Spanish government, Major was forced into an embarrassing climbdown, which risked not only the future of Douglas Hurd but also brought fresh demands for his own resignation. The eleventh hour compromise, agreed at the end of March, raised the blocking majority to 27, but allowed for a legally enforceable pause in decision making when states mustered between 23 and 27 votes. Major made play of the 'root and branch' review of qualified majority voting which would take place in 1996, and the assurance he had received from the European Commission that it would not seek in future to circumvent the British Social Chapter opt-out. The political backlash from Major's U-turn on majority voting was not confined to Eurosceptics. Whilst sceptics, such as Tony Marlow, demanded that Major should 'stand aside', Eurorealists again voiced concern over Major's credibility. The position was well summarised by Roy Jenkin's depiction of 'the pathetic spectacle of a weak man trying to behave like a strong man' (*Financial Times*, 29.3.94; 31.3.94).

Major's apparent 'achievement', namely Britain's opt-out from the Social Chapter, also represents muddled thinking on Major's part. Evidence provided by the government's Department of Trade and Industry on the competitiveness of UK manufacturing drew attention to the fact that relatively low labour costs in Britain are partly offset by low levels of productivity, so that unit labour costs are much higher than in the USA, Japan, Germany or France. Moreover, Japanese inward investors do not cite low labour costs as a main reason for investing in the UK, which in any case cannot compete on labour costs alone with the states of East Asia or Eastern Europe. In summary, government claims that low labour costs offer Britain a competitive advantage are highly dubious. The all-party committee on UK competitiveness concluded that, 'the efficient use of labour and the raising of its value through better education and training ultimately matter far more than low labour costs' (Department of Trade and Industry, 1994, p. 38).

As the Summer of 1994 wore on, uncertainty over the role Britain would play in a future united Europe began to intensify. In late June, seeking the support of Tory Eurosceptics, Major vetoed the European Council's choice of Jean-Luc Dehaene as successor to Jacques Delors as President of the European Commission. Furthermore, in a move calculated to outflank Major's vision of Europe as a 'sophisticated, free-trade area of loosely knit states', Edouard Balladur praised Helmut Kohl's plans, unveiled in September, to push ahead at full speed with European integration based on a three-tier, 'variable geometry' or multi-speed approach.[17] The German Christian Democrat's (CDU) proposal contained in *Reflections on European Policy*, envisaged Germany and France forming the 'hard core of the hard core' surrounded by a group of states (including Belgium, the Netherlands and Luxembourg) committed to full-blooded monetary, military and social union. The second circle would include states, such as Britian, Spain and Italy, in a slow lane on particular economic or foreign policy issues. An outer tier would consist of more unstable states possibly drawn from central and eastern Europe. Although the realisation of Kohl's ambitious plan was fundamentally dependent on the conclusion of the French presidential election in Spring 1995, Kohl's re-election to a fourth term of office in October 1994 and the decision of Austria, Finland and Sweden to join the Union, placed increasing pressure on Major's decentralised 'sovereignty based' model of Europe.

Assessing Major's attempt to depoliticise economic policy: from the ERM to the low wage economy

Any assessment of the political economy of the recession of the early 1990s must give pride of place to an analysis of the ERM. For the first two years of Major's premiership, it constituted the 'central discipline underpinning UK macroeconomic policy providing the framework for monetary policy and the operation of the UK economy' (Grant, 1993, p. 57). As a strategy of depoliticisation, membership of the ERM was highly successful for the Major administration. It is important, however, to be aware that Major deserves no credit for discovering the benefits of an automatic pilot. Depolitisation has a long history as an instrument of governance in British politics and it is perhaps best exemplified by Britain's return to gold under Stanley Baldwin in the 1920s.

In May 1925, Britain returned to the gold standard at the prewar parity of £1 = $4.86. The move was subjected to a devastating critique by John Maynard Keynes who argued, in a variety of publications,[18] that the prewar parity was too high and would impose painful and useless deflation on the British economy (Block, 1977, p. 17). Leading supporters of the return to gold, in particular John Bradbury and Otto Niemeyer in the Treasury, were adamant that the gold standard would make the British economy 'knave-proof', free of manipulation for 'political or even more unworthy reasons' (Rukstad, 1989, p. 440). In effect it was judged that the gold standard with its 'automatic corrective mechanisms' was the best guarantee against inflation. Contrary to classical liberalism, Keynes believed that the working class would resist a direct reduction in

its real wages and so even colossal unemployment would fail to
bring down wages and prices to an internationally competitive
level. Keenly aware of the political dimensions of economic
policy, Keynes concluded that the main result of the new parity
would be intensified class conflict and escalating
unemployment.

The parallel between Britain's return to gold in the 1920s and
Major's determination to depoliticise economic policy making
by joining the ERM in 1990 is striking. Both 'regimes' seemed
to offer an automatic corrective to inflation and both, in the
short term, were successful in delivering their promise.
Although unemployment increased in the 1920s, those countries
which had returned to gold at prewar rates of exchange saw a
reduction of wages and prices sufficient to reverse much of the
wartime inflation. By contrast, countries such as France,
Belgium and Italy which ultimately returned to gold at parities
below those prevailing before the war, 'were unable to prevent
inflation from continuing into the mid-1920s' (Eichengreen,
1990, pp. 25-6).[19] In this light, the now familiar view that
joining the ERM was 'one huge and recognizable mistake' (Jay,
1994, p. 202), is to miss the point that it helped the government
to cut inflation by almost a third between October 1990 and
September 1992. In other words, the decision to join the ERM
should be seen as a governing strategy whose success in the
short term outweighed the political embarrassment it caused
Major once he had attained his election victory. Moreover, as
with the return to the gold standard, many commentators also
maintain that the rate on entry to the ERM was much too high.
This, however, is to overlook that participation in the
mechanism was not motivated by the desire to compensate
inflation, wage increases, and sluggish productivity, by a lower
exchange rate. The argument that the rate was too high seems to
imply that a devaluation of sterling would have been desirable.
However, the purpose of joining the ERM was to exert a
disciplinary impact on labour and capital, ostensibly imposed
from the outside, forcing them to achieve downward pressure on
wages and increased productivity, in short, lower unit labour
costs. Stevens (1991, pp. 26-7) summed up the experience of the
1980s when he suggested that,

> arguably the most disappointing feature of the past
> eleven years of attempted price restraint has been the
> fact that wage inflation has persistently outstripped
> general inflation ... It is now clear that merely a portion

of these greater labour costs were justified by improvements in productivity. Only an exchange rate policy ... can constitute sufficiently obvious discipline, even for the dullest of wage negotiators, to break this trend that has bedevilled us for more than a generation.

Against the background of the anti-poll tax revolt, Britain's hard pressed policy makers gained an important degree of freedom in joining the ERM since initially, membership removed the risk of a drastic decline in the value of the pound and improved Britain's credit-rating.[20] The ERM did not of course reduce deficits. The condition of sustained membership was primarily a reduction of unit labour costs through wage reductions and the intensification of work. The Bank of England made this quite clear:

> The Governor has emphasized that henceforth companies can have no grounds for expecting a lower exchange rate to validate any failure to control costs. The greater stability which ERM membership offers sterling against other European currencies should in itself be welcome to business as it will enable firms to plan and invest with greater certainty. If companies recognize that they are now operating under a changed regime the benefits of lower inflation will accrue sooner, and at a lower cost in term of lost output, than could otherwise be expected. But if they fail to recognize the constraints under which they now operate the outcome will prove painful to them (quoted in Smith, 1993, p. 187).

The success of the new-found monetary anchor depended on the establishment of a stronger link between exploitation and money: deficits had to be brought down and inflation had to be brought under control. Against the background of bad debt and huge balance of payments deficits, ERM discipline involved a painful adjustment process. This discipline meant a prolonged period not merely of living on less but also encouraged individuals to work harder in the face of declining conditions. Thus, the ERM demanded a closer tie between consumption and productive work. The ERM sanctioned repayment of colossal debt, thereby reinforcing bankruptcies, failures and liquidations. In short, ERM membership saddled the property owning democracy of the 1980s with costs which could no longer be corrected by a devaluation of the pound. Furthermore, unlike the situation in the early 1980s, by the end of that decade producers and consumers were much deeper in debt and so found it much harder to withstand the monetary discipline of the ERM.

Initially, Britain's membership of the ERM was widely seen as an economic success. It was proclaimed that 'sterling's years of living dangerously are over' (*Financial Times*, 29.4.91) and that the UK was 'about to enter a period when making things is more important than moving paper' (*Financial Times*, 8.2.91). These assessments focused primarily on the decline of speculative pressure against the pound. However, these early assessments missed an important point. During the 1980s there had been a dramatic shake out of labour, trade union bargaining power had been weakened and the Keynesian nexus between wages and public expenditure had been attacked. There had not been, however, a breakthrough in productivity, productive investment or a reduction in average wages relative to other European states. In fact, by 1990, the growth in unit labour costs in the UK stood at 12.5 per cent compared with an European average of 5.7 per cent (Deakin, 1992, p. 185). The depth of the recession of the 1990s was to a great extent a response to the ballooning of debt which accommodated the failure to make the working class a much more profitable labour force. The anti-inflationary discipline of the ERM deepened the recession and thus led to a renewed 'shake out' of labour as unemployment soared and company liquidations and bankruptcies increased. As David Marsh put it, 'Britain faced a milder form of the those [pressures] born by east Germany' (*Financial Times*, 12.3.91). During membership of the ERM real interest rates remained high. The UK joined with interest rates at 14 per cent (down from 15 per cent) while inflation was at 9.5 per cent in 1990 (up from 7.8 per cent in 1989). During 1991 interest rates declined further from 13.5 per cent in February to 10.5 per cent in September compared with an inflation rate of 5.9 per cent. Throughout 1992, interest rates declined dramatically, especially after the suspension of ERM membership on September 16th, 1992. However, they still stood at 7 per cent in November 1992, compared with an inflation rate of 3.7 per cent. Real interest rates therefore remained high. Consequently the monetary squeeze on debtors was enormous. Unemployment increased from the official rate of 5.9 per cent in 1990 to 8.3 per cent in 1991 and approximated 10 per cent in 1992.[21] Bankruptcies increased dramatically, per year, from 9,365 in 1989 to 35,940 in the first nine months of 1992. During the same period, company liquidations rose from 9,427 to 24,825. Manufacturing output contracted and the volume of retail sales declined dramatically. GDP dropped from 2.1 per cent in 1989 to -2.2 per cent in 1991 until it 'recovered' to -0.6 per cent in 1992. The PSBR which had shielded the pound in the late 1980s from sustained speculative pressure, moved from minus 14 per cent in 1988-89 to a staggering 36.5 per cent in 1992-3. At the same time, the amount of outstanding bank and building society lending increased year by year, reaching £622.8bn in 1992 compared with £504bn in 1989. House prices collapsed, leaving many with a mortgage which was much higher than the value of the property ('negative equity'). The number of repossessions reached staggering proportions: 75,540 properties were repossessed in 1991 and 68,540 in 1992, compared with 15,810 in 1989. This 'socialisation' of the debt problem was reinforced by an equally dramatic increase in mortgage payment-arrears: the number of mortgages in arrears (6-12 months) rose from 66,800 in 1989 to 205,010 in 1992. The property owning democracy collapsed under the threat of debt, eviction and homelessness - between 1979 and 1991 homelessness increased in England by 160.3 per cent, the number of households in bed and breakfast accommodation by 578.7 per cent and the number of households in hostels and women's refuges by 159.5 per cent. According to the *Independent* (19.7.93), around 150,000 young people were becoming homeless each year. The recession of the 1990s represented a dramatic shake out of labour. Yet, average wage increases declined only slowly during the early part of the recession from 9.5 per cent in January 1990 to 7.25 per cent in January 1992.[22]

It was against the background of this recession that many observers thought the entry rate of DM2.95 was too high. However, there is no doubt that the anti-inflationary discipline worked. As the recession deepened and consumer spending was capped, the rate of inflation declined from 9.5 per cent in 1990 to 3.7 per cent in 1992. The then chancellor, Norman Lamont was quite clear on this: 'Rising unemployment and business failures "were a price worth paying" for the defeat of inflation' (Smith, 1993, p. 188). Although hampered by bad debt problems, ever increasing balance of payment deficits and a rising PSBR, the pound was shielded against speculative pressure through high interest rates and fiscal tightness. Despite an increase in unemployment, public expenditure as a proportion of GDP was constrained and increased only slightly, remaining well below the levels of the early 1980s. The containment of public expenditure as a proportion of GDP was particularly impressive for the government against the background of a negative GDP.

The *sine qua non* of the pound's stability within the ERM was a reduction in unit labour costs and increased productivity. Failure to achieve this would have made it unlikely, as indeed was the case, for the pound to survive inside the ERM. The continued decline of the strength between money and exploitation made the devaluation of sterling look more and more likely during 1992 in spite of ERM membership. During the early 1990s the volume of activity on world currency markets expanded dramatically (Busch, 1994) as financial markets were looking for 'profitable' outlets outside the arena of productive investment where profits had fallen and bankruptcy spread. Indeed, there was a growing concern about a 'credit-crunch'. The level of lending decreased on a global scale (Harman, 1993). However, the availability of money was not in question. There was simply a lack of profitable opportunities to spend it (ibid., p. 44). Low levels of lending and a global shortage of capital occurred at the same time as companies required additional credit to maintain solvency. While credit was hard to come by, past debts became due. Further, the Deutschmark which had been the long-term guarantor of stability, was suddenly inflation-prone. As the costs of German unification rocketed, the Bundesbank sought to balance the fiscal expansionism of the federal government through a tight monetary policy, driving German interest rates up. The Deutschmark appreciated pushing its partner currencies to the lower end of the fluctuation margin. Money fled to Germany, putting pressure on the exchange rate of the pound and making it impossible to reduce interest rates in Britain at a time of deepening recession. The loss of stability in Germany meant that the exchange rate of the pound to the dollar increased, so putting an extra burden on dollar exports. Members of the ERM no longer benefited from the disciplinary effect of the German mark.

The loss of the Deutschmark as a guarantor of anti-inflationary stability made it harder for ERM countries to maintain exchange rate stability and to fend off speculative pressure. During the recession, governments became increasingly vulnerable to a sharp rise in interest rates, and public spending pressure increased as unemployment rose. High real interest rates, persistently slow economic growth, public spending pressure and loss of revenue intensified the fiscal crisis of the state. Budget deficits increased at the same time as the guarantee of global credit relations through central bank reserves and state revenue decreased in strength. As argued in chapter 3, the growth of global credit markets had been so dramatic during the previous decade that central banks could not hope to resist speculative attacks on a particular currency or currencies by exchange markets. As a consequence speculative policing of domestic attempts to safeguard currencies through deflationary control of social relations increased, reinforcing global pressure on expansionary policies through speculative runs, leading to a drain on the reserves. Against the background of both huge balance of payment deficits and budget deficits, as well as sluggish economic growth and a stumbling banking system, the pound became a target in financial markets. Even an increase of interest rates to 15 per cent on 16th September, 1992, credit-support by other European central banks, and the spending of billions of pounds to maintain the pound inside the ERM, could not rescue the pound. The policy of sacrificing social relations on the altar of deflation 'was thus shattered by Black Wednesday' (Wilks, 1993). The 'ERM-crisis' of September 1992 had its roots in the failure of successive postwar governments to increase the competitiveness of the British economy. In the short term this crisis was exacerbated by the serious conflict between Britain and Germany over macroeconomic interests (see Sinclair, 1994, p. 226). Exit from the ERM allowed a resolution of the short term conflict but could do little to address, what the government perceived to be, the underlying weaknesses of the British economy.

Future political commentaries on Major will no doubt draw attention to his role in attempting to end the 25 years of conflict in Northern Ireland which, by 1994, had claimed over 3,000 lives. Such commentaries are less likely to focus on the impact Major's economic policies had on recasting class relations in Britain. Despite the rhetoric of classless Britain, Major followed Thatcher in consolidating the relative impoverishment of the working class in the first four years of his premiership. As the following chapter demonstrates, people's experience of the Major government was profoundly disillusioning, and for the working class in particular, Major's Britain was synonymous with job insecurity, personal debt, pauperisation, and the intensification of work. The increase in unemployment and the risk of personal bankruptcy supported a dramatic squeeze on both private and public sector wage levels. According to CBI calculations, pay rises in the manufacturing sector between April and June 1993 were the lowest since the wage squeeze under Callaghan in the late 1970s (see German, 1993, p. 17). In the public sector, excluding managers and administrators, pay increases were very low and were held back by a public sector wage freeze at 1 - 1.5 per cent for 1993-95.

Kenneth Clarke made much of Britain's economic recovery. However, the government's own Department of Trade and Industry concluded with 'alarm', that 'urgent action' was necessary to tackle 'the continuing low level of labour productivity and the remaining deep rooted problems in areas such as investment, finance for industry, training and the rarity of strategic alliances between firms' (Department of Trade and Industry, 1994, p. 123). Although Major had been relatively successful in imposing financial discipline on the working class, his confrontational policies had failed to raise productivity to the levels of other EU states and thus to secure a more favourable foothold for Britain in the hierarchy of the price system. As the competitive deregulation dynamic in global finance, and liberalisation in production and trade, continued unabated, Major's attempt to construct a competitive advantage for Britain on the basis of low labour costs smacked of desperation. To the working class it was evident that Major's solution to crisis meant cheap labour, diminishing employment rights and the intensified imposition of work in the guise of a more 'efficient' competition state.

In the wake of Britain's exit from the ERM, Major's economic policy had three distinct, though interrelated, elements. Firstly, realising the benefits of depoliticisation, he attempted to continue the strategy albeit in a much weaker form by restructuring the relationship between the Treasury and the Bank of England. By gradually giving a much larger role to the Bank in the formulation and execution of monetary policy, Major sought to effect a permanent domestic depoliticisation of economic policy making. Secondly, after the crisis of the ERM, Major was forced to attempt to contain inflation by focusing on its 'domestic' conditions. In particular this meant a closer scrutiny of wage demands, except for top executives, and a further restructuring of the labour market. Finally, Major placed his faith in the benefits of the Social Chapter opt-out. As EU states followed a trend towards a shorter working week and

110

increased job sharing, European Commission statistics revealed that Britain in 1992 was the only member state where the length of the working week had increased over the decade since 1983 (CSO, 1995, p. 71; *Guardian*, 24.1.95).

In both economic and political terms, depoliticisation through the ERM had been extremely successful for the Conservative government. However the discipline of the ERM had now sunk without trace. For the rest of his premiership Major sought to build a more competitive economy on the basis of the low inflation that the ERM had delivered. As the following chapter demonstrates, labour market strategies and reforms in education, training and welfare, were at the forefront of Major's economic policy.

---

1 Unless otherwise stated, the statistics in this chapter are drawn from OECD (1994); CSO (1994); *Eurostatistics* (1994); and the United Nations (1994).

2 For a discussion of this issue, see Smith (1993).

3 For an extensive discussion of the historical nature of these constraints, see Hall (1986).

4 For a more general discussion of the relation between policy and ideology, see Burnham (1991).

5 See, for instance, Peter Norman in the *Financial Times*, 27.10.89, p. 25.

6 M. Thatcher, BBC World Service broadcast, May 1989, quoted in the *Financial Times*, 27.10.89.

7 Major's single-minded determination to lower inflation was emphasised in his first public speech as chancellor on the 27.10.89 in Northampton. He argued, 'the problem is inflation. I have no doubt that the central task before us is the reduction and elimination of rising prices.' For further elucidation of this point, see Jay (1994, pp. 200-4).

8 These are purchasing power parity estimates taken from Crafts (1994, p. 210). For a wider statistical analysis, see van Ark (1993).

9 For an analysis of the restructuring of the Civil Service as employer, see Fairbrother (1994).

10 Lawson (1992, pp. 499-501) notes that copies of *Britain's Economic Renaissance* were circulated in draft form to Thatcher prior to the

ministerial meeting of the 13th of November 1985 where Thatcher issued the ultimatum, 'if you join the EMS, you will have to do so without me'.

11 For an analysis of the concept of 'statecraft' and a study of statecraft under Thatcher, see Bulpitt (1986).

12 This situation was considered so serious that some commentators, for instance Anthony Harris, advocated bank nationalisation as a solution. See *Financial Times*, 19.10.92.

13 For the text of Lamont's speech, and commentary, see *Financial Times*, 27.5.92.

14 For an overview of the Italian events, see Smith (1993, pp. 239-43).

15 See Busch (1994a) and Alesina (1988) for a critical discussion of how an independent central bank would, in theory, reduce the general inflationary tendency which results from 'political manipulation' of monetary policy.

16 After the collapse of the Bretton Woods system in the early 1970s, a so-called 'dirty floating' regime emerged wherein central banks intervened in the foreign exchange market but without a fixed rate to defend. For details, see Tomlinson (1990, p. 314).

17 For details of the Christian Democrat document *Reflections on European Policy*, see *The European*, 2-8.9.94.

18 See Keynes (1981).

19 Also see, C. H. Feinstein (1972, table 65) for an analysis of the movement of average wage earnings and retail prices.

20 This section draws on Grahl (1990).

21 For a comparison of the rate of unemployment with the UK's main competitors, see McKie (1993, p. 49).

22 The data in this section is drawn from McKie (1993), and Smith (1993).

5 A Major Agenda: Labour Market, Welfare and the Local State

This chapter explores the impact of government policies under John Major's leadership in the areas of labour market, welfare and central/local government relations. In chapter 2 we outlined our theoretical approach to analysing British politics in the 1990s before locating the experience of Major's government in the context of the crisis of Keynesianism and monetarism (Ch. 3). We moved from our theoretical discussions to chart the political economy of the recession in the 1990s, looking specifically at the crucial role of Britain's membership and later withdrawal from the ERM. Being forced to leave the ERM when pressure on the pound could no longer be contained, the government had no alternative but to intensify its domestic policies with the aim of keeping inflationary demands low, decreasing wage costs and increasing productivity. The erosion of collective rights and rejection of 'corporatist' relations have gone hand-in-hand with a growing emphasis on individualism, most directly exemplified by John Major's 'big' idea of the Citizen's Charter, and the exclusion of the trade union movement from the policy arena. Commenting on domestic policies such as the Citizen's Charter and the push towards greater managerialism in the public and the private sectors, Atkinson and Cope (1994, p. 51) conclude that, 'in this area,

Major may have been more radical than his predecessor, pushing neo-liberal reforms further than she was willing or placed to so'.

With the replacement of Margaret Thatcher as leader of the Conservative Party in 1990 by the more 'caring' John Major, it had been anticipated by some that the more confrontational, divisive and 'ideological' aspects of government policy would also change. For example, Andrew Gamble (1991, p. 15) was of the view that 'under Major ideology can be expected to play a much smaller part in the Conservative Party.' In rhetoric at least, John Major appeared to offer a more conciliatory and less confrontational approach, and reformed some of the more unpopular aspects of policy under Thatcher, most notably the highly contentious poll tax. However, the 'consensus' option was closed to him especially after Britain's departure from the ERM. Instead the government has strengthened its resolve to compete in the global price hierarchy on the basis of a low wage, deregulated and flexible labour market, explicitly rejecting labour market policies associated with the social contract aspects of the EU. The pursuit of greater productivity, lower wages and reduced government spending has resulted in further labour market and welfare benefit reforms, which in turn have exacerbated social conflict and division.

In this chapter we discuss the experience of labour market restructuring, reforms of the welfare system and changing local/central government relations, and the inter-relationship with other policy areas including privatisation, the 'agencification' of the civil service, the changing role of government as provider of services, the drive towards greater 'managerialism', and the emphasis on 'individualism' and the Citizen's Charter. Further we explore the relationship of these policies to law and order issues as well as discussing the consequences of policy with respect to increasing levels of personal debt. These policies are not exhaustive but are key to understanding the government's attempt to improve its position in the global price hierarchy, to depoliticise its domestic policy and to reshape the relationship between the state and the civil society. The language of agencification, consumer choice and citizens' rights has been used to defend and legitimise labour market and welfare reforms and the restructuring of local government. These reforms are concerned with reducing public expenditure as a proportion of GDP, providing incentives to work and streamlining the delivery of services. Our main focus is on policy under the premierships of John Major, but the roots of these policies are to be found in the Conservative administrations of the 1980s.

Labour market policies

The labour market policies pursued by the Major governments in the 1990s have to be viewed within a framework of reforms initiated under the Thatcher administrations in the 1980s. While the 1974-79 Labour administration made a last ditch attempt at accommodation with the trade unions, particularly in the area of social policy, this approach was rejected by the new Conservative administration under the leadership of Margaret Thatcher. As we have argued in chapter 3, since 1975 the priority of governments was to defeat inflation and to create the right conditions for private sector business and investment. Since 1979 an extensive array of supply-side changes have been implemented in respect of taxation, benefits and labour market reforms in conjunction with a programme of deregulation and privatisation. In the early days of the first Thatcher government, strengthening the supply-side of the economy was deemed to require an increase in incentives to work through reducing direct taxation, the value of unemployment benefits and trade union powers (Brown, 1988; Gamble, 1994; Rowthorn, 1992). The contradictory nature of arguing that some sections of society would have a greater incentive to work if their taxation levels were reduced and their income increased, while others would have a greater incentive to work if their benefits or wages were lowered and their rights at work reduced, did not appear to trouble government ministers in defending their strategy.

The Thatcher government's pursuit of monetary targets and reductions in public expenditure in the early 1980s was felt in terms of dramatic rises in unemployment. By 1985, and after the criticism of some government ministers over the 'unacceptable' level of unemployment, the government published a White Paper on Employment (Department of Employment, 1985).[1] Direct contrast can be drawn with the famous White Paper on Employment published in 1944 which, a number of commentators argue, helped form part of the so-called postwar social democratic consensus (Addison, 1977; Kavanagh, 1990). In the 1985 version, it was asserted that governments could not be held responsible for the level of employment or unemployment: 'the key contribution of government in a free society is to do all it can to create a climate in which enterprise can flourish, above all by removing obstacles to the working of markets, especially the labour market' (Department of Employment, 1985). It was argued that unemployment is not caused by lack of demand, lack of public sector investment or technological change, but rather by deficiencies in the labour market: 'the biggest single cause of our high unemployment is the failure of our jobs market, the weak link in our economy' (ibid.). In order to improve the functioning and efficiency of the labour market, the government proposed supply-side reforms under four categories - quality; cost and incentives; flexibility; and freedom. These objectives can be translated into the policies directed at improving quality and skills through education and training reforms; reducing costs to employers and increasing incentives to work through downward pressure on wages, benefits and taxation; increasing flexibility [2] by passing legislation designed to remove the perceived obstacles to change placed by the trade union movement; and enhancing freedom in the labour market and employers' room for manoeuvre through policies of deregulation, contracting-out, privatisation and the removal of wage and employment protection for workers. Brown (1988) illustrates the way in which these different policies were combined in an attempt to reduce the control exercised by organised labour over a whole range of areas including the apprenticeship system, collective bargaining, industrial action, tripartite organisations and public sector employment.[3]

In the 1980s government ministers continued the trend set in the 1960s which identified the trade union movement and the industrial relations system as the cause of Britain's poor economic performance. They capitalised on opinion polls which recorded the unpopularity of trade unions and the disciplining force of mass unemployment to justify and pursue many of their labour market reforms. However, with the return to recession in the 1990s, and having claimed success in 'defeating the unions' during the 1980s (Lawson, 1992), this explanation for Britain's economic failure had lost its credibility. Also, it was clear that public opinion towards the trade unions has shifted. In 1979 over 80 per cent of people polled thought that the trade unions in Britain were too powerful. By 1987 this percentage had dropped dramatically to just under 40 per cent (Crewe, 1990; Monks, 1994). It had been anticipated that John Major, as the new prime minister, would take a different and less confrontational approach to trade union reform. Any such expectations could not be sustained, however, following the publication of the 1991 Green Paper, *Industrial Relations in the 1990s*, the 1992 White Paper, *People Jobs and Opportunity*, and the subsequent trade union legislation of 1992 and 1993. The 1992 White Paper made it clear that the government continued to reject 'collectivist' solutions and had no intention of allowing unions a political role. Rather labour market policies of the 1980s were applauded and the government claimed success for making business more efficient and productive, for helping enterprise to flourish, and in giving individuals at work greater opportunities and choice. Emphasis was placed 'on the role and importance of the individual employee in business performance [as] individual achievement and national prosperity go hand in hand' (Department of Employment, 1992, pp. 5-6). The White Paper set out the government's plans for further changes to the law, incentives to individuals, and action to encourage 'progress' in the 1990s. The document reaffirmed the government's rejection of the approach taken by the EC noting its preference for a 'lightly regulated, decentralised and flexible approach to employment and labour market issues' which it contrasted with the 'centralist and regulated model based on single solutions and uniformity' being pursued, at least in theory, by other European states (ibid., p. 71).

By examining the different aspects of policy which influence the operation of the labour market - legislation; wages, benefits and taxation; education and training; and privatisation and deregulation - it is possible to illustrate the way in which the Major government intensified its attempt to discipline and reduce the power of organised labour and restructure social relations. Common themes in the government's approach include the attempt to restrict the role played by trade unions in the workplace, intensify the work process, keep downward pressure on wages, discourage trade union recognition, decentralise wage bargaining, deregulate the labour market, promote individualism at the expense of collective rights, and to extend the policies of 'agencification' of the civil service, 'marketisation' of training, and 'managerialism' in the workplace. In its capacity as a major employer, the state has been able to have direct influence over such policies in the public sector at least (Fairbrother, 1994).

Trade union legislation

Given the adherence to the 'voluntarist principle' in Britain and the accepted orthodoxy in the 1970s that industrial relations could not be changed through legislative means, the extent of the state's legal intervention in the 1980s and 1990s is perhaps surprising. The incoming Conservative government in 1979 made no secret of its view that they considered the trade union movement to be a major obstacle to labour market flexibility and industrial renewal. The stated aim of the 1979 manifesto and subsequent manifestos has been to change the balance of power away from 'irresponsible' trade unions and back towards management. The Thatcher governments implemented no less than five pieces of trade union legislation - the Employment Acts 1980 and 1982, the Trade Union Act 1984, and the Employment Acts of 1988 and 1990. The key features of these Acts are summarised by Dorey (1991) and Marsh (1991, 1992). The legislation covered most of the criticisms which had been levelled at trade unions in relation to picketing, industrial action, union democracy, and secret strike ballots of members. The legislation sought to abolish the closed shop, and undermine the payment of the political levy to the Labour Party. In removing certain employment rights from individuals the legislation gave individual union members the right to claim compensation if they refused to join a trade union, made it unlawful to dismiss an employee for refusing to join a trade union, even where 80 per cent of the workforce had voted for a closed shop, made it unlawful to take disciplinary action against any member who refused to participate in legal strike action, and made it unlawful for an employer to refuse employment to job applicants on the grounds that they did not belong to a trade union. Most importantly the labour legislation subjected the trade unions to financial penalties should they be found in breach of the law. This legislation made it possible for trade union funds to be open to sequestration. As indicated by Smith and Morton (1993, p. 100), the 1980s legislation denied 'workers access to resources of collective power, thereby commensurately increasing employers' discretion to determine the terms of the employment relationship both within and outside collective bargaining.' Although the authors capture significant aspects of Thatcher's industrial relations policies, it is important to be aware that the legislation had effects which were sometimes contrary to the government's expectations (Elger, 1994). For example, the 1984 Act required unions to hold ballots before taking strike action. More than 90 per cent of ballots supported industrial action. This 'success' was often used by unions to strengthen their bargaining and negotiations with employers as an alternative to the use of strikes themselves. This point is made in the Advisory Conciliation and Arbitration Service's (ACAS) 1986 Annual Report: 'it seems clear that on a number of occasions ballots have been used by trade unions to demonstrate the strength of feeling among their members in ways which some managements have found difficult to counter' (quoted in Marsh, 1992, pp. 201-2).

The Conservative governments of the 1980s also made it clear that they did not intend to include trade union leaders in discussions over pay or other issues, rejecting the politics of inclusion. The politics of monetarism were to operate on the basis of exclusion. The consent of trade unions to proposed changes was not sought. Instead the market was to discipline relations between employees and employers, and corporatist relations were rejected in favour of a dualist approach to state management of labour relations (Brown and King, 1988; Goldthorpe, 1984). The restructuring of the economy away from heavy, traditional industry which was male dominated and highly unionised towards an expanding service sector which was female dominated and non-unionised, took place within the context of a general attack on collective rights and traditional forms of trade unionism (Evans, Ewing and Nolan, 1992).

The Thatcher governments adopted an incremental approach to reform. Against the background of mass unemployment and several confrontations with the organised labour movement, especially in the early 1980s, the law was used to consolidate a shift in the balance of class forces. As the 1980s wore on, trade union membership levels fell as did the incidence of strike action. In 1979 13,289 million people were members of trade unions, a density rate of 54.1 per cent. By 1988 the membership had reduced to 10,238 million, a density rate of 44.1 per cent (Bird, 1990). The number of reported stoppages of work in 1979 was 2,125, but by 1989 it had been reduced to 701 (Bird, 1990a). However, looked at in isolation, these bald statistics are misleading. In spite of the rise in low paid jobs, real wages increased in the UK on average by 28 per cent between 1979 and 1988, an increase that outstripped real wage increases in competitor countries (*Financial Times*, 14.10.89). This trend implied, as indeed the *Financial Times* suggested, that

119

'Thatcherism' had not defeated the trade unions. Not only was there little evidence that employers in manufacturing industry made extensive use of the new powers given to them by law, there was also a 'bargain' between trade unions and employers in that productivity deals and intensification of work were compensated for by increased wages. Such developments prompted Hyman (1989, p. 192) to observe that, 'as the dust settles after the initial experience of Thatcherism, what is perhaps most striking is the persistence rather than the eclipse of established industrial relations institutions.'

It can be argued that the sustained rise in real wages and the role still played by organised labour help to explain why there was no slackening of the policy towards trade unions and industrial relations reform after John Major became leader of the Conservative Party. In July 1991 Michael Howard, as Employment Secretary, published proposals for further reform of trade unions in the Green Paper, *Industrial Relations in the 1990s*, followed by the 1992 White Paper, *People, Jobs and Opportunity*. Reviewing these government papers, Smith and Morton (1994, p. 4) note that, 'both documents embody an individualist ethos which was utilised to justify further measures to restrict and regulate unions.' On re-election, Major's government pressed forward with its legislative proposals, resulting in the Trade Union and Labour Relations (Consolidation) Act (TULRA) 1992 and the Trade Union Reform and Employment Rights Act (TURERA) 1993, a move described by Painter and Puttick (1993, p. 3) as 'more of the same.' Smith and Morton (1994, p. 3) argue that the government has intensified its commitment to union exclusion policies stating that

> we can no longer talk of Thatcherism as if the policy of the Conservative government during the 1980s were intrinsically identified with the personality of the former Prime Minister. Analysis of this policy's origins must be situated within the objective contemporary imperatives of competitive accumulation and the Conservative government's appropriation of "free market" assumptions and theories as to the operation of a capitalist economy and society.

Many of the provisions of the 1980s legislation are incorporated into TULRA 1992 and have been extended under the TURERA 1993. The new legislation seeks to remedy some of the anomalies and inconsistencies in the 1980s legislation, but also represents a strengthening of policy under Major with the inclusion of components which the Thatcher governments held back from enacting, for example the balloting of members in their own homes and making shop stewards legally responsible for unlawful strike action. Links are also made with other aspects of policy such as the Citizen's Charter with the inclusion of new rights for citizens to claim damages against unions for any costs incurred during a strike. In other words, the language of citizenship and consumer rights was used to disguise the attack on the ability of trade unions to provide collective protection for their members.

The provisions of the 1993 Act place further restrictions on the ability of trade unions to call strikes. The Act establishes a legal right to individuals to join a trade union of their choice where more than one union exists, thus challenging the Bridlington rules (ACAS, 1980) which regulated inter union rivalry. As another way of undermining the membership levels of trade unions, the Act stipulates that individual workers are required to consent to deduction of their union subscription from their pay by their employer. The worker's agreement to the 'check-off' system has to be given every three years. Extended powers have been given to the certification officer to make investigations into a trade union's internal affairs, and customers of public services now have the legal means to restrain unlawful strike action in certain circumstances. The Act fell short of accepting all of the proposals in Howard's 1991 Green Paper, for example it did not include provisions for legally enforceable collective agreements (Taylor, 1994). However, it included provisions for the abolition of Wages Councils, a process which had begun earlier in the 1980s (Brown, 1988a).

The 1990s labour legislation which aimed at curbing collective power, went hand-in-hand with other attempts to restructure the state's relations with organised labour, for example the abolition of the tripartite National Economic Development Council (NEDC) in December 1992. Significantly, the 1993 Act also revised the original terms of reference of another tripartite organisation, ACAS, by removing the clause in their remit which relates to 'encouraging the extension of collective bargaining'. At the end of 1992 the government announced that state funding for trade union postal ballots and trade union training and health and safety at work courses were to be phased out within four years, and John Major refused to end the ban on trade unionism at GCHQ (Taylor, 1994). The appointment of the new general secretary of the TUC, John Monks, in September 1993 did result in an invitation to the then Employment Secretary, David Hunt, and Stephen Dorrell, to speak at TUC events. However, David Hunt made it clear that this development did not herald a return to what he described as the 'discredited corporatism' of the 1970s (McKie, 1994). This sentiment was reinforced by John Major's decision to appoint Michael Portillo to the Ministry for Employment in the Cabinet re-shuffle of 1994, which did not signal a more conciliatory approach to the relationship with trade unions.

The impact of industrial relations legislation has attracted conflicting interpretations and has to be analysed in conjunction with other labour market changes.[4] Without doubt certain trends have continued in the 1990s with respect to the reduction in trade union membership levels and the number of strikes. The costs imposed on trade unions are so punitive that alternatives to strike action are normally sought. In the context of high unemployment and job insecurity, workers, especially those who have been encouraged to buy their own homes, are particularly reluctant to risk the loss of their jobs by taking industrial action. Although statistics demonstrate a reduction in official strikes, resistance has found other forms of expression. Increasing stress levels have resulted from the restructuring of work and pressures to increase productivity, and as a result the level of absenteeism has increased sharply. Recent calculations illustrate that 80 million days are lost every year in Britain through stress related illnesses, which costs British industry an annual figure of £3.7 billion.[5] In 1993 the CBI reported that absenteeism was 'one of the biggest blights on UK business', in its calculation costing employers around £13 billion every year. It is estimated that absence rates are currently running between 4 and 5 per cent. Employers are looking for ways to reduce the level of absenteeism and its associated costs, particularly as from 1994 most large UK employers are responsible for meeting the full burden of sick pay (*Financial Times*, 28.3.94).

Wages and benefits

From the election of the first Thatcher government in 1979, the Conservative Party has pursued a policy of making wages more responsive to market conditions and reforming the benefits and taxation system. The intention to improve the labour market through altering wage costs and incentives to work is very clearly stated in the government's 1985 White Paper which outlines the policy to ensure 'that people are neither prevented from pricing themselves into jobs nor deterred from taking them up' (Department of Employment, 1985). The 'rewards and incentives for individuals' at work theme is developed in the 1992 White Paper (Department of Employment, 1992). The government cites the decline in the number of people whose pay is now determined by national collective agreements, the move away from collective bargaining, the shift towards decentralisation of pay determination, the adoption of new forms of performance related pay and other payment incentives, and a widening in pay to reflect skill differentials as evidence of positive developments in the 1980s. The 1992 White Paper sets out the government's plans for the 1990s to advance these trends, to continue to oppose any proposal for a national minimum wage, and to give priority to setting an example on pay flexibility in its capacity as an employer through changes in civil service pay determination and the role of Pay Review Bodies.

In rhetoric, at least, the Major government continues to oppose legislative intervention in pay determination. The 1979 Conservative government had specifically rejected the imposition of a formal incomes policy, arguing that such devices were part of the bankrupt policies of the postwar period. Nevertheless, during the 1980s and now in the 1990s, Conservative governments have operated an indirect incomes policy in the public sector through the setting of cash limits on government departments and local authorities, reducing public expenditure and recommending the rate at which wages should grow in any one year. McKie (1994, p. 69) notes that the Chancellor, Kenneth Clarke, confirmed in his November 1993 Budget that the norm in the public sector was effectively nil, and that he intended that the freeze on wages should last for three years. Also the ability of Pay Review Bodies to award pay rises was restricted by ensuring that no new money would be available. The Major administration has continued to articulate the party's opposition to the concept of an annual pay round, to national bargaining and to comparability and job evaluation exercises in the public sector, and is promoting a system under which wage levels should be based primarily on performance, merit, profitability, and demand and supply in local labour markets. The government's approach to wage claims in the public sector was tested in the 1994 rail dispute when Ministers intervened in an attempt to prevent Railtrack settling at a figure above what was acceptable to the government.

The Major government's view on the relationship between wage levels and employment can be illustrated most directly in its decision to abolish the remaining Wages Councils in 1993, in spite of strong opposition from a broad spectrum of opinion including many employers. When the government first made the case for abolition in a consultative document issued in 1985, it was on the grounds that such bodies contributed to labour market inefficiency and inflexibility and were one of the causes of unemployment, particularly youth unemployment. This view was supported by a study carried out by the Department of Employment's own Market Research Unit which concluded that 'increasing real labour costs, of which minimum wages and non-wage costs are an important part, have acted to decrease employment over the period 1950-70 for both males and females' (quoted in Brown, 1988a, p. 71). Ignoring evidence from respondents to the consultative paper, who put forward a contrary view, the government nevertheless reduced the scope of Wages Councils and their coverage under the 1986 Wages Act. Therefore, under Thatcher, Wages Councils were not totally abolished. The decision to proceed with abolition in 1993 symbolised the Major government's approach to labour market restructuring.

The consequences of the government's approach to wage determination are reflected in the rise of low pay in Britain. The abolition of the Wages Councils is likely to exacerbate this trend. Just three months after abolition in 1993, a survey conducted by the Low Pay Network found that a fifth of Jobcentre vacancies in former Wages Council jobs were paying below the previous Wages Council rate (Cox, 1994). At the other end of the scale, the wage levels of top earners have increased substantially. The earnings of top directors in the privatised water, gas and electricity companies is reported to have risen by 52.3 per cent over 1993, and in June 1994 the Guardian Index of top executive pay recorded average increases of almost 25 per cent over the year (McKie, 1994, p. 69). Other studies confirm the disparity in pay awards. One survey carried out by Hay Management Consultants in November 1994 showed that directors of UK-listed companies have received larger pay rises than their counterparts in foreign-owned companies (*Financial Times*, 16.11.94).

The gap between the lowest and highest paid workers in Britain has grown significantly. According to Glyn (1992, p. 81) aggregate real wage incomes fell during the 1980s by 5 per cent. 'Those workers who kept their jobs, however, saw a substantive (28%) increase in their real wages'. The Report of the Commission on Social Justice (1994) records that the gap between the earnings of the highest-paid and those of the lowest-paid workers is now greater than any time since records were first kept in 1886; that the pay of company directors continued to rise even as profits fell after 1988, and that despite the recession the very highest-paid people in London and the South-East increased their earnings by an average of £22,000 a year between 1989 and 1991, while the bottom 50 per cent of earners took an average pay cut of more than £200 a year; and that by any measure poverty has risen rapidly since 1979, affecting in particular families with children (ibid., pp. 28-31).[6]

Linked to the downward pressure on wage rates, is the reduction in the real value of welfare benefits. The government's willingness to allow freedom to employers to offer low wages, does of course put an additional cost on the benefits system, and operates as a subsidy for some employers and an indirect tax on taxpayers. Given the government's contention that some unemployment is due to people choosing not to work on the grounds that they are better off claiming benefit, a key element of the government's strategy has been to reduce this so-called 'voluntary unemployment' by reducing the real value of unemployment benefits. Thus although overall government spending in this area may have increased because of rising unemployment, the relative value of benefits paid to individual claimants has decreased (McGlone, 1990; Rowthorn, 1992). Throughout the Thatcher administrations, the conditions for entitlement to benefit were tightened, including the exclusion of married women from claiming most benefits, thereby removing them from the official unemployment statistics. Those claiming benefit have been subject to increasing scrutiny and harassment, and their availability for work questioned. Increasing the incentive to work through benefit changes and other reforms is still central to the Major government's approach and there are no signs of this policy being slackened in spite of rising unemployment in the early 1990s.

The number of people claiming benefit rose as the official

unemployment rate increased from 5.9 per cent in 1990 to 10.3 per cent in 1993. The attack on one particular group of claimants, young unmarried mothers, in 1994, added a distasteful element to the debate. Controversy surrounded the claims that many young women were deliberately becoming pregnant so that they no longer had to live with their parents, but instead could be housed, clothed and fed by the state (McRobbie, 1994). This view was reinforced by research produced by such bodies as the Institute of Economic Affairs, which correlated rising levels of crime with single parenthood (Dennis, 1993; Dennis and Erdos, 1993). In response to the moral panic concerning the growing numbers of single mothers, the government considered proposals for encouraging them back to work and decided on a modest scheme, announced by the Social Security Secretary, Peter Lilley, just before the 1994 party conference. The 'childcare disregard' scheme will allow single mothers to earn an extra £40 a week towards the cost of childcare before their social security benefits are cut. Children have to be placed with registered child minders, nurseries or other approved places for which receipts of payment must be produced. Where such places are to be found for £40 per week is a question left unanswered by the Minister.[7]

In October 1994 plans for a new Job Seeker's Allowance were announced by Peter Lilley to replace the combination of unemployment benefit and income support for the unemployed. The allowance is to be means tested after six months. 'Helping the job seeker and motivating the job shy' are the declared objectives behind this policy initiative on the grounds that 'these proposals will help Britain generate even more jobs. They will help unemployed people find work, they will strengthen Britain's economy and give better value for taxpayers' money' (*The Scotsman*, 25.10.94). Against the background of mass unemployment, the attempt to force people into low paid jobs is indicative of the government's approach of securing integration into the world market through low wages and deteriorating working conditions.

In his 1994 Budget, the Chancellor, Kenneth Clarke, announced further benefit changes and measures to tackle long-term unemployment with the aim of reducing the costs to employers and creating incentives for the unemployed to accept work. From April 1995, the government intends to cut the lower rates of employers' national insurance contributions for every employee, and from April 1996, employers who give work to someone who has been unemployed for two years will receive a full national insurance rebate for up to one year. New pilot schemes under the 'Workstart' programme which provides a grant to employers to recruit people who have been unemployed for over two years are to be developed, and the 'Work Trials Scheme' which allows unemployed people to try out a new job for three weeks is to be expanded. To encourage the unemployed back to work, the chancellor intends to continue the 'Community Action' scheme for the long-term unemployed, and to extend the concept of 'Restart', which requires people who are on benefit to attend an interview, to young unemployed people under similar schemes called 'Workwise' and '1-2-1'. Further measures are proposed in the form of payments of family credit and housing benefit, assistance with rent and council tax, and provision of a jobfinder's grant to encourage the unemployed to move from dependency on benefit to low paid work. In making these proposals the chancellor acknowledged that 'unemployment remains far too high' and that 'demand expansion on its own is not enough to produce a sufficient fall in unemployment' (*The Times*, 30.11.94). Since the early 1980s, it can be argued that the government's approach has had more to do with disciplining the unemployed and forcing them to take jobs at any price, rather than with the creation of new jobs (Benn and Fairley, 1986; Finn, 1987; Mizen 1994, 1995).

If ostensibly high levels of unemployment benefit were said to be acting as a disincentive to work, so too, the government contended, were high levels of taxation. As we have shown in chapter 4, the Major administration continued to shift the tax burden away from direct to indirect taxation, that is from taxes on earnings to taxes on spending, with the result that the general tax burden for the majority of families in Britain has increased. Further, the growth of additional jobs which were supposed to flow from the government's reduction of income tax and greater incentives for some taxpayers has not materialised. Nevertheless, the rhetoric of tax reduction remains, with John Major stating in his New Year message to the country in 1994 that, 'the Conservative party remains the party of the lowest possible tax, the party of low income tax and the only party whose instinct is to cut tax and leave money with individuals and families and not take it for the state' (quoted in McKie, 1994, p. 39).

The Thatcher government claimed Britain's labour market suffered from the low quality and inadequate skills of its labour force. This perceived problem was to be tackled through education and training reforms. The government criticised standards in education and claimed that the education system was failing to provide the skills which young people require to compete in the labour market and thus failing to meet the needs of the economy (McVicar and Robins, 1994; Scott, 1994). Previous governments were also criticised for sacrificing high attainment in their search for equality, as were teachers for emphasising the more liberal aspects of education, adopting new teaching methods and devaluing teaching of the 'three Rs', and for not giving sufficient attention to the views of parents. The government sought to gain working-class support for its proposed education reforms on the grounds that the current system was academically elitist and did not value other, more vocationally orientated, skills.

What followed during the years of the Thatcher governments were a number of radical reforms directed at introducing a new 'vocationalism' into education including the introduction of the 16+ Action Plan in Scotland, the Technical and Vocational Education Initiative, the establishment of City Technology Colleges for Science and Technology subjects, the proliferation of national vocational qualifications (NVQs, GNVQs, SVQs and GSVQs) and the introduction of a national curriculum for schools in England and Wales. The government ran into major controversies with the establishment of school boards in England and Wales, their attempts to introduce school testing and examination league tables, the closure of small schools in England, the proposed privatisation of the schools inspectorate, and their policies to encourage schools to opt-out of local authority control. They encountered particular difficulty in this regard in Scotland, where testing was rejected by both parents and teachers, and where only one school in the whole of Scotland made the decision to opt-out of local authority control (Brown, Breitenbach and Myers, 1994). Linked to education reforms have been policies targeted at changing the remuneration and working conditions and rights of teachers (*Guardian*, 7.2.95).

Schools were not alone in being subject to criticism and radical change, as further and higher education institutions have experienced similar pressures. Reductions in resources, increases in student numbers, staff appraisal, attempts to remove tenure and other pressures to make the college and university systems more relevant to perceived market needs continued throughout the Thatcher years (McVicar and Robins, 1994). Thus, administrations since 1979 restructured the educational system both north and south of the border, although their attempts in Scotland have been thwarted by the strength of the educational community operating within a different education system and the opposition of a large majority of voters and parents.

It was anticipated that the Major administration would avoid the more controversial aspects of educational reform. However, trends started in the 1980s have continued unabated. In his role as the Secretary of State for Education, Kenneth Clarke, put forward proposals in 1991 to remove further education colleges from local authority control, a move which Scott (1994, p. 338) describes as 'a continuation of the Thatcherite prejudice against local government'. He also announced plans to allow polytechnics to become universities with degree awarding powers, thus ending the binary distinction between the two sets of institutions. Following the 1992 General Election, Kenneth Clarke's successor, John Patten, introduced further measures to cajole more schools to opt-out of local authority control under the provisions of the Education Act 1993 for England and Wales. His next move was to publish yet another Education Bill 'aimed at traditional Tory targets - student unions and teacher training' (ibid., p. 346).[8]

The government has, however, been forced to make some concessions to its proposals in response to criticism from parents and the concerted opposition of teachers and their trade unions. Modifications to the national curriculum (England and Wales) and testing were announced in 1993. Patten also 'accepted his critics' case that league tables of school performance based on raw figures did not tell the whole story' (McKie, 1994, p. 90). Furthermore, he had to abandon the proposal for a 'mum's army' to supplement staff in primary schools and had to water down his plans to give students the right to opt-out of student unions. In addition, in spite of the government's incentives to schools to opt-out of local authority control, the numbers deciding to do so did not reach the minister's predictions (ibid.).

The government has not been entirely successful in meeting

its objectives for post-school education. Far from making an elitist system more open to a wider range of students, spending cuts and reduction in the value of grants and other social benefits, have made the attainment of a further or higher education qualification more difficult for many students. The expansion of places in further and higher education can be interpreted as an indirect way of reducing pressure on unemployment figures, particularly as dependency on parents is now deemed, as far as grants and benefits are concerned, to continue until 25 years of age. For those students already in education, the government's policy has trapped them in debt. During the 1980s, their financial resources declined while costs central to their education, such as books, have risen. By the late 1980s, students were denied access to housing benefit and were expected to meet additional costs such as the poll tax. Since October 1990 the student grant has been frozen and a complementary 'loan system' instituted (McVicar and Robins, 1994). From the time it was set up, the company charged with providing student loans has loaned £700 million plus (*Guardian*, 2.8.94). By 1993-94, 20 per cent of students were reported to have considered abandoning their studies because of financial hardship. Debts amounting to several thousand pounds are common. This situation is likely to deteriorate further following the decision to cut maintenance grants by 10 per cent a year for the next three years, with effect from September 1994 (*Observer*, 21.8.94). The costs of sustaining a university education for young students are especially painful for working-class parents lacking the means of supplementing grants, and for middle-class families whose earnings are just too high for their children to qualify for a student grant and who are, at the same time, trapped with mortgage debt which they find difficult to service.

Linked to the many educational reforms and the new vocationalism in schools, are changes to the training system in Britain. Initially the incoming Thatcher government in 1979 had no immediate plans to involve itself in training programmes. The government had argued that training is the responsibility of individual employers and it did not anticipate the need to increase public spending in this area. But employers in Britain have a longstanding record for their unwillingness to train and they compare unfavourably in this regard with many of Britain's industrial competitors (Anderson and Fairley, 1983; Department of Trade and Industry, 1994). The government's approach changed quite dramatically in response to rapid increases in youth unemployment, to the inner city riots of 1981 and to rising crime rates, when it committed resources in excess of £1b per year to training and introduced the Youth Training Scheme in 1983 (Benn and Fairley, 1986; Finn 1987). However, the way in which the scheme was introduced and the conditions under which it operated reinforced other aspects of the government's labour market policy, namely downward pressure on wage rates, changing expectations about wage rises, breaking the traditional links with the trade union movement and the apprenticeship system, abolishing the tripartite Industrial Training Boards, and reducing the role of local authority education input in favour of private sector provision. The scheme was managed by the Manpower Services Commission (MSC), a quango which was set up in the early 1970s and which was to find its influence enhanced considerably in the 1980s. The MSC was subsequently replaced by the Training Agency before responsibility for training was transferred to the Department of Employment in England and Wales and Scottish Enterprise and Highlands and Islands Enterprise in Scotland (Brown and Fairley, 1989).

During the 1980s the number of special training programmes expanded, both for young people and unemployed adults, and there was an expectation that the government was moving increasingly towards the 'Workfare' system practiced in a number of states in the United States, where welfare payments are made dependent on the participation of claimants on training schemes. John Major voiced his own attraction to the idea of 'Workfare' in a speech given in 1993 when he stated: 'Increasingly, I wonder whether paying unemployment benefit, without offering or requiring any activity in return, serves unemployed people or society well' (Atkinson and Savage, 1994, p. 13). The government guaranteed a YTS place for all 16-18 year olds and withdrew their right to benefit if they refused to participate on the scheme. Participants have often been forced to take training schemes which provided little, if any, training and which exploited the labour of young workers. Those who do not comply become dependent on their parents for financial support. Young people without a family, or where family relationships have broken down, have no source of income if they are unable to find employment. The dilemma facing young people in this situation is, 'if you don't have a job, you can't get a house', but 'if you don't have an address, you can't get a job'. Thus a vicious circle has emerged where many young people have been forced to sleep and survive on the streets.

The Major government proceeded with the transfer of responsibility for training to the employer led Training and Enterprise Councils (TECs) in England and Wales and the Local Enterprise Councils (LECs) in Scotland, and set out its priorities for training and vocational education in the White Papers, *Education and Training for the 21st Century* (Department of Employment, 1991) and *Access and Opportunity: A Strategy for Education and Training* (Department of Employment, 1991a). The trend towards increasing the influence of local employers and private provision of training, and decentralising training budgets has continued under Major's government. Farnham and Lupton (1994) comment on the dominance of employers in the design of programmes and the tailoring of work placements to meet their needs as resulting in the subjugation of the scope and content of training to the operation of market forces. Peck (1991) refers to this development as the 'enforced marketisation' of training.

The TECs and LECs have been subject to much criticism in relation to their use of funds and the quality of training, but also as part of wider criticism of the enhanced role given to unelected and unaccountable quangos. The 1992 White Paper, *People Jobs and Opportunity*, gave an indication of Major's approach to 'marketisation' through such proposals as the introduction of training credits to 'place in the hands of young people the power to purchase the training they want from the provider of their choice', and tax relief for individual investment in skills and career development loans 'to help individual people pay for their own training' (Department of Employment, 1992, p. 25-6). A new initiative on training, announced by the former Employment Minister, David Hunt, in 1994 was the introduction of a modest apprenticeship scheme for young workers. This initiative is ironic given that it was the Conservative government who dismantled the traditional apprenticeship schemes in Britain in the 1980s. It is a tacit admission that the YTS has been less than successful in providing the skilled young workforce which industry needs.[9]

The Major government's rhetoric on improving skills has not been matched by a willingness to direct resources to a sustained programme of improving the quality of training in Britain. In 1983-84 the government was spending £4.3 billion in real terms on employment and training schemes, and it is estimated that the figure will be reduced to £3.5 billion for the year 1993-94. This spending amounted to just 2.2 per cent of general government expenditure in 1983-84 decreasing further to 1.4 per cent in 1993-94 (McKie, 1994). It is in line, however, with the argument that it is not central government's role to pay for training and that this should be the responsibility of employers and individual workers. Extending the principle of 'marketisation' of training, the 1994 Budget includes a provision for changing the funding arrangements of TECs and LECs. In the future, funding will be linked to performance, in that funding will reflect the number of people starting on programmes, and the outcome of their training (*The Times*, 30.11.94).

Labour market deregulation and privatisation

The government's policies of privatisation and deregulation are intrinsic to other aspects of its labour market policies (Smith and Morton, 1994). John Major has built on the argument of New Right theorists that employers' freedom to hire and fire workers was removed by postwar governments in Britain, and that legislation to improve working conditions and health and safety have acted as a disincentive for employers to employ more workers. In addition, it is contended that the size of the public sector in Britain has acted as a considerable barrier to private investment and job creation. The solution, therefore, is to privatise industry, deregulate aspects of public sector markets, and decrease workers' rights. Conservative governments accepted this line of reasoning and used the small firms' lobby to argue the case for 'freeing the market'. Policies to reduce employment protection, unfair dismissal, maternity and other rights at work, and the powers of the health and safety executive have been pursued actively since 1979.

This approach is also shown in the Major government's negotiation of the Social Chapter opt-out. Major is attempting to gain a competitive advantage for British employers by deregulating the labour market and encouraging a low wage economy. Nevertheless, the government has had to concede the influence of Europe on labour market issues and workers' rights. For example, the TURERA 1993 included a provision for the introduction of the legal right to fourteen weeks' maternity leave, the requirement on employers to provide a written statement of particulars in the employment contract of every worker, and the implementation of health and safety at work rights. The government also faced defeat over two other issues. The first related to the decision of the European Court of Justice in 1994 which ruled in favour of the rights of workers in contracted-out organisations, and the second to the ruling of the House of Lords in the same year that, in accordance with European law, part-time workers must have the same redundancy and unfair dismissal rights as full-time workers. However, the government successfully resisted pressures from Brussels to adhere to the EU's working time directive in 1994, and the Employment Secretary, Michael Portillo, made clear his rejection of rights for paternity leave. Nevertheless, it is evident, that one route to increasing market flexibility by reducing workers' rights is constrained by the EU's social programme.

Privatisation of parts of the public sector, is an area where the Conservative governments have claimed considerable success. The selling of public sector assets was, of course, a useful way of raising revenue and allowing the government to maintain its pledge to reduce income tax and cut the size of the PSBR. In addition to privatisation through the sale of assets, services provided by local authorities and government departments have been deregulated and so made subject to market forces. The adverse effects of competitive tendering and contracting out of services on the quality of provision, the conditions of work, wage levels and trade union organisation have received much publicity from opponents of this policy (Ascher, 1987; Stoker, 1991). The main industries which could be sold off readily have been privatised. The government under John Major has shown its intention to continue with privatisation and deregulation. In spite of strong opposition, the government proceeded with privatisation of the coal industry and is continuing its policy of privatising the railway industry. One area where it has had to make a tactical retreat, however, is in its plans to privatise the Post Office. But for many workers, the result of the government's approach to increasing freedom in the labour market through privatisation and deregulation, has been job loss, job insecurity, poorer working and safety conditions, longer hours and less pay.

Summary

Labour market reforms have been central to the Conservative

governments' policies to restructure social relations and reduce the role of organised labour in the 1980s and 1990s. But how successful have these policies been? Government ministers use every opportunity to congratulate themselves on 'improving efficiency' in the labour market, reducing industrial unrest, and achieving a real breakthrough in productivity to internationally competitive levels. An assessment of the changes in industrial relations is provided by information and data from the Workplace Industrial Relations Survey conducted in 1990 (Millward et al., 1992). The authors conclude that there were major changes in employee relations during the 1980s including the decline in the representation of workers by trade unions and a decline in collective bargaining particularly in the private sector. However, in workplaces where trade union representation and collective bargaining persisted, very little has changed in industrial relations practices. They were unable to identify any new patterns of employee representation to replace trade union representation and attributed many of the changes which had taken place to major structural changes in the economy and their impact on the types of workplaces and jobs available. In summarising their findings Millward et al. (ibid., p. 352) state that 'the structures of collective bargaining remained in many respects similar in character to those at the start of the 1980s, but they were present in fewer workplaces and affected fewer employees'.

Evans, Ewing and Nolan (1994) challenge the claim that industrial relations have been improved and that the government achieved important advances in industrial performance in the 1980s. They do not subscribe to the 'new revisionism' which 'celebrates Thatcher's industrial relations policies but attributes Britain's faltering growth performance and prospects to her mishandling of technology and training policy' (p. 583). They counter the view of a productivity 'miracle' and conclude that there has not been a sustainable improvement in competitiveness. Instead they argue that inequalities in the labour market have widened substantially as a result of the attack on trade unionism and other regulatory bodies, and that there has been no improvement in investment in 'human capital.' For them the prospects of industrial renewal in Britain look more remote as Britain tries to compete in the market on the basis of cheap labour (ibid., pp. 586-7).

The recession of the early 1990s contradicted any claims that the government's labour market and supply-side policies had solved the problems of unemployment. Unemployment rose dramatically, but what was significant was that groups of workers, especially white-collar workers and the professional middle-class, who had earlier been relatively protected from unemployment in the 1980s, found that they too were vulnerable to fluctuations in the labour market. Thus white-collar workers as well as blue-collar workers faced redundancy and the replacement of 'jobs for life' with temporary contracts. Hutton (1994, p. 2) estimates that 'full-time jobs only represent three fifths of Britain's jobs' and only 'a fifth of new jobs are the full-time pensionable jobs that the middle classes used to cherish.' The government responded to criticism by arguing that unemployment is a problem throughout Europe and is worse in countries, such as Spain and France, where a minimum wage rate is in operation.

The official statistics on unemployment published by the Department of Employment have always understated the actual level of unemployment in Britain. More accurate figures are provided by the Unemployment Unit index,[10] which measures the unemployment count on the pre-1982 basis and which takes account of government changes to the system of counting. The government may have changed the official measure of unemployment on as many as thirty occasions since it came into office in 1979, but such manipulation has been insufficient to hide a very real problem faced by families in Britain. Average figures also underestimate the consequences for specific groups, the regional impact, and the knock-on effect on rising poverty levels and social deprivation. Unemployment, or the fear of it, is being experienced by those who previously felt fairly secure in job market terms. Unpublished figures from a Department of Employment database show that unemployment has affected as much as 40 per cent of the workforce over the period 1989-94 and that the impact is felt by people both in and out of work (*The Times*, 29.12.94).

There is, therefore, support for Robert Taylor's (1994, pp. 264-5) view that John Major

> may have talked calmly and occasionally with sympathy about the social consequences of the recession. ... But none of this made any noticeable impact on his government's employment and industrial relations strategy. In this policy area at least, prime ministerial words of compassion were often belied by harshness of executive action. The creation of a

flexible, more deregulated labour market was one subject on which all sections of Mr Major's Cabinet could find common agreement. Mrs Thatcher's labour market strategy was indeed safe in their hands.

Welfare policy

In pursuing their policy priority of lowering inflation, Conservative governments in the 1980s and 1990s have attempted to reduce public expenditure, but have experienced some difficulty in achieving this objective. The rapid increase in unemployment in the early 1980s and the continuation of high unemployment into the 1990s contributed to the government's difficulties in decreasing the level of public spending. The attempts to reduce pressure on the public purse went together with a major restructuring of the relationship between the state and civil society.

The incoming Thatcher government in 1979 continued the systematic restructuring of the welfare state begun in 1975. Conservative governments in the 1980s subjected the welfare state to significant and far-reaching reforms including education, benefits, pensions, public housing, health and family policy. In assessing the social policy legislation of the Thatcher years, Howard Glennerster (1994, p. 322) argues that, 'taken together this legislation was the biggest break with social policy tradition since 1945'. He identifies common themes across the different legislative changes, namely the devolution of budgetary responsibility to schools, to care managers, to housing estates and to general practitioners; the introduction of competition between public services for public funding; and the capacity of different agencies to free themselves from local political control - 'this collection of "quasi-market" reforms were intended to improve the efficiency of these services short of full privatization' (ibid, p. 323). In analysing Thatcher's legacy for the British welfare state, Paul Wilding (1992) summarises the key elements as a challenge to collectivism, the promotion of private provision, the implementation of spending cuts, support for a new managerialism, an attack on local government, a move to welfare pluralism, a change in the rights of citizenship, and the growth of the regulatory state. All these changes exacerbated social divisions.

In the early years of his government, John Major was

responsible for implementing much of the legislation which passed through Parliament in the 1980s (Pierson, 1993), but has pursued restructuring with renewed vigour. As Glennerster (1994, p. 319) points out, Major may have shown more passion and sincerity in defending the NHS than his predecessor, but midway through his premiership at the Conservative party conference in 1993, he 'allowed certain members of his orchestra to start experimenting with another tune altogether. Such improvisations lead to a diverting little movement variously called "Back to Basics" or "family values blues"'. At the same time, in his role as Chief Secretary to the Treasury, Michael Portillo, with Peter Lilley, as the Secretary of State for Social Security, began to re-think the government's plans for social policy and its funding. Their response to the fiscal crisis of the state meant that service provision and standards of delivery could no longer be maintained in their present form.

The government defends its welfare state reforms on the basis of targeting the most needy, stressing the advantages of self-help and individual responsibility. This approach illustrates the government's attempt to legitimise and depoliticise its policy, individualising the solution to welfare 'problems'. In this short section, it is not possible to analyse all of the areas of welfare policy in depth. By examining a few key policy reforms and initiatives of the Major government, it is possible, however, to provide some assessment of the government's approach. John Major's key contribution to the welfare state debate is the Citizen's Charter.[11] In discussing the rationale behind this new initiative, Kavanagh (1994, p. 9) states that 'John Major's search for mechanisms other than privatization to empower people, giving them more opportunity and choice, resulted in the Citizen's Charter in early 1991'. On the basis that the 'consumer' had been ill-served by public services in the past, the public sector is now required to define and set standards and targets for provision and delivery of services - for example in education, health, and transport - and to publish their success in achieving their stated aims. However, there is little evidence that people have been 'empowered' as a result. As Atkinson and Cope (1994, p.49) indicate, 'it appears that the Citizen's Charter is increasingly being used as a vehicle, and a justification, for a major restructuring of the state, ie what it does and how it does it'.

This section, therefore, illustrates our analysis of the depoliticisation process through the growing 'marketisation' and 'agencification' of service delivery, the split in the function between the provider and purchaser of services, and the emphasis placed on the individual citizen and 'consumerism'.

Health policy

The principle of free health care to those in need regardless of ability to pay is strongly defended in Britain. The Thatcher governments encountered concerted opposition to suggestions that the health service should be included in their early privatisation programme. In reply to fears and claims that the NHS was to be privatised, Margaret Thatcher declared in 1983 that the health service was safe in her hands. By 1987, in a manner somewhat contradictory given its stance on reducing public expenditure, the government boasted that it had increased spending in the National Health Service. At the same time, Thatcher defended her own decision to use private health care on the grounds that, 'I want (to enter hospital) at the time I want and with the doctor I want. ... I exercise my right as a free citizen to spend my money in my own way' (quoted in Kavanagh and Morris, 1989, p. 88).

Although the government may not have been able to proceed with overt privatisation of the health service, or to cut spending in this area, the 1980s witnessed important changes in the administration and management of the service, the contracting-out of ancillary services, increased prescription charges, the end of free dental and eye tests, tax relief for those who contribute to private and occupational health schemes, the restoration of pay beds in NHS hospitals, and the role given to the voluntary sector in the provision of care. Health care was increasingly assessed as a business and a new managerial culture was introduced (Kendall and Moon, 1994).

In response to growing public concern about the future of the health service, the Thatcher government undertook a review of the NHS following its victory at the 1987 General Election. The key findings of the review were published in the White Paper, *Working for Patients* in 1989 (Department of Health, 1989). 'Radical' measures included the proposal that hospitals were to manage their own affairs independent of local health authorities through hospital trusts and that general practitioners should be given budgets which they could spend on purchasing care for their patients. In order to discourage the formation of cartels, the government's solution was the 'functional separation of purchasing - buying health services to satisfy local need - from providing - the day-to-day business of delivering that care' (Kendall and Moon, 1994, p.167). The key aims were thus to create an internal market based on privatisation principles, and to introduce the concept of purchaser and provider functions. However, the review conceded that care should continue to be free at the point of use and should be funded through general taxation. According to Glennester (1994, p. 324), 'the central idea that underpins the new NHS is the distinction between the purchaser and the provider of services. The latter compete for the contracts set by the former.' The government was forced to increase spending on the health budget in order to counter the widespread opposition to its proposed reforms.

The key proposals of the White Paper were implemented in 1991 and were followed by the development of a health strategy for England, *The Health of the Nation* (Department of Health, 1991) and the introduction of the Patient's Charter. Kendall and Moon (1994, p. 170) outline the shift from the strategy of 'steady state' in the period up to the 1992 general election where the changes were modest, to the development of 'managed competition' within the NHS after the election through 'the emergence of NHS trusts as the dominant form of provider unit, the development of the purchaser role, the growth of GP fundholding, continued debates over the structure of the service, and the impact of the operation of the internal market itself.' The Major government has continued to meet opposition to its proposals from the general public, health service professionals and from trade unions (Pierson, 1993). The key concerns are that too much influence is being given to managers, that funding is being directed away from patient care to administration, and that the service is increasingly being run on narrow 'economic' criteria. John Major's speech in 1992 singling out the free NHS as a symbol of the caring post-Thatcherite society (Kavanagh and Seldon, 1994, p. 468), and his decision to replace William Waldegrave as Health Minister with the 'softer' touch of Virginia Bottomley, have been insufficient to counter resistance to restructuring of the health service.

There is considerable disagreement over the impact of the health reforms and disputes over the accuracy and interpretation of data on spending levels, waiting lists, availability of beds, and staff costs. In relation to spending, the percentage of expenditure on health has increased from 12 per cent in 1979-80 to 14.1 per cent in 1990-91, and it is estimated that the figure for 1993-94 will be roughly the same (McKie, 1994, p. 99). The 1994 Budget contained plans to increase spending on the NHS in England in cash terms by 4.2 per cent (*The Times*, 30.11.94). However, increased spending has to be seen within the context of rising demands on the health service from a growing population of the elderly, the increase in demand on the service as a consequence of advances in medicine made possible by new technology, and the increase in the cost of drugs. In addition to growth in spending, the government claims success in reducing waiting lists, but the figures are subject to dispute because of the method of calculation. It is possible, however, to demonstrate the fall in the number of available beds from Department of Health statistics. Looking at England, there were 355,978 available beds on average in 1980, by 1990-91 this had decreased to 255,438, and by 1992-93 it had decreased further to 231,363 (McKie, 1994, p.101). Another area of criticism of the government's record surrounds the number and cost of managerial staff employed in the health service. In a written answer to Alan Milburn MP in November 1993, the salary costs of managerial staff in hospital and community health services were judged to have risen from £158.8 million in 1989-90 to £494.2 million in 1992-93 (McKie, 1994). Thus, the government has continued to come under attack for closing local hospitals, creating a two tier health system, and for discharge procedures which are alleged to result in a tendency to release patients early in order to keep down costs. One particular aspect of public concern has surrounded the policy to release an increasing number of mentally ill patients to live in the community. The King's Fund health institute report, published in January 1994, 'found that standards of care and patient choice had not been greatly enhanced' (ibid., p. 95), and despite the implementation of the Patient's Charter, 'genuine involvement of consumers remains rare' (Kendall and Moon, 1994, p. 179).

Linked to government health reforms was the introduction of the community care scheme. Although the National Health Service and Community Care Act of 1990 contained provisions for community care, these were not implemented until 1993. The foundations of the system were, therefore, laid down in the Thatcher era but implemented under John Major. The scheme involved removing community care from the responsibility of the health service and transferring it to local authorities and shifting from a provider-led service to a needs-led service. Six objectives were set out in the 1989 White Paper, *Caring for People, Community Care in the Next Decade and Beyond*, namely to promote the development of domiciliary services and to enable people to live at home where possible; to prioritize support for carers; to stress the importance of assessment and care management; to promote the independent sector; to clarify the responsibilities of the agencies involved in community care; and to introduce a new funding structure. Critics, for example Lewis (1994), have pointed to the increasing responsibility being placed on already hard-pressed local authorities, the lack of sufficient funding of the system, the reduction in the quality of care being provided for many patients, and the implications for women who already undertake the majority of caring within the community. Although the government announced an increase of £20 million in funding for community care for the year 1994-95, local authorities will have insufficient resources to ensure the achievement of agreed standards (McKie, 1994), reinforcing the view that the government is cynically trying to reduce the cost of care with little regard to the personal costs experienced by patients and carers.

Since gaining office, John Major has not only implemented many of the policies on health care which were planned under Margaret Thatcher's administrations, but the resolve to increase competition and marketisation of the health service has been intensified. The government has also been caught in the contradictory position of arguing on the one hand that it is increasing spending on health, while on the other trying to reduce the cost of the health service as part of its overall plans to reduce public expenditure. It has attempted to overcome this contradiction through the introduction of internal markets on the grounds of greater efficiency and by contracting-out aspects of the service. By giving greater responsibility to Hospital Trusts and Boards for decision-making, and introducing the purchaser/provider relationship, the government is also attempting to depoliticise its stance and to distance itself from responsibility and criticism. In other words, it hopes to redirect this criticism to the new boards, hospitals and their managers, and away from the government itself. The government aims to overcome opposition from the public through the introduction of the consumerist Patient's Charter, a strategy which so far has been less than successful.

In launching its manifesto for the 1987 General Election, the Conservative party described its policy of home ownership as 'the greatest success story of housing policy' since 1979 (Kemp, 1992, p. 65). Indeed many commentators cite housing as one area of policy where the Thatcher governments were successful in meeting their objectives, increasing the level of owner occupation, minimising local authority housing provision and decreasing public expenditure.[12] Administrations in the 1980s were less successful, however, in revitalising the private rented sector. Also the political sensitivity surrounding mortgage tax relief, meant that the government's desire to reduce this subsidy and stimulate market forces was constrained. The continuing drive to encourage home ownership was included as one of the principal items of the Conservative Party's 1992 general election manifesto, *Best Future for Britain* (Seldon, 1994, p. 36). The policies pursued by the Conservative governments of the 1980s and 1990s have involved a restructuring of roles within the state sector and a restructuring of housing expenditure (Atkinson and Durden, 1994).

During the 1980s and 1990s, there have been cuts in public spending on housing, a fall in the number of houses built by local authorities, a shift in ownership away from local authorities, and a dramatic rise in homelessness. The percentage of government expenditure allocated to housing was 7.2 per cent in 1979-80, it had dropped to 2.9 per cent by the time Margaret Thatcher left office in 1989-90, and was set to drop further to 2.1 per cent in 1993-94 (McKie, 1994, p. 117). Similarly the amount of local authority spending on new house building in England fell in real terms (1992-93 prices) from £2,547 million in 1979-80, to £841 million in 1990-91 and to £116 million in 1992-93 (ibid., p. 118). Atkinson and Durden (1994, p. 185) quote Housing and Construction Statistics for 1981-91 to show the drop in local authority dwellings completed in the UK in the period from 45,948 in 1981 to 8,073 in 1991. The transfer of some responsibility for housing to Housing Corporations has, in contrast, resulted in an increase in gross capital spending. In real terms (1992-93 prices) spending of Housing Corporations in England increased from £957 million in 1979-80 to £1,115 million in 1989-90 and further to £2,369 million in 1992-93 (McKie, 1994, p. 118). These figures demonstrate that trends which began in the 1980s have continued into the 1990s.

However, care should be taken in assessing the impact of government policy in different parts of Britain, and the differences which exist between housing tenure and policy in England and Scotland. Sales of council houses took off much more slowly in Scotland (Atkinson and Durden, 1994). To some extent this can be explained by the dominance and particular character of Labour councils in Scotland, which meant that local authorities were able to sustain their resistance to government policy for a longer period.

One of the consequences of the government's housing policy and other policy changes in welfare provision has been the dramatic increase in homelessness in Britain. The reduction in local authority provision and availability of low cost rental dwellings in the private sector, the increase in levels of low pay and poverty, and the change in benefit rules which have forced many young people on to the streets, have all contributed to the growing problem - 'sadly the main visible legacy in housing from the 1980s, at least in the capital, was the growth in vagrancy and rough sleeping among young people' (Kemp, 1992, p. 80). The number of households applying to local authorities in England and Wales as homeless increased from 249,100 in 1986 to 339,400 in 1993 (CSO, 1995).

It is extremely difficult to provide an accurate estimation of levels of homelessness in Britain. Research in this area has indicated that official statistics underestimate the true level, especially in relation to the amount of 'hidden' homelessness amongst people who may be sharing accommodation with relatives or friends but wish to find or are in need of a home. The 'unofficial homeless' both actual and potential in England in the 1990s is judged to be approximately 1,712,000 (Burrows and Walentowicz, 1992). This estimate includes people sleeping rough (c. 98,000), unauthorised tenants or squatters (c. 50,000), single people in hostels (c. 60,000), single people in lodgings (c. 77,000), insecure private tenants (c. 317,000), and the hidden homeless (c. 1,200,000).[13] Homelessness also impacts differentially on men and women. For example, figures published by the London Housing Unit in 1989 showed that some 70 per cent of households registered as homeless are headed by women (Atkinson and Durden, 1994, p. 194); and a report carried out for the Equal Opportunities Commission (EOC) (Brown, Breitenbach and Myers, 1994) cites evidence from different studies of homelessness and access to housing among women in Scotland which highlight some of the problems faced by women in relation to housing.

Two other consequences of government housing policy have been the increase in the use of temporary bed and breakfast accommodation and the impact on poverty and inequality. The former development was described by the National Audit Office in 1991 as a waste of taxpayers' money. They claimed that it was more cost effective for the government to build two new houses than provide poor quality bed and breakfast accommodation for a family in an inner-city hotel. In addition a report published by the Joseph Rowntree Foundation has shown how the increase in housing costs in Britain has driven more families into poverty, and evidence from the British Social Attitudes Survey demonstrates the way in which the sale of council houses has accentuated social and economic differences between council tenants and others (McKie, 1994).

But it is not just the poor who have been affected by the restructuring of housing policy. For those who were able to participate in Thatcher's 'property owning democracy' there have also been problems of keeping up with mortgage repayments and living with the consequences of negative equity. As Hutton (1994, p. 2) states, with 'personal debt in relation to post-tax income now the highest in the industrialised West and house prices drifting, nobody can be carefree'. As we discussed in chapter 4, the number of re-possessions and mortgages falling into arrears reached staggering proportions in the 1990s. For example, the number of mortgages in arrears in 1989 stood at a level of 80,600. By 1992, this figure had increased dramatically to 352,000 and had reduced slightly to 295,500 mortgages in arrears by 1994 (CSO, 1995). Further, it is estimated that by the fourth quarter of 1994, 1,300,000 households were in a position of negative equity (*Observer*, 22.1.95). For those who have managed to keep their houses, the level of mortgage interest tax relief has been reduced (McKie, 1994, p. 115). Atkinson and Durden (1994, p. 198) locate these developments within the context of the government's economic policy:

> With the onset of a savage and lengthy recession in the late 1980s the house price inflation bubble burst and the "chickens came home to roost" in a quite devastating fashion. Conservative voting middle-class owner-occupiers suddenly found themselves suffering from unemployment and reeling under the effects of apparently ever increasing interest rates as the government attempted to maintain its membership of

the Exchange Rate Mechanism (ERM). The result was that most dreaded of outcomes: repossession.

Benefits and pensions

We have already discussed the relationship between labour market policy and the restructuring of welfare benefits aimed at increasing incentives to work. We noted the replacement of unemployment benefit by the new Job Seeker's Allowance announced in the government's 1993 Budget and outlined the further initiatives proposed in the 1994 Budget. These new benefit changes are in line with policies introduced by the Thatcher governments which denied benefits to striking workers, removed young people from benefits if they did not participate on a training scheme, and which tightened the eligibility rules for the unemployed. Benefit changes have not been confined to areas affecting the labour market, and in the 1980s and 1990s the young, the old, the disabled, the homeless, the sick, the unemployed, have all been adversely affected. Other welfare payments have also been subject to attack, including state pensions, child benefit, and opting out from National Insurance contributions. During the Thatcher years and also under John Major's premiership, those on the right of the Conservative government have been keen to scapegoat so-called welfare 'scroungers' as a drain on the public purse. Given the percentage share of total government expenditure allocated to social security, the drive to reduce spending in this area is unsurprising. Although the Conservative Party was unsuccessful in cutting public expenditure on social security in general because of the rise in claimants, there were cuts in particular benefits and in the relative value of individual benefits, such as the changes to uprating rules so that benefits were no longer inflation-proof, cuts in insurance and means-tested benefits, changes in the rules of entitlement, controls on payments to the unemployed, and measures to increase contributions from absent fathers (Hill, 1994).

A major review of the social security system was undertaken in 1985 and resulted in the Social Security Act 1986. The Act contained provisions for the development of a new structure and brought together the renamed benefits of Income Support and Family Credit with Housing Benefit - 'all based upon broadly similar principles' of means-testing and targeting (ibid., 1994, p. 248). Hill lists four key themes of social security reform. First, in the spite of its commitment to reduce public expenditure, the government has found the growth in social security difficult to curb. Secondly, the government's approach to cutting income maintenance expenditure has involved an attack on 'universalism' and an increasing emphasis on targeting and means tested benefits and the encouragement of private provision. Thirdly, the government's social security policy has to be placed within the context of 'Conservative acceptance, and indeed often encouragement, of an increasingly unequal society' (ibid, p. 242). And lastly, consideration has to be given to the extent to which social security changes are affected by the process of institutional change, namely the process of 'agency' creation including the Benefits Agency, the Contributions Agency and the Child Support Agency.

The last theme is explored in some depth by Peter Fairbrother (1994). Fairbrother shows that, in line with other sections of the civil service, Department of Social Security (DSS) offices were transformed during the 1980s and 1990s, and past practices and arrangements rejected. One central aspect of change was the transformation of one section of the DSS into the Benefits Agency in 1991 under the control of a chief executive, 'since then, the senior management of the Agency sought to establish the Agency as a "consumer"-focused organization, with a devolved managerial structure. For workers this has meant insecurity, uncertainty and growing workloads' (ibid, p. 89). 'Improving customer services' was a core value of the business plan which was drawn up for the Agency, and a report from the Treasury and Civil Service Committee in 1991 quoted the chief executive as stating, 'I think our staff are beginning to call the people who come through the door customers rather than claimants, although that has been dismissed by some as superficiality' (quoted in Fairbrother, 1994, p. 82). The shift in emphasis from claimant to customer demonstrates the government's encouragement of market relationships and so-called consumer sovereignty.

Another key area of social security reform, which had already been included in the Fowler Review of 1985, was pensions. The Fowler Review had argued that the State Earnings Pension Scheme (SERPS) would impose a financial burden on future generations because of demographic changes and increases in life expectancy. This line of argument has been sustained under Major's administration. The substantial cost of providing pensions for the elderly of the future has been used as a way of challenging the state pension and encouraging private provision, again reflecting the government's concern that 'individuals' not the state should make provision for their old age. The private pension industry was not slow to capitalise on this rhetoric and the decline in the value of the state pension. However, scandals over private pension funds have proliferated in the 1990s. In December 1993, the Securities and Investment Board, found that as many as half a million workers who had switched to personal pension plans were worse off as a result (McKie, 1994). Another change, which impacts specifically on women workers, is the proposed equalisation of the pension age at 65. Although this is welcomed by some women because it allows them longer to work and earn money to compensate for years they may have lost in having and looking after their children, the government is accused of making the decision to round up to 65 rather than round down, for both men and women, to 60, on the basis of cost alone.

Another embarrassing episode for the Major government in 1994 surrounded the fate of the Civil Rights (Disabled Persons) Bill. The private member's bill was talked out of the House of Commons by the large number of amendments proposed by Conservative backbenchers. Initially, Nicholas Scott, the minister responsible for disabled people, denied any link with the amendments, but just a few days later he apologised to the House for misleading them on this issue. The government was again accused of putting cost before the rights of disabled people (McKie, 1994).

Research evidence shows that the many welfare changes have reinforced social division. For example, two reports published by the Joseph Rowntree Foundation in June 1994 highlighted the fact that incomes of the poorest have dropped, not just in relative terms, but in absolute terms during the Conservative years. It was estimated that the real income of the poorest 10 per cent fell from a peak figure of £73 a week in 1979 to £61 in 1991. One of the adverse effects of increasing poverty on health is that the life expectancy for some of the poorest in Britain has been declining for the first time in 50 years (Wilkinson referred to in McKie, 1994). For families on benefit or low income, forced into debt, the pressures are enormous and manifest themselves in physical and mental illness (Kempson et al., 1994).

Increasing unemployment, low wages for those in work, low benefits or no benefits for others, have all contributed to rising poverty and debt in the 1990s. The number of households falling below the official poverty line is growing and they are now paying a relatively larger proportion of their income on tax, both direct and indirect, than other groups in society. Because of their poverty, lack of assets and poor employment prospects, they do not have the same access to credit which is available to others. Existing evidence supports the association between poverty and credit and low income and debt (Ford, 1991), and German (1993, p.13) notes that, 'total personal debt trebled between 1980 and 1992, from £100 billion to £300 billion', making 'actual wage levels today lower than they might at first seem'. Debt and poverty is reinforced and perpetuated through a vicious circle of obtaining loans from disreputable loan companies charging exorbitant rates of interest (Ford, 1991). The problems are particularly acute for women in low paid, temporary and part-time jobs, and especially single mothers dependent on benefits (Alcock, 1993). Because of their lack of economic independence and their disadvantaged position in the labour market, women as a group are much more likely to be poor at different stages of their lives. One study (Kempson et al., 1994) shows that half the mothers in low-income families regularly go without food to secure the basic needs of their children.

After sixteen years of Conservative government, the social security budget remains a substantial part of public expenditure. Yet, for an increasing number of people dependent on benefits and pensions, their situation has deteriorated. Although the government has not been successful in reducing expenditure, it has attempted a major restructuring of relations by shifting responsibility to agencies and in 'individualising' problems associated with unemployment, homelessness, disability, youth and old age. The result has been growing inequality and despair.

Family policy

The 'moral' panic about growing crime rates, drug abuse, sexual behaviour and the role of the family led some to fear the disintegration of society, and prompted John Major, to make his famous 'back to basics' speech in 1993. He stated 'it is time to return to core values, time to get back to basics, to self-discipline and respect for the law, to consideration for others, to accepting responsibility for yourself and your family - and not shuffling it off on other people and the state' (quoted in McKie,

1994, p. 122). A central concern was the disintegration of the traditional family and its socialising roles and the erosion of so-called family values. The fall in marriages, the rise in divorce rates, and particularly the increase in one-parent families fuelled the debate. Young, single mothers became scapegoat number one (McRobbie, 1994). By 1991, one parent families accounted for 19 per cent of all families with children, compared with 10 per cent in 1976. Approximately 900,000 lone parents, 90 per cent of them women, claimed income support in 1992 and a Cabinet paper estimated that the number of lone parents would grow by around 50,000 annually to the end of the decade (McKie 1994, p. 127). One of the government's responses was to consider schemes for encouraging young, single mothers back to work thus reducing their claim on state benefits.[14]

Another controversial policy development was the Child Support Act of 1991 which came into force in 1993. The principle underlying the Act was to make fathers take financial responsibility for their children. The way in which the government approached this objective led to vehement criticism and opposition. One of the strongest areas of protest came from fathers themselves, particularly men who were in a second relationship and responsible for both families. A key criticism related to the policy of pursuing fathers who were already paying maintenance and the absence of the right to appeal, and the government was accused of again being concerned with reducing costs rather than with protecting the interests of those involved. Towards the end of 1993, a Commons select committee demanded changes which provoked a modest response from the government. In its first annual report in 1994, the Child Support Agency had to admit that the benefit savings achieved by the policy were more than 20 per cent below the target set, and that child maintenance had been arranged in only 31.5 per cent of cases compared with the target of 60 per cent (McKie, 1994, p. 129). Peter Lilley, the Social Security Secretary, was finally forced into 'a shake-up of the controversial and politically catastrophic Child Support Agency' (*The Scotsman*, 23.1.95). The White Paper published in January 1995 includes a provision for a limited right of appeal for absent fathers but fails to meet the criticisms levelled at the agency from pressure groups such as the Child Poverty Action Group (CPAG) (*The Scotsman*, 24.1.95).

The rehabilitation of child benefit was one of John Major's particular contributions to family policy (Lister, 1994). His retreat on the provision of universal nursery education on the grounds of its impact on public expenditure, not only indicates the government's unwillingness to pay for nursery provision, but reinforces its endorsement of the traditional role of women within the family. As indicated by Ruth Lister (ibid., p. 363), the Major government has worked largely within the framework of the agenda set by the Thatcher governments, and 'it is more likely to be remembered for the "moral panic" about the state of the "family" and the backlash against lone parent families that it helped to unleash, together with the legacy it inherited in the form of the Child Support Act, than for any distinctive policies of its own directed towards families and women.'

Combating crime

Increasing concern about law and order issues in the 1970s was highlighted by the Conservative Party in their election campaigns and election manifestos throughout the 1980s. Law and order reforms are a central part of the party's agenda for change associated with their politics of austerity. 'Welfarist' and 'liberal' solutions adopted by previous administrations were rejected on the grounds that they exacerbated a growing problem.

In spite of the fact that the Thatcher governments provided more resources aimed at controlling crime and public order problems and rewarding the police with pay increases, notified offences have been rising steadily, the rate of detection has been declining as has public confidence in the police (Morris, 1994).[15] In the 1990s the number of reported crimes continued to rise, and the Major government seems no more successful than its predecessor in curbing public order problems. There are two opposing interpretations of the reasons for the rising crime level. One lays the blame directly on the policies pursued under the Thatcher and Major governments which are said to have created a society of 'haves' and 'have nots' and to have cultivated an ethos and culture of 'individualism' and 'selfishness'. The result has been a growing number of disaffected people, particularly the young, who, unable to make ends meet, find alternative ways of coping through crime and drug abuse. The opposite point of view is put by others on the right, who use gurus such as Charles Murray, to substantiate their analysis.[16] Under this scenario rising crime is caused by a growing number of people in society who will not take responsibility for their actions and who have been encouraged to abdicate responsibility because of a state welfare and penal system which is too lenient (Murray, 1994). The solution, therefore, is to be less generous in providing welfare benefits and payments and to give custodial and harsh prison sentences to those who break the law. John Major has associated himself with this latter view, identifying crime as a characteristic of socialist-governed inner cities. As he sees it, 'there is no excuse for crime. Society is not to blame and individuals are' (quoted in Morris, 1994).

Major's sentiments found expression at the Conservative Party Conference in 1993, when the Home Secretary, Michael Howard, returned to the early 1980s with a speech which outlined 27 new 'get tough' measures and reaffirmed the party's commitment to deterrence and imprisonment - 'prison works ... it makes many who are tempted to commit crime think twice' (Nash and Savage, 1994, p. 159). This statement directly contradicted the government's own White Paper published in 1990 which explicitly denied the effectiveness of deterrence and imprisonment.

John Major has returned to the tactics of the early Thatcher governments arguing for a tough stance on detention. Only this time, unlike Thatcher, Major is not rewarding the police with rises in pay and promotion prospects. Instead the service underwent two reviews leading to the publication of White Papers in 1993 which included far-reaching proposals to change both the governance of the police and their relationship with local and central government, and planned to restructure their pay and conditions of employment. These proposed changes went hand-in-hand with other moves to contract-out or privatise the prison service and restructure the probation service and the courts and legal services, making all these services more subject to market criteria and the '"three E's scrutiny" - Economy, Efficiency and Economy' (Nash and Savage, 1994, p. 142). As Morris (1994, p. 301) argues, 'the most profound shifts in the direction of penal policy have occurred during these last four Major years.' The White Paper, *Police Reform: A Police Service for the Twentieth-Century,* included proposals to measure the performance of police forces and compare 'league tables', to devolve budgets, to decrease local political representation on local police authorities, and to encourage the participation of the business community, with the chairs of the new authorities being appointed by the Home Secretary. The second White

Paper, the Report of the Sheehy Committee, *Inquiry into Police Responsibilities and Rewards*, contained other initiatives such as performance related pay and fixed term contracts of employment.[17] In the face of opposition, the government was forced to abandon some aspects of the more controversial plans, for example the proposal for fixed-term contracts for police contained in the Sheehy Report, Michael Howard's insistence that chairs of police committees should be chosen by Whitehall, and proposals to allow the home secretary to appoint one third of police committee members (McKie, 1994, pp. 139-40). The intention to contract-out and privatise prisons was also constrained by resistance from the Prison Officers Association.

The government's tough stance backfired when the Labour Party captured the debate with the 'tough on crime and tough on the causes of crime' speech made by Tony Blair, then as shadow minister and later as leader of the Labour Party. In addition the government, and Michael Howard in particular, have been subject to vigorous criticism because of the poor security provided by the private security company, Group 4, in transferring prisoners, the highly publicised escape of prisoners from prisons, and the unrest and riots in the prisons (McKie, 1994).

The party of law and order is in some difficulty when its record on law and order is examined. The most recent controversy surrounds the Criminal Justice and Public Order Bill introduced in December 1993.[18] Nash and Savage (1994) argue that the Bill is a reflection more of the mood of the Conservative Party conference than the findings of the Royal Commission on Criminal Justice carried out in 1993. The Bill contained changes to the right of silence, new powers for the police to take DNA samples from suspects without consent, new custodial centres for 12-14 year olds, extended sentences for young offenders, reduction in the right to bail, and the prohibition of 'rave' parties as well as trespassing. Under the guise of protecting private property, the Bill restricts lawful demonstrations and protests. The dilemma at the heart of the government's 'get tough' stance, however, is that, 'increasing resort to carceral solutions for social problems is often equally lacking in effect but ruinously expensive' (Morris, 1994, p. 306). By rejecting the evidence that economic and social factors also have a substantial impact on the level and types of crime committed in society, the government is digging itself into a deeper hole. The same point is made most succinctly by Nash and Savage (1994, p. 161):

> An intelligent observation of these figures (growing law
> and order expenditure and rising crime rates) would be
> that law and order and criminal justice policies
> themselves can only ever have a marginal impact on
> crime – social and environmental factors such as
> unemployment are far more significant. The paradox is
> that it has been the Conservatives above all who have
> dismissed such factors as accounting for crime. In the
> light of the evidence of increasing crime, the
> Conservatives have rejected their only viable defence.

Summary

The approach of the Major government is a continuation of
many of the policies and trends established in the Thatcher
years. The so-called 'caring' John Major has presided over
rising homelessness, deteriorating standards in health for the
poorest in society, the removal of benefits, a rise in absolute
poverty, and more stress on women who have traditionally
played a greater role in providing welfare for others. The
government's welfare policies also represent an attempt to
restructure social relations and the state's relationship with its
citizens. The government has promoted the growth of agencies,
market relationships, means testing and individual
responsibility, with the aim of reducing its own responsibility in
the area of welfare. Yet it has done so in ways that have
intensified social divisions, centralised government power, and
involved a return to a 'tough' approach to combating crime. The
language of citizenship and choice has been employed to
legitimise the government's approach, including its stance on
law and order. However, it should be remembered that a central
objective was also to reduce public expenditure in the
government's fight against inflation. As Pierson (1993, p. 266)
so aptly notes, 'for all the rhetoric of choice and citizenship, the
single most important political consideration surrounding the
welfare state over the last 20 years has been its cost'.

Restructuring local government

Tensions in the relationship between central and local

154

government are not unique to the Conservative governments of the 1980s and 1990s. Faced with growing pressure from local authorities on public expenditure and conflicts between local and central government on policy issues, previous governments have initiated plans to reorganise local government and to impose restrictions on local government spending.

During the 1980s and 1990s there have been significant and far-reaching changes in the relationship between central and local government. Local authorities constituted a major constraint for Conservative governments in curtailing public expenditure. They were also seen as the site of sustained, and often highly successful, political opposition to government policy. Authorities, including the GLC, Liverpool and Edinburgh, regularly hit the headlines in their attempts to disregard central government policy and the financial squeeze. The GLC and the Metropolitan Areas paid a heavy price for their opposition when they were abolished by the Thatcher government in 1986. Governments have been concerned not only to contain local government spending, but to control the power of local authorities and undermine the influence of the large, unionised workforce through contracting-out of services (Ascher, 1987; Stoker, 1991). Both the Thatcher and Major administrations have been highly active in restructuring the central state (Fairbrother, 1994), and its relationship with local government and between local government and the people.[19] In general, central government has sought to change funding arrangements between central and local government, decrease the power of local authorities in favour of the private sector and newly established agencies and quangos, emphasise the role of the 'individual' and 'consumer', drive down costs in the name of greater efficiency, increase the sphere of the market and competition in the operation of the local civil service and delivery of services, and shift the role of the local authority from the 'provider' of services in the local area to the 'enabler' function.

Local government finance

The poll tax is now legendary as one of the crucial factors which led to the demise of Margaret Thatcher as leader of the Conservative Party in 1990.[20] The introduction of the poll tax has to be assessed within the context of the replacement of the old Rate Support Grant with the new Block Grant system in

1980 and growing discontent, mainly from local businesses and the small firms' lobby, as local authorities attempted to meet their commitments by increasing local rates. The government's proposals for the abolition of the rating system and its replacement with a new local tax, officially termed the community charge, were set out in the Green Paper, *Paying for Local Government*, published in 1986. The rationale behind the introduction of the new tax was not strictly financial. The Green Paper and subsequent speeches by government ministers were explicit in making the connection between the 'accountability' of the local state and the 'consumer' of local services. The idea was that the policies of high spending councils would be judged at the ballot box (see Department of Environment, 1986, p. vii).

The government's argument was that many local voters did not pay rates and thus they had an incentive to vote for high spending councils which provided local services. It was contended that, as a result, the ratepayer subsidised services for non-ratepayers. Another spurious argument, made on the grounds of 'fairness', was that pensioners living alone were said to be paying the same rates for a property as a household possibly containing more than two adults in full-time employment. On these and other grounds, the government introduced its community charge - popularly labelled the poll tax - which was levied equally on every person of voting age in the locality with each local authority having the power to set its own rate. As Des King (1993, pp. 197-8) notes, 'the poll tax changed the basis of local taxing in Britain by shifting from a property-based tax to an individual one, ending the progressive element of local taxation and increasing considerably those eligible to pay the local levies irrespective of income'.

The tax attracted fierce opposition, and not just from opponents of the government. For example, the uniform business rate which was part of the poll tax and which applied to commercial and industrial properties, attracted opposition from the business community who organised 'a revolt of its own' (Stoker, 1991, p. 190). The key objections to the poll tax and the level of opposition have been discussed extensively by commentators.[21] The levying of a 'head' tax created considerable practical difficulties for collection, but the main criticism surrounded the 'unfairness' of a tax which was to apply to every adult in Britain regardless of ability to pay or level of income and wealth. Others objected to the potential effect on local services and jobs, the loss of local council control over their financial resources, and the threat to civil liberties posed by the poll tax register.

Scotland was the test-bed for the new tax, which was introduced in 1989, one year before its introduction in England and Wales. The adverse impact of the poll tax was soon felt. For example, in Scotland the average tax per person rose by nearly 40 per cent in the first two years of operation (McCrone, 1991). The negative redistributive effects also became apparent at the very earliest stage. As opposition grew, local authorities found it increasingly difficult and costly to collect the new tax. Many people, particularly the young, simply did not bother to register, thus excluding themselves from the voting register. The result was that the anti-poll tax campaign flourished with the establishment of a Scottish Federation of local groups, and later a British Federation. In Scotland, action groups were set up in middle-class, inner city areas as well as council housing estates on the periphery.

In introducing the poll tax in England and Wales, John Major, as Chancellor of the Exchequer, offered modest concessions to assist the passing of the legislation. He did not apply these concessions to Scotland, which led to further discontent north of the border, with the Scottish Secretary of State having to make the same concessions from within his own budget. Further, opposition to the poll tax suddenly emerged from some rebel Conservative MPs representing English seats, who had been only too happy to vote for the legislation when it affected Scotland. David McCrone argues that the real difference between Scotland and England 'came to a head in April 1990 in the so-called Battle of Trafalgar Square in London, when a poll tax protest turned to violence, described by *The Scotsman* newspaper as "quasi-revolutionary" class war' (McCrone, 1991, p. 448). The poll tax debacle was one of the key reasons for the forced resignation of Thatcher later in 1990, and an example where a keynote policy of the government was defeated in the streets (ibid.).

It came as no surprise, therefore, that abolition of the poll tax was one of the first areas of policy to be tackled by the incoming Major administration. Michael Heseltine was appointed as Environment Minister and put in charge of the introduction of the new council tax. The first move was to announce additional government finance to keep the level of the poll tax down. The cost of this was met by the taxpayer in another form through the raising of VAT by 2.5 per cent from

15 per cent to 17.5 per cent in March 1991 (King, 1993). At the same time financial difficulties over collection of the old poll tax remained, and local authorities are still engaged in the collection of unpaid tax. For example, in Scotland the oustanding debt on the poll tax stood at £780.1 million in 1993, the year the poll tax was replaced by the council tax. It is estimated that the figure for 1995 will remain dramatically high with around £595.8 million still outstanding in unpaid poll tax bills. The view from the Scottish Office is that local authorities should continue in their attempt to collect outstanding tax and it has stated that, 'there is no intention to stop pursuing debtors at any given date' (*The Scotsman*, 30.1.95).

Proposals for the new council tax were contained in the Local Government Finance Act 1992. The council tax, which came into effect in 1993, retains elements of the old rating system (a tax on property) and elements of the poll tax (a personal tax). The property element of the tax was based on the notional capital value of property which is divided into 'bands' (the rates had previously been based on notional rental value), and the personal element was based on the assumption of a two-person household with discounts available for those living alone. The business rate remained unaltered. To some extent, the new tax offset many of the criticisms of the old poll tax, but there was significant controversy over the banding of property values which favours those who own high valued property. The tax impacts differentially on the rich and poor and people in different parts of the country. As Young (1994, p. 88) indicates, 'whatever the score on the criteria of fairness and accountability set down by Heseltine for a better local tax, the council tax and its associated adjustments secured the government's over-riding aim: the tighter control of local authority spending. In this regard John Major and Michael Heseltine shared Mrs Thatcher's preoccupation with restraining spendthrift, generally Labour, local authorities'.

Local government control

Over the last decade the power and influence of local government has diminished substantially as councils have lost control in key areas such as education, housing and health, have had aspects of their functions privatised or contracted-out, and have experienced large scale job losses (Davies, 1988, Stoker 1991). Increasingly they are under pressure to move from the 'provider' of local services to the 'enabler' role, where the private sector competes for local government work, a development which is analogous to the Next Steps initiative implemented in the civil service (Fairbrother, 1994; King, 1993). 'For some, the notion of an "enabling" authority is little more than a euphemism for the "end of local government"' (Cochrane, quoted in Atkinson and Cope, 1994).

The impact of central government legislation post-1979 on local government can also be seen in terms of the establishment of an 'informal local government' (King, 1993). Many of the functions previously carried out by local councils are now undertaken by agencies. In contrast to local authorities, which are subject to local elections, 'informal local government agencies are not directly accountable to local voters (and are indirectly accountable in only a few cases) yet they shape many of the policies - such as education, health, urban regeneration and training - which affect citizens' (ibid., p. 207). Examples of the informal local government system include Urban Development Corporations (UDCs) set up to regenerate urban areas (Duncan and Goodwin, 1988); the transfer of responsibility for training provision by the replacement of the Manpower Services Commission (MSC) with the new Training and Enterprise Councils (TECs) and Training Agency in England and Wales, and Local Enterprise Councils (LECs), Scottish Enterprise and Highlands and Islands Enterprise; the encouragement given to schools to opt-out of local authority control with managerial and financial functions being devolved to individual schools; the creation of a new Urban Development Agency to coordinate urban regeneration work and the introduction of the City Challenge programmes; the fostering of private-public partnerships with a view to revitalising economic development in the inner cities; the setting up of 'US-style' regulatory authorities to act as watchdogs of consumers' interests in the provision of services such as electricity, gas and water; and the creation of Hospital Boards and Trusts which has meant the replacement of locally elected political representatives by the government's political appointment of those supportive of its policies.

The process of 'agencification' has a number of common features such as the centralisation of power to the central state at the expense of local government autonomy, and the enhanced role given to private sector business interests at the expense of public sector provision and trade union involvement. Stewart (quoted in Atkinson and Cope, 1944, p. 43) characterises this trend as the creation of a 'new magistracy' which

> is being created in the sense that a non-elected elite are assuming responsibility for a large part of local governance ... Accountability such as it is rests upon the accountability of these bodies to central government, although even that appears uncertain in the case of the governing bodies of, for example, hospital trusts and grant maintained schools.

Local authorities are also subject to performance indicators with the Citizen's Charter being used as a means by which their 'customers' can assess their performance (Young , 1994). At the same time, the extensive use of agencies and quangos in local government is severely restricting the scope and scale of local government, thus reinforcing central government's ability to by-pass local authorities unsympathetic to their aims (Stoker, 1991).

Local government reorganisation

A proposal which took many politicians and commentators by surprise was the government's plans, announced in 1991, to reorganise local government. Opponents and supporters of the government have questioned the reasons behind the government's intention to proceed with a major and costly reorganisation, for which there is little demand even within the Conservative Party (Young, 1994). The rhetoric supporting reorganisation is very familiar, with its stress on too much government and bureaucracy, the need for greater accountability, cost saving and efficiency, and for a enhanced role for local people and local communities. These objectives are to be achieved by replacing the two-tier local government system in favour of unitary authorities.

The government set up an independent Local Government Commission - the Banham Commission - to take evidence from interested parties and to undertake a review of English local authorities with a view to moving towards a unitary structure. The relationship between the Banham Commission and the government has run into difficulties, especially at times when the Commission made recommendations which did not find favour in government circles (ibid.). The final recommendations of the Banham Commission are due to be published some time in 1995. In Scotland and Wales, no such Commission was established. Instead the respective Secretaries of State published consultative documents setting out the government's intention to move to a single-tier structure of local government.[22]

In spite of concerted opposition to its plans, the government is proceeding with local government reform in Scotland. The Local Government etc. (Scotland) Bill received Royal Assent in November 1994 and includes provisions to replace the existing two tier structure of local government in Scotland and its 9 regional councils, 53 district councils and 3 island councils with 32 all-purpose local authorities (Fairley, 1995). The Act also includes measures to transfer responsibility for water and sewerage from local authorities to three newly appointed water authorities and to give Joint Boards responsibility for services including Joint Police and Joint Fire Boards.[23] The new councils will come into being on the 1st of April 1996, with transitional arrangements being made for the transfer between the two systems and for elections to the shadow councils taking place in April 1995. The government's decision to push through reorganisation at such speed and against public opinion in Scotland has been heavily criticised, and the government has also been accused of manipulating the new boundaries to maximise its potential electoral support in Scotland. Summarising the key implications of the new Act, the Scottish Local Government Information Unit (1994) concluded:

> The Act gives the Secretary of State substantial new powers. It tightens the Secretary of State's control over local government and limits the discretion available to elected members to make local decisions. The Act reduces the role of local government by creating new areas of public service and public spending controlled by unelected bodies appointed by, and responsible to, the Secretary of State.

It is estimated that the number of councillors will be reduced by one-third as a result of reorganisation. Trade unions are concerned about the potential impact on the terms and conditions of employment and job security of their members following such a major restructuring process. Also there is controversy surrounding the costs of the whole exercise. There is little evidence to suggest that greater efficiency and accountability will be achieved in the process. Rather, the aim would appear to be to make local government more accountble

161

to central government's dictate. As in the case of the poll tax, the government is provoking opposition which it may find difficult to contain.

Summary

Local authorities have been subject to sustained attack on their powers and their ability to raise local taxation under both the Thatcher and the Major governments. The Conservatives have implemented legislation which has promoted the role of the market, greater competition, and increased managerialism, at the same time as transferring local government powers to newly created agencies and quangos, and local government service delivery to the private sector. The restructuring of central and local state relations and the relations between the local state and local people has continued into the 1990s with new proposals for full-scale reorganisation. These policies have inevitably drawn the attention of critics to the consequences for local democracy, accountability and decision-making and the dangers of the growing centralisation of power (Stoker, 1991). Opposition to the government's approach was reflected in Conservative losses in the local elections of 1994 and 1995. In assessing the 'Major effect' on local government, Young (1994, p. 96) comments, 'Major's electoral honeymoon proved short-lived. ... The track record so far suggests that there is little to distinguish between the actions taken under Major and those which might have been expected from a fourth Thatcher government'.

The government is still faced with the need for an effective policy to control public spending. In this context the reorganisation of local government amounts to a institutional restructuring of the state with the object of cutting public expenditure and undermining local resistance to government policy. In comparison with other European states, Britain already has one of the weakest forms of local government in the EU, and wholescale reorganisation will make it *the* weakest form.[24]

---

[1] Sir Ian Gilmour was one of the most outspoken critics of the Thatcher government's adoption of New Right theories and its approach to the problem of unemployment, publishing such books as *Inside Right* and *Britain Can Work*.

2   See, for example, Pollert et al. (1991) and Gilbert et al. (eds.) (1992) for an assessment of the concept of flexibility.

3   See diagram in Brown (1988).

4   For example, Longstreth (1988) provides a useful summary of the different interpretations of the impact of so-called Thatcherism on trade union strength and organisation. Other useful sources are Evans et al. (1994), Kelly (1990), Marsh (1992), Millward, et al. (1992), and Smith and Morton (1994),

5   Information from BBC2 programme, *Open Space*, 29.11.94.

6   The media has given a great deal of publicity to high level pay awards causing some embarrassment to the Major government. Following controversy over salary increases given to top executives, including the pay settlements for chief executives in the privatised utilities, the business community felt it necessary to respond by launching a City 'taskforce' to investigate and monitor executive pay and to draw up a code of practice. The 'taskforce' is backed by the CBI, the Stock Exchange, the Association of British Insurers and the Institute of Directors. The chairman of Marks and Spencer is to lead the 'taskforce' which is expected to issue its report after a six month period (*The Times*, 17.1.95).

7   Ironically, this proposal has met with most criticism from the right within the Conservative Party as demonstrated by a comment from the Conservative Family Institute, a rightwing think tank: 'This is a retrograde step and will yet again favour single mothers. We shouldn't be encouraging single mothers to work anyway. Their place is at home looking after their children' (*The Times*, 3.10.94).

8   McKie (1994, p. 94) provides details of the Bill which received Royal Assent in July 1994.

9   Farnham and Lupton (1994) discuss the decline in government support for other forms of training including the traditional apprenticeship, and refer to a study by Finegold and Soskice (1988) which noted that over the Conservatives' first term in office they cut the number of engineering and technician trainees by nearly half.

10 Unemployment Unit Briefing papers and the Unemployment Bulletin are available from the Unemployment Unit, 9 Poland Street, London, W1V 3DG.

11 For a discussion of the Citizen's Charter and its application to different areas of policy see contributions to the edited volumes by Kavanagh and Seldon (1994) and Savage et al. (1994).

12 Kemp refers specifically to the work of Hills (ed.) (1990), *The State of Welfare*. See also Atkinson and Durden (1994) for a summary of the development of housing policy before and after 1979.

13 These figures are quoted and discussed in Atkinson and Durden (1994, pp. 193-4).

14 See our earlier discussion on the introduction of childcare allowances for young single mothers.

15 Information on the level of government spending on crime, and details of the numbers of those in custody, can be found in McKie (1994).

16 See, for example the report in *The Sunday Times* (18.9.94), on Charles Murray's contribution to the Forum on the Underclass in September 1994.

17 Full details of the two White Papers and the government's proposals are set out in Nash and Savage (1994, pp. 147-8).

18 For full details of the Bill see McKie (1994, p. 148).

19 Des King (1993) provides details of selected legislation affecting the powers of local government from 1980-1992. See also Stoker (1991).

20 For a discussion of the forced resignation of Margaret Thatcher as leader of the Conservative Party, see Alderman and Carter (1991) and Wickham-Jones and Shell (1991).

21 See, for example, Dunn (1990), McCrone (1991) and Stoker (1991).

22 The consultative process in Scotland was in two stages and was monitored by the Convention of Scottish Local Authorities (COSLA). Surveys commissioned by COSLA demonstrated that there was no significant support for moving to a single-tier system of local government without broader constitutional changes and the establishment of a Scottish Parliament. See, McCrone, Paterson and Brown (1993).

23 The government abandoned plans to sell off the water industry in Scotland. Strathclyde Region conducted a referendum on the future of the water industry in 1994 and over 95 per cent of voters expressed their opposition to the government's privatisation proposals (Fairley,

1995).

24 Paper presented by John Fairley to conference on Local Government Reorganisation held in Lothian Regional Council, Edinburgh on 24 January 1995, and organised by the John Wheatley Centre.

6 Conclusion: The Major Government and the Crisis of the Postwar British State

Any attempt to assess economic policy under Major must avoid the temptation of just comparing Major with the Thatcher administrations. Although political commentators, particularly those on the left, became obsessed with the 'iron lady' in the 1980s, from the viewpoint of the 1990s the significance of 'Thatcherism' appears to have been somewhat overplayed. A much more fruitful interpretation can be gleaned if we place Major in the context of all postwar British governments.

Foremost among the constraints with which policy makers in the postwar period have had to grapple, are those deriving from the state's management of labour power, the state's management of money, and the opportunities and constraints provided by inter-state relations. In the case of Britain, these constraints have been identified firstly, as the 'British worker problem' (industrial militancy, low productivity and wage inflation); secondly, the problematic position of sterling within international markets (and the relationship between the City of London and British industry); and finally, the issue of the relationship between Britain and Europe (played out for most of the postwar period in terms of the Anglo-American 'special relationship').[1] This chapter looks at these constraints and illustrates their impact on British governments in the postwar period. The aim is to show how this legacy limited the room for manoeuvre of postwar governments. In focusing on these particular constraints we have, of course, been selective and thereby omitted many other factors, such as military spending, which are highly relevant to debates on 'Britain's decline' (Coates, 1994). Nevertheless, we consider that by highlighting these three areas, we can establish a solid base for a historically grounded assessment of the economic policies pursued by Major between 1990-94.

Industrial militancy, productivity and inflation

The election of the first Labour government with an overall majority in July 1945 was seen as a turning point by the organised labour movement in Britain. The consolidation of the welfare state, including Labour's public commitment to the 1944 Employment White Paper, and the nationalisation measures of 1945-48, were capped by the institutionalisation of forms of bargaining and consultation with the official trade union movement. However, the popular view that the Attlee government's main domestic economic problems in the period 1945-51 lay with capital and not labour is grossly simplistic. Since 1940 economic policy had been dominated by the issue of how to avoid a repetition of the rampant inflation which occurred after 1918. Given that a situation of high demand was expected straight after the war, the control of inflation became a major preoccupation. The Attlee administration responded to this threat in two ways. Firstly, the government retained (and in some areas increased) the level of direct control over the economy. Consumer rationing was increased between 1945-48 and controls existed over investment, imports, raw materials, prices and, also, foreign currency exchange. Secondly, in an attempt to tackle the problem of rising wages (wages rose almost 9 per cent annually over the period 1945-47), the government sought to convince the unions to exercise voluntary wage restraint (Cronin, 1991, p. 179). With the decontrol of prices and rationing at the end of 1948, Cripps stabilised the cost of living through food subsidies, rent control and a rigourous budgetary policy. In this way he gained TUC approval for the introduction of a one-year pay freeze beginning in 1949. The period 1948-50 was, therefore, characterised by a quasi-incomes policy concerned with aggregate incomes, not the regulation of relative wages or wage planning as later developed under Macmillan. As clarified by Panitch, 'this was not a wages policy which set out to establish wage differentials as part of a programme of manpower planning. It was expressly a policy of wage restraint' (Panitch, 1976, p. 22; Tomlinson, 1991, p. 100). As a consequence, from 1948 to 1950, the increase in wage rates dropped to a little over 2 per cent a year (see Jones, 1987, pp. 36-40; Howson, 1993, p. 214) and 'real wages probably fell slightly for most workers' (Cronin, 1991, p. 179).

Labour's policy of limiting opposition by using its links with the leadership of the official labour movement to the full, prevented a serious confrontation with the working class in the immediate postwar period. However, working days lost through industrial dispute averaged 1.9 million per year between 1946-51.[2] In October 1951, the incoming Churchill government reverted to Attlee's policy of moral exhortation rather than introducing an official incomes policy. In the wake of a slender overall majority of just 17 seats, Churchill pursued a policy of 'industrial appeasement', aptly conveyed by Walter Monckton, as the Minister of Labour, who recalled, 'Winston's riding orders to me were that the Labour Party had foretold industrial troubles if the Conservatives were elected, and he looked to me to do my best to preserve industrial peace' (quoted in Cronin, 1991, p. 215). The Conservatives, however, could not extract the same level of commitment from the official union movement as Labour. By 1955 real wages had increased to a level 7 per cent above that of 1950-51. Industrial disputes increased, with 8.4 million working days lost in 1957 alone, and the Churchill and Macmillan governments found themselves unable to resist unions in the public sector, thereby weakening the hand of private capital. In sum, during the 1950s, output per worker rose by on average 2 per cent per year. Between 1948 and 1958, the average annual increase in wages and salaries per head of the civilian labour force was 6.5 per cent.[3] Thus, by the late 1950s, the institutionalised power of labour, contributing to increased inflation, was seen as the main threat to the stability of the British economy.

The run on the pound, which occurred in Autumn 1957, brought the issue of inflation to a head. Peter Thorneycroft, Enoch Powell and Nigel Birch sought to temper Macmillan's Keynesianism with the announcement of the infamous 'September measures' (Brittan, 1964, p. 192). Couched in monetarist rhetoric, Thorneycroft advocated severe public expenditure cuts, and set up the Council on Prices, Productivity and Incomes (CPPI) to explore the relationship between wages and inflation. The resignation of Thorneycroft, Powell and Birch, in January 1958, did little to halt the mounting criticism of Macmillan's conciliatory approach to the unions. In February 1958, the CPPI reported that wage increases were responsible for inflation and only sound monetary policy (wages freeze, high interest rates and public spending cuts) would cure the ills of the British economy. Further, in November 1958, the classic anti-labour formula, the 'Phillips curve', was published, and calls for the implementation of a strict incomes policy began to intensify (see Cronin, 1991, p. 227). In this climate Macmillan ordered a full investigation into the factors limiting economic growth in Britain. In a prescient report submitted to the Cabinet in 1961,[4] Treasury officials concluded that

> the disparity between the rate of increase of average earnings and of GDP per worker is the biggest single danger to healthy growth in the future. The rise in prices in the UK has been greater than in most other countries and has gradually eroded the benefits of the 1949 devaluation. If British costs go on rising at the present rate, not only will this country be unable to sell enough exports to pay for the rising volume of imports required by the potential rate of growth, but even in the home market British goods will become less competitive, so that imports will rise still further. The deterioration of the balance of payments shows the need to prevent this continuing. Looking ahead there can be no doubt that a continuation of past experience will carry with it a very real possibility of devaluation being forced upon this country. *The essential need is to find a means whereby the national interest is brought to bear on wage negotiations* (emphasis added).

For Macmillan, and for successive governments up until the first Thatcher administration, wages were to be contained by appeals to the 'national interest' expressed in the form of indicative planning and official incomes policies.

In this vein, Macmillan presided over the first formal incomes policy of the postwar era with the creation, in 1962, of the NEDC. Its twenty members were drawn equally from the Treasury, the Federation of British Industry and the TUC and it provided a forum for tripartite debate but had no executive powers. Aided by its policy making office and flanked by twenty-one main Economic Development Committees, the NEDC, in collaboration with the National Incomes Commission, sought to gain trade union agreement on pay policy. In essence, the strategy was to reach a consensus on expected rates of economic growth which would enable the NEDC to recommend 'acceptable' wage rates. However, this attempt to impose wage restraint on the working class proved futile. The NEDC was neither well integrated into the policy making process nor did the initiative command the wholehearted support of the TUC (see Cronin, 1991, p. 231; Tomlinson, 1990, p. 271). Above all, the effort to regulate wages was rejected *in toto* by the rank and file of the labour movement. In a context where industrial relations was dominated by shop stewards and the emergence of local systems of collective bargaining and job control, national agreements policed by the TUC were of limited significance (Goodman and Whittingham, 1969). This was a lesson well learned by the Wilson governments 1964-70.

In February 1965, Wilson replaced the National Incomes Commission with the National Board for Prices and Incomes. A pay norm of 3-3.5 per cent was set in April 1965, which could only be exceeded if productivity gains were made (see Cronin, 1991, p. 234). This effort to control wages on a voluntary basis collapsed in July 1966. Following the seamen's strike in May, the government introduced a six-month statutory pay freeze along with a set of deflationary financial measures. This was followed by the establishment of wage norms between 3 and 4 per cent from July 1967 to the fall of the government in 1970. Although Wilson had argued that incomes policies would be pursued alongside controls over profits, dividends and rents, it was evident, by 1969, that incomes policies were being used to hold back inflation and maintain profit margins by reducing labour costs. The 1969 White Paper on *Productivity, Prices and Incomes Policy* stated clearly that the government did not believe that any general reduction in the rate of return on private capital would be helpful to the modernisation of the economy.

Most studies of the Wilson period conclude that the government's attempt to hold down wages and reduce the significance of the shop stewards' movement was a failure (Coates, 1975; Coopey et al., 1993). A number of factors contributed to this failure. The institutionalised forms of bargaining and consultation, which successive postwar governments had set up to contain and co-opt the working class, had, in fact, strengthened the bargaining power of work groups and their shop stewards. This needs to be seen against the background of twenty years of relatively full employment, and the degree of job control that local unions had achieved. The strength of labour was evident in wage drift, that is, the difference between national rates and actual local earnings, which characterised the car industry, the docks, shipbuilding and engineering. It was also evident in the growing pattern of short, local, unofficial strike action which spiralled in the Wilson years; and in the control exercised by the workforce itself over the pace of work and job security. By the mid 1960s, inflation continued to erode the value of real wages. The Retail Price Index increased by 35 points between 1963 and 1970 (Butler and Butler, 1986, p. 382). Over 90,000 shop stewards in engineering, docks and building, produced a wave of unofficial industrial action which testified to the inability of the Labour Party or the TUC to control working class resistance. This set the scene for the infamous report of the Donovan Commission on Trade Unions and Employers Associations which influenced the strategies adopted by both Wilson and Heath to tackle the 'problem' of industrial relations.

Researchers for the Donovan Commission reported that shop stewards 'were active in most industries and firms where unions are recognised', and that most stewards had 'established their right to bargain with management about most of the main aspects of their members' working lives - wages, conditions, hours of work, disciplinary matters and employment issues' (McCarthy and Parker, quoted in Coates, 1994, p. 106). This situation was characterised by the Commission as one of 'parallel unionism'. In effect, a two-tier bargaining system had been created. The upper tier was the formal structure recognised by law, where negotiation took place between paid union officials and management at an industry level, which the government sought to regulate. The lower tier was informal, not subject to regulation by law, highly decentralised and in the hands of workplace leaders (Jones, 1987, p. 78). A 1968 report of the National Board for Prices and Incomes portrayed this situation as follows,

> the essence of the problem of applying the incomes policy to Payment by Result (PBR) Systems is that a large part of the increase in earnings under them does not arise from 'claims' or 'settlements' in the accepted

sense of the word, and they are often negotiated by individuals or small groups of workers with foremen, rate-fixers or first-time management ... Thousands of such bargains are struck every day ... we came across only one instance where a firm was attempting to apply the (incomes) policy to PBR earnings in any way (quoted in Jones, 1987, p. 77).

In short, union officials found themselves with no means of implementing the national agreements they signed. Donovan's conclusions echoed the findings of Board of Trade studies into the first shop stewards' movement which grew out of the 'great unrest' prior to the first world war (Aris, 1994). Official trade unions could no longer contain the power of labour. Disorder in factory and workshop relations threatened to undermine management prerogatives and, in extremis, undermine the ability of the state to regulate labour power.

Building on the work of Tolliday and Zeitlin (1986), David Coates (1994, p. 109) has recently added some important qualifications to the picture painted by the Donovan Commission. Not only were there wide variations in the influence and activities of stewards in different plants, but there were also significant variations in degrees of management control even within the car industry, which is normally cited as the most prone to workgroup power. Nevertheless, in the upper echelons of the state, the power of labour was viewed with increasing dismay. Government perception was of an impending political crisis produced by the working class whose decentralised form of action seemed increasingly beyond government or official trade union control.

The Donovan Commission's solution was for management to take the lead. In the Commission's view the shift in power to the lower tier should be recognised and effective procedures developed voluntarily to regulate actual pay, constitute a factory negotiating committee, and cover the rights and obligations of shop stewards (Jones, 1987, p. 78). Through the centralisation and formalisation of steward organisation, the shift to plant and company bargaining would be recognised and the link between wages and productivity strengthened. However, in the event, Wilson disregarded Donovan's preference for voluntarism and opted, instead, for legislation to contain the strength of the shop stewards in the form of the 1969 White Paper, *In Place of Strife*. The White Paper sought to formalise the informal sector and to provide the government with the legal authority to call a twenty-eight day 'cooling off' period for each unofficial strike and compulsory balloting for 'official' disputes. These initiatives foundered on the rock of rank and file militancy, central trade union opposition and employer indifference. However, as earnings increased by over 14 per cent in 1970 and as the number of days lost in industrial dispute over the period 1968-70 topped eight million (see Jones, 1987, p. 79; Hawkins, 1976, p. 136), the incoming Heath government attempted to push through, what has been described as 'the greatest revolution in legal thinking about trade union laws since the Trade Union Act of 1871' (Kidner, 1979, p. 17).

Heath's Industrial Relations Act 1971, had two, now familiar, objectives. Firstly, it sought to consolidate union organisations as disciplining agencies, by conceding specific bargaining rights in return for 'responsibility'.[5] Secondly, it proposed a range of legislation which aimed at strengthening individual rights against unions, enabling penalty clauses and criminal sanctions to be applied against irresponsible unions (thereby restoring the principle of Taff Vale)[6] and 'unconstitutional strikers', all to be regulated under the jurisdiction of a distinct Industrial Relations Court. In this way it sought to undermine the organisational strength of workers and, by establishing the right not to belong to a union, it aimed to undermine the closed shop (Lewis, 1983; Bain and Price, 1983).

Whereas the Donovan Commission believed that reforms could be accomplished without destroying the 'British tradition of keeping industrial relations out of the courts' (Lewis, 1983, p. 370; Heath, 1971), the 1971 Act made the law the main instrument of solving the 'problem' of labour. The legislation, however, proved to be of 'very limited value' as the TUC instructed its members not to register under the new Act and most employers, anxious not to fan the flames of unrest, neglected to use its provisions (Jones, 1987, p. 86). Heath's attempt to tackle wage inflation through a policy of 'de-escalation', which had replaced a formal incomes policy, also came to grief.[7] The Conservative's 'quiet revolution' in government which looked for market based solutions to the 'inefficiency' of the British economy, formally ended in November 1972 after failing to tame the mineworkers. In conditions of rising unemployment and inflation, Heath's strategy from November 1972 to his fall in February 1974 was to pursue expansionary policies (culminating in the Barber boom) together with a firm incomes policy.

Drawing on initiatives adopted in the United States by Richard Nixon, the Conservative's introduced a three-stage statutory incomes strategy which began with a three-month wages and prices freeze, and thereafter sought to moderate wage claims within limits set by the Prices Commission and Pay Board. Although Heath's first phase was relatively successful, Russell Jones correctly argues that the government's strategy of combining 'rapid expansion, depreciation of the exchange rate, and statutory incomes policy was fundamentally flawed' (ibid., p. 96). In the context of a worldwide commodity price boom, a fourfold increase in oil prices at the end of 1973, and the downward float of sterling following the introduction of the floating rate system, any attempt to peg wages within a narrow band was bound to end in disaster, particuarly without TUC endorsement. When the end arrived in early 1974, the Wilson government found it relatively easy to repeal Heath's Industrial Relations Act[8] but experienced more difficulty, as the 1970s wore on, in controlling wages and inflation.

Labour entered office emphasising its special relationship with the official trade union movement. To blunt the rank and file militancy which had created problems for Labour in the 1960s and brought down the Heath government, the Wilson/Callaghan administration made the fullest possible use of policies of co-option and co-operation. Through the rhetoric of the 'Social Contract', Labour invoked the ideology of worker participation, endorsed arbitration and conciliation procedures through, for example, the establishment of ACAS, enacted legislation to uphold employment rights, used productivity deals to promote sectionalism, encouraged the TUC to police 'irresponsible elements', and finally used troops to break strikes (Coates, 1980). Above all, Labour skilfully deployed the threat of imminent economic crisis to gain TUC backing for policies designed to drive down wage costs.

By the first quarter of 1975, 500,000 civil servants had negotiated wage increases of 32 per cent, 100,000 power workers of 31 per cent (matching the miners 31 per cent rise in March), and gas manual workers of 34 per cent (see Coates, 1989, p. 72). In the face of rampant inflation and a deepening balance of payments problem, which had not been corrected by Healey's $3.7 billion loans from private banks and the Shah of Iran in 1974, TUC leaders agreed in the Summer of 1975 to impose voluntary pay restraint. Complementing Healey's infamous deflationary budget of April 1975, the government urged rank and file compliance with the pay norm. By the third quarter of 1976, the inflation of basic wage rates had dropped from 33 per cent in 1975 to just 18.7 per cent. Over the same period price inflation fell from 26.6 per cent to 13.7 per cent (see Jones, 1987, p. 107). However, as the social and industrial 'benefits' of the Social Contract failed to materialise, and prices continued to rise, Labour's ability to control working-class resistance ebbed away. As Coates (1989, p. 74) explains, the rising tide of unemployment and the persistent fall in living standards that accompanied Labour's policies towards the end of the 1970s, ate away at the loyalty shown to trade union officialdom, and undermined its credibility and role as advocate and enforcer of pay restraint.

By the summer of 1977, the government sought to impose a pay limit of 10 per cent. This came on the back of a 40 per cent depreciation in sterling in 1976, which caused import prices to explode. At the same time, unemployment reached 1.37 million, and inflation outstripped average wages by 8 per cent (see Jones, 1987, pp. 110-1; Coates, 1989, p. 72). This 8 per cent gap between prices and earnings prompted sporadic industrial unrest, culminating in the 'winter of discontent' in 1979 which saw 29,474,000 days lost, the largest number of days lost in industrial disputes since 1926 (see Bain, 1983, p. 211). The sense of bitterness and despair experienced by the labour movement in the closing months of Callaghan's premiership is well captured by Coates (1989, pp. 75-6) who argues that

> as one stage of the incomes policy followed another, the willingness of Labour ministers to castigate trade unions and attack working class power increased. A Labour Prime Minister ended up urging trade unionists to cross picket lines during the lorry drivers' strike, a Labour chancellor repeatedly lectured the unions on the evils of secondary picketing, and the Labour Cabinet as a whole persistently argued that high wage settlements threatened price stability, employment levels and the possibility of adequate welfare provision.

The popular image of the 'winter of discontent' is one of mass radicalism dominated by trade union 'power' which was then defused by the Thatcher government. In retrospect, the surge of industrial unrest in 1979 is more accurately portrayed as the high point of a receding tide of conflict (see Cliff and Gluckstein, 1988, p. 344) with an embittered labour movement struggling to come to terms with rising unemployment, de-industrialisation and the language of monetarism.

In chapter 5 we outlined briefly Thatcher's approach to the 'problem' of industrial relations. The lesson Thatcher had learned from the failure of Heath was that legislation alone could not undermine the organisational strength of the working class. Thatcher pursued a policy of head-on confrontation with sections of the trade union movement, whilst backing so-called 'macho management' in disputes, for example, at British Leyland, News International and P&O Ferries. In line with the ideology of monetarism, Thatcher eschewed formal incomes policies, although the government took a particularly hard line on public sector pay (Jones, 1987, p. 120).

Economic policies which reinforced mass unemployment and the devastation of manufacturing heartlands, resulted in a fall in union membership weakening the bargaining power of unions and forcing shop-floor unionism in the direction of bureaucratisation and centralisation (Bonefeld, 1993; Elger, 1994a). Although steward organisation was not destroyed, shifts in the labour market increased employment in areas where neither stewards nor unionism had much of a foothold. The main exception to this trend was the public sector, where the 1980s saw a growth in branch based union organisation (Fairbrother, 1994). In addition, the bureaucratisation of workplace unionism made senior stewards more responsive to management dictates, prompting them to give way to managerial policies and pressures. Working class militancy was weakened in the context of unemployment, which had reached the figure of 12.5 per cent of the total workforce in 1983 and which remained high throughout the 1980s. The rate of inflation dipped to 3.4 per cent in 1986, before once again beginning to rise steadily (see Tomlinson, 1990, pp. 334-9).

The popular image that Thatcher 'tamed the unions' is grossly over-simplistic. In addition to political factors, it is long-term secular trends, those associated with the organisation of capital and the competition between and within classes, that shape industrial relations (Coates, 1989, p. 134). Thatcher accentuated some of these trends for example by promoting individualisation and enforcing the rule of money through law. However, efforts to enhance market conditions to reassert managerial prerogative had begun well before Thatcher came to power. As William Brown revealed, attempts to reduce the degree of worker resistance to new techniques and the introduction of greater flexibility were widespread by 1978, by which time single-employer agreements were the norm in manufacturing industry (Brown, 1981; Coates, 1989, p. 139).

A large body of evidence has recently emerged which challenges the conventional view that the 'British worker' is primarily responsible for Britain's relatively low level of productivity (Coates, 1994; Tomlinson, 1991a; Tiratsoo and Tomlinson, 1993). Nevertheless, the important point for this study is that all governments in the postwar period have been convinced that 'union power' is a major source of economic underperformance. Accordingly, governments since the war have sought, through numerous strategies, to make all workers limit their wage increases (Jones, 1987, p. 129). This concentration on wages produced a situation in the early 1970s which gave Britain the dubious honour of being the industrialised country in Western Europe with the lowest labour costs, with the sole exception of Ireland (Ray, 1987). As Coates emphasises, 'the data on low wages is quite remarkable, and seems to be little known outside the specialist literature' (Coates, 1994, p. 115). By 1970, average labour costs in Western Europe were 60 per cent higher than in the UK. This represented a change, from the position in 1960, when British costs had exceeded those in France, Italy, Germany and Belgium. By 1980, as Ray (1987, p. 72) reports, the European average level of total labour costs was 40 per cent higher than the British level. In sum, the purchasing power of British workers, in comparative terms, fell steadily from 1960.

This evidence does not bode well for the low-wage economy model held in such high esteem by the Major administration. Major has continued to follow the trend set by governments since the 1960s of keeping real wages low whilst presiding over the decline of UK-based manufacturing industry. In the face of overwhelming evidence which points to the difficulty of maintaining the productivity increases of the 1980s (see chapters 3 and 4), Major's low-wage strategy seems increasingly unrealistic. Moreover, the star in Major's economic firmament - low inflation - is once more in jeopardy as Britain's exit from the ERM weakened the government's hand in relation to organised labour. Further, as argued in chapter 3, the deregulation of financial markets and their enhanced importance in the global economy, means that inflation is very much an international phenomenon - beyond the ability of any one national state to control whatever its domestic policies. The familiar characteristics of the British economy, in particular relatively low productivity levels and deindustrialisation, continue to pose major problems for any government. The attempt to gain a competitive advantage by opting-out of the Social Chapter offers little basis for the resolution of these difficulties. As the next section of this conclusion will indicate, the question of competitiveness has shaped Britain's policy towards Europe since 1945. The inability of the British state to resolve its relationship with Europe since the war is at the heart of Major's current dilemma which threatens to split the Conservative Party.

The management of sterling and Britain's relationship with Europe

At first sight it may seem strange to link a discussion of the management of sterling to Britain's policy towards Europe in the postwar period. However, the link becomes clear if we stand aside from those shibboleths which have equated closer European economic integration with the creation of a supranational state form. Throughout the postwar period the management of sterling has been a central preoccupation of British governments. This preoccupation largely determined Britain's strategy towards Europe up until currency convertibility at the end of 1958. Since that date, governments have found themselves buffeted by the pressures which the international use of sterling place on the British economy. The Major government is the current heir to this legacy and, as the experience of the ERM illustrates, it has found itself unable to cope with these pressures in the absence of a clear commitment to full European economic integration.

Britain ended the war in 1945 with the largest external debt in history.[9] In June 1945, with gold reserves standing at just over £500 million, Britain's liabilities totalled over £4000 million (Cairncross, 1985). Preventing bankruptcy by whatever means available, therefore, became the principal objective of the Attlee government. In economic policy terms, the depleted reserves of the entire sterling area constituted the most significant constraint on achieving economic growth. In this climate, the management of sterling was at the heart of governing Britain until conditions allowed the convertibility of the currency in the late 1950s. Accounts which argue that British productive capital was sacrificed on the altar of finance in the postwar period (Fine and Harris, 1985), misinterpret the situation facing the economy after the war. Securing the import of raw materials, whose trade was obviously regulated internationally by the availability of foreign currency, was fundamental to the expansion of productive capital. In the context of government controls, industry required an immediate solution to the problem of depleted foreign currency reserves. The interests of the Treasury and the Bank of England were not therefore opposed, in this instance, to those of productive capital.

Keynes' description of the situation in 1945 as a 'financial Dunkirk' was no exaggeration (R. Clarke, 1982). The volume of Britain's exports in 1944 was only 30 per cent of the amount exported in 1938 (and less than half the value). By contrast, the volume of Britain's imports still stood at 60 per cent of the 1938 figure and, once peacetime conditions were restored, they were expected to exceed the prewar level. With the British economy a net importer of 55 per cent of total food supplies and almost all raw materials (other than coal), the key question facing the government was how to fund its existing balance of payments deficit in addition to finding extra dollars to pay for the import of essential raw materials that were abundant only in dollar markets. Postwar planners estimated that the deficit on the external balance of payments over the first three years of the reconstruction phase would amount to £1.2 billion. In addition, the government had sold over £1 billion of assets to fund the war and accumulated debts as a result of military expenditure overseas totalling £3.3 billion. To complicate matters further, Britain's continuing world wide military presence was costing the government an annual figure of £800 million (Robinson, 1986).

The fundamental point to grasp regarding this situation is that the physical reconstruction of cities and output depended absolutely on the more subtle diplomatic reconstruction of international trade and payments systems. The British government sought agreements that would enable dollars to flow to Britain whilst restricting the convertibility of sterling in domestic and foreign hands (hence the Washington Loan Agreement, the Marshall Plan and the military assistance programmes which encouraged a continuous flow of dollars to Britain). In terms of Britain's trade strategy, the government placed particular emphasis on exports to the dollar area (dollar-earning exports), with sterling area exports deemed next in importance and those to Western Europe running a poor third. Similarly, imports were encouraged from the sterling area whenever possible in preference to those from Western Europe. In 1950, 45 per cent of the merchandise trade of the UK was with the Commonwealth, with the EEC 'Six' absorbing only 12 per cent (see Nevin, 1990, p. 15). This tendency to trade in 'soft', protected markets clearly affected the competitiveness of British industry - but in the immediate postwar years it was a strategy forced on Britain by the lack of foreign currency reserves.

By 1950 it seemed that the reconstruction tasks of the Attlee government had been successfully completed. Despite a 30 per cent devaluation of the pound in September 1949, occasioned by repeated sterling crises, the balance of payments was now back in surplus, the sterling area was still intact and the state had managed to extend the restrictions on the international use of sterling, despite unremitting pressure from the United States government. However, in retrospect, 1950 represented one of those quiet turning points in Britain's relationship with Europe which would rebound with serious consequences for the British state under the Eden and Macmillan governments.

The crisis which prompted devaluation in 1949 had its roots in the 'inventory recession' which took place in the United States in the first part of that year (Milward, 1984). American imports from the Organisation for European Economic Cooperation (OEEC) nations declined almost continuously from January 1949. Whilst this had only a marginal impact on the total value of Western Europe's foreign trade, for Britain the effect was devastating. American imports from Britain dropped almost 40 per cent between July 1948 and July 1949. In effect, the structure of trade established under Attlee meant that Britain was alone among the major Western European states in experiencing a severe crisis in 1949. Western European economies were booming since they had embarked upon a vigorous pattern of intra-European trade. Intra-Western European exports increased in value between 1948 and 1949 by 28 per cent (see ibid., p. 349). Of all the West European countries, only the exports of Austria grew more strongly to the rest of the world than to Western Europe. However, the increase in value of British exports to Western Europe in the period 1948-1950 was a mere 4.9 per cent compared, for instance, to French exports which were up 41 per cent. As Milward (1984, p. 350) clarifies, 'all other Western European countries had a higher proportion of their exports going to Western Europe than had France and Britain'. Although this was important in itself it demonstrated something much more significant to the United States and the French and German governments. It indicated clearly that a Western European economic unit was both politically feasible and economically viable *without the participation of the United Kingdom.* As long as Britain concentrated on sending its exports to traditional markets with very different requirements and low effective demand for high levels of manufactured goods, the British economy would be prone to the consequences of US recession and insulated from economic expansion in Europe.

Throughout the early 1950s, the governments of 'Little Europe' set about institutionalising closer economic relations, in the form of the Schuman Plan in May 1950 and the Treaty of Paris in 1951 (which brought the European Coal and Steel Community into existence in 1952). Throughout these negotiations Britain refused to be treated as 'just another necessitous European nation' and continuously staked its claim for difference on the 'unique pressures' which sterling placed on the economy. In discussions on a proposed Council of Europe, Gaitskell spoke for Attlee (and later for Churchill) when he announced in August 1949, 'the UK by reason of its geographical position and of its political and economic relations with the Commonwealth and the United States could not enter into any exclusive political or economic association with Continental countries' (Burnham, 1990, p. 133). In various memoranda to the OEEC, British state officials pointed to sterling's role as a world reserve currency which set up special difficulties for the UK since large holdings of sterling by individual states subjected the pound to wider variations than the generally small holdings of the other currencies of Europe. The result was that sterling was particularly sensitive to adverse movements in world trade. Similar considerations emerged when the Treasury met in January 1952 to discuss how to halt the latest sterling crisis which took place in the closing months of 1951. The Overseas Finance Division of the Treasury advocated the introduction of immediate sterling convertibility on a floating rate system (the so-called Operation Robot initiative) as a means of enhancing and maintaining the international position of sterling. As one Treasury official outlined, 'the loss of gold reserves is the one national disaster in peacetime which is comparable with the loss of a war ... with sterling reduced to a domestic currency like the franc or the lira, our entire standing and economic fabric would be permanently changed'.[10]

Although the Robot scheme was abandoned, after the Economic Section of the Cabinet Office managed to persuade government ministers that it would probably increase pressure on the pound, Conservative governments throughout the 1950s set about reasserting the international status of sterling and the importance of the City of London as the world's premier financial centre. In 1953, commodity markets and exchanges for raw materials were reopened in London. March 1954 saw the long awaited return of the London Gold Market - open to all non-residents of the sterling area. Changes were made in currency regulations in 1955 which allowed the partial convertibility of the pound for non-sterling area residents and non-dollar area residents. This was followed finally by the full convertibility of sterling in December 1958 and by the Bank of England's decision in 1962 to provide cheap foreign exchange cover and allow non-residents to hold dollar balances with the Bank of England (thus signalling the beginning of Eurodollar markets). Dollars could now be deposited with the Bank of England, in an external account, thereby escaping US exchange regulations and earning a higher rate of interest than obtainable in the US. The aim here was well calculated. London's position as the main financial centre would be re-established and the City would quickly become the world's leading Eurodollar market.

Although it is easy to see these events as being driven by their own internal logic, to view their real significance, they must be set in the context of the negotiations which took place between Britain and Europe in the mid 1950s. In the summer and autumn of 1955, Britain was invited to discussions on closer European economic integration by the six nations which eventually signed the Treaties of Rome in March 1957. After a flurry of activity in Whitehall, the Cabinet Office circulated the Trend Report which pointed to four decisive considerations against membership (Burgess and Edwards, 1988, p. 407). Firstly, the Cabinet Office and the Treasury had concluded that membership would weaken the UK's economic and consequently its political relationship with the Commonwealth and the colonies. Secondly, it was judged that the UK's economic and political interests were worldwide and that a European common market would be contrary to the approach of freer trade and payments. Thirdly, it was thought that participation would gradually lead to political

182

federation, which was unacceptable to Britain. Finally, the Cabinet Office concluded that membership would be detrimental to the British economy since it would involve the removal of protection for British industry against European competition. When placed alongside the earlier considerations relating to sterling, the Trend Report convinced the Eden government that Britain should withdraw from the Messina talks. Instead of negotiating with the Six, Thorneycroft at the Board of Trade convinced the Cabinet to launch an alternative non-discriminatory scheme aiming to wean the Six away from the idea of the common market. This scheme, labelled *Plan G*, later developed into Britain's free trade area proposals, which became the basis of the European Free Trade Area established after the Stockholm conference in 1959 (Camps, 1964). Whilst *Plan G* proposed a free trade area designed to eliminate industrial tariffs, it carried no further implications regarding wider economic integration. Within a free trade area, Britain could retain its traditional trading structure, and as Board of Trade reports concluded, this would be entirely different from a European discriminatory bloc in which Britain came under the domination of Germany.

The successful conclusion of the Treaties of Rome in March 1957 came as a major surprise to the British state. It was fundamental to British thinking that the Six would not go ahead without the participation of the UK. In a frank memorandum titled, 'What went wrong?', the Treasury surveyed the scene in July 1959, and concluded that the government had made a number of serious errors.[11] Britain had misunderstood the US position not realising that the US State department would always back the Community given its political and defence implications. It had made a number of tactical errors, in trying to divide the Six, in believing that the UK would be allowed to join at any stage once the Community was formed and in failing to establish a negotiating machinery to match that of the French. Finally, the British government had continued to pursue the half-hearted 17-nation EFTA strategy when it was clear that neither the French nor the Germans were attracted by the idea, which in any case the Treasury concluded, 'does not bear examination for five minutes'. The next 14 years would be spent struggling with the legacy of the British state's failed attempt to prevent the creation of the Community.

Whilst it is easy to criticise Eden and Macmillan for short-sightedness, a more rounded explanation must make reference to the form of Britain's postwar integration into international trade and money markets. Although a number of events began to weaken Britain's position in the global political economy (Suez and the relentless process of decolonisation), access to privileged markets had enabled the economy to reconstruct and prosper in the early 1950s. Moreover British governments could utilise the international prestige of sterling and the City of London to counter, at least in theory, the effects of balance of payments deficits. Once it became clear that de Gaulle would not sanction UK entry to the Community, Britain was caught in a bind and was forced to pin its economic hopes on the revival of the City of London.

In the nineteenth century, it was the competitiveness of 'British industry' which led to the international use of sterling. By the late 1950s, the lack of competitiveness of Britain's industrial base (particularly vis-á-vis Europe) now meant that the international use of sterling could quickly turn from an asset to a liability. As sterling was made convertible, short term capital inflows and outflows increased in volatility. In these circumstances, the Bank of England found it increasingly difficult to defend the exchange rate - the slightest rumour could lead to massive speculation against the pound, destabilising the domestic economy. Although these pressures were seen to exist even as early as 1956 (when sterling was only partially convertible) - over the first two days of Britain's invasion of Egypt there was an outflow of $50 million - they became more acute over the next 20 years (Milward, 1992). From the early 1960s, the 'British economy' was dominated by a pattern which saw rising levels of imports, falling exports, and when the balance of payments surplus diminished the introduction of high interest rates to attract short term capital (hot money) to London (see Milward, 1992, p. 387; Browning, 1986, p. 254).

On entering office in 1964, Wilson found that convertibility and the establishment of the Eurodollar markets had produced a situation whereby financial markets could validate or disapprove of policy measures within hours. In many ways the story of the Wilson government is one of speculative action against the pound followed by international rescue operations to shore up the sterling exchange rate. Deflationary measures pursued throughout 1965 and 1966 failed to stem the tide of speculation, forcing the government to devalue in November 1967 and to negotiate a $1.5 billion standby credit from the IMF (Browning, 1986). Although devaluation had been foreseen as early as 1961, Wilson agreed with Bank of England and Treasury opinion that it was a strategy to be avoided unless Labour was willing to destroy confidence in sterling and the City as the premier financial centre.

The crisis which beset international money markets in the early 1970s, enabled Heath to consolidate his new relationship in Europe with Pompidou (entry to the Community had been negotiated in 1970). Heath joined with the French premier in thwarting Nixon's attempt to push for a revaluation of European currencies. With the US now unprepared to subsidise a British presence East of Suez, the Community offered, in Heath's view, an opportunity for Britain to continue its world role, but as part of a European mission (Blackburn, 1971). By the early 1970s, EC membership began to have a significant impact on the structure of Britain's trade. By 1973, 26 per cent of the UK's merchandise trade was with the Six (compared with 12 per cent in 1950), and trade with the Commonwealth had fallen to 17.7 per cent (from 45 per cent in 1950) (Nevin, 1990, p. 14). However, the 1970s were a dormant decade as regards initiatives concerning closer economic union. Across Europe, states were struggling to cope with raging inflation, rising unemployment and fiscal crisis. Whilst deflation was the European norm, in Britain, the 1974 Wilson government began by trying to expand the economy. The result was a collapse in profits, a further decline in competitiveness, low productivity, rising unemployment, and low levels of inward investment, topped by deeper balance of payments problems.

By 1978, it was evident that Britain was determined to distance itself from a number of the integrative ideals which flowed from Brussels. Heath had already stood out against common policies in the areas of industry, social policy, science and technology. Moreover, his pursuit of a common regional fund did not imply support for integration, but rather sought to secure a subsidy for the government's existing regional development policy (George, 1991, p. 51). In the face of speculative pressure in July 1972, Heath had withdrawn sterling from the 'snake in the tunnel' agreement, and the Treasury refused further negotiation unless the German government would agree to underwrite its value (Tsoukalis, 1977). As the 1970s wore on, Britain began to pursue a determined policy of minimising the economic costs of British membership. Callaghan refused to take sterling fully into the European Monetary System in the light of numerous studies which predicted that the move would have damaging results for the British economy (see George, 1991, p. 56; Statler, 1979). Britain reached the end of its period of transitional membership in 1978. The renegotiation of Britain's net contribution was imperative since, despite having the third lowest GDP per capita in the EC, the UK was set to become the second largest net contributor to the budget. Whilst Thatcher struggled with budget considerations, the election of Jacques Delors as President of the Commission in 1985 signalled an attempt to push for closer integration in Europe. The creation of a genuine internal market, through the Single European Act, was embodied as a formal objective by 1992, and the powers of the European parliament were extended. As with other integrative initiatives, these proposals were viewed with some scepticism. The deregulation of finance and the creation of a common market in services was deemed to be beneficial for the City of London. However, as was indicated above, the issue of monetary union and the single currency represented a dilemma for the state since it was unclear how such initiatives would affect the international role of sterling. Proposals to seek a 'level playing field' in other areas affecting economic policy, such as the Social Chapter, were perceived to be particularly damaging to the competitiveness of the economy.

The issue of the role of sterling has been at the heart of British economic policy in the postwar period. It has dominated policy towards Europe and conferred both costs and benefits on the 'British economy'. The issues which have preoccupied, and divided, the Major administration (ERM, monetary union and the single currency) have been raised, in many guises, on numerous occasions in the postwar period (Milward, 1992, p. 441). The legacy not only of the postwar period, but of the nineteenth century, continues to make its presence felt on current governments which are now confronted with the deleterious consequences of Britain's industrial and financial dominance in the last century.

Britain in the global economy: finance and industry

The relative economic decline of the UK is often viewed as resulting from the dominance of financial over industrial capital. Proponents of this view such as Anderson (1987), Fine and Harris (1985), Coakley and Harris (1983) and Ingham (1984) interpret this divide as an expression of the peculiarities of British capitalism. This situation, it is argued, has undermined attempts to arrest the relative decline of the British economy.[12] There is no doubt, that within the global circuit of capital, Britain is a low-wage and low-productivity country and a centre of global finance (see Fine and Harris, 1985; Fine and Poletti, 1992). This integration of Britain into the global circuit must be traced back to the commercial and financial dominance of the UK in the last two centuries as expressed in the power of the City as an international clearing house, the creation of an internal market (i.e. the British Empire) and the transnational organisation of 'British' capital associated with the British Empire (see Gamble, 1986; Elbaum and Lazonick, 1986).

The differentiation between the global role of the City and the declining competitive strength of industry does not mean that British industry has been undermined as a consequence of financial interests and policies favouring the concerns of financial markets. Although the global role of the City *has had* a detrimental effect on British industrial development, the decline of Britain has by no means been matched by a decline in the power of 'British' capital. As indicated by Rowthorn (1975, p. 175), 'the overseas strength of British big *capital* has compounded the debility of British *capitalism*'. This has not changed during the 1980s (Overbeek, 1990). While the City responded to the decline of the pound by detaching its operations from reliance on the domestic currency, productive capital, in the face of domestic mergers and monopolisation (Gamble, 1986), has taken advantage of the global strength of the City. 'British' capital has expanded business to international markets. This expansion has been based on multinational companies. 'It helps to account for one of the great paradoxes of British decline - why an economy performing so poorly should nevertheless have produced more multinational companies than any other country apart from the United States' (ibid., p. 109). The global orientation of 'British' capital involves more advanced industrial capitals being less affected by domestic constraints at the same time as their competitive position on the world market depends on a policy of financial stability to maintain and improve conditions of exchange on the world market itself.

The thesis then, that in Britain the dominance of financial capital over productive capital expresses the incompleteness of capital organisation in the UK, is misleading. Advocates of the finance/industry divide fail to see that the transnational organisation of 'British' capital and the development of London as the centre for the global circulation of capital expresses the organisation of 'British' capital at the most developed level of global capitalist relations (see Ch. 2). Rather than signifying the incompleteness of the organisation of capital, the international orientation of 'British' capital expresses its organisation at the most fundamental level of the world market: i.e. the integration of productive and money capital on the basis of financial capital and the operation of capital dissociated from domestic constraints. The international role of the City and the detachment of productive capital from domestic constraints corresponded with a decline in the productive power of the UK. This resulted in continuing balance of payments problems and difficulties in stimulating domestic expansion through deficit financing because of constant pressure on exchange rates. After the first world war, the pound was no longer backed by the UK's industrial strength. This condition was exacerbated in the stop-and-go cycle of the 1960s. 'Given the inadequacy of the reserves, every balance of payments crisis caused a run on sterling and produced measures to deflate demand and cut credit and investment' (Gamble and Walton, 1976, p. 156). Following the breakdown of Bretton Woods, the domestic management of capital accumulation was much more directly exposed to the global movement of money.

During the postwar era, the divorce of financial markets from productivity growth manifested itself, so far as the UK was concerned, in a further dissociation of 'British' capital from domestic constraints. Since 1978, the UK has experienced an enormous increase in the net outflow of capital (Coakley and Harris, 1983; Harris, 1983). This development was fostered by the abolition of remaining exchange controls in 1979 and the Big Bang in 1986. The abolition of already liberal exchange controls permitted multinational companies to shift production into different areas. The global relocation of production is 'the basis of trade union fears that the production abroad induced by direct investments is being used to substitute former export of commodities, and hence endanger jobs at home' (Olle and Schöller, 1982, p. 52; see also Picciotto, 1984 and Soskice, 1984).

However, this development must be treated with caution since high interest rates attracted money capital to London and since the UK is one of the main countries attracting productive investment, particularly from US-based multinationals. In the 1980s, the bulk of the inflow of productive investment contributed to a geographically uneven recomposition of accumulation (deindustrialisation of the old heartland of heavy engineering and the opening up of greenfield sites). Following the breakdown of Bretton Woods, various financial deregulations aimed at recouping a central role for the City in global financial networks (Coakley, 1984, Coakley and Harris, 1992). The principal motive behind the deregulation of the City in 1986 (the Big Bang) was the realisation that the London Stock Exchange was in danger of losing ground to other centres. 'The Big Bang has afforded London one major advantage over its two main competitors' (Coakley, 1988, p. 18). The City 'does not restrict the securities activities of its commercial banks and grants banking licences to investment banks. That is, London is the only centre which offers free trade in all types of international securities and banking markets to both commercial and investment banks' (ibid.). The lifting of exchange controls and deregulation underpinned the credit-sustained boom and reaffirmed the form of Britain's integration into the world market.

Financial policy and the working class

During the 1980s, the widening gap between productive accumulation and monetary expansion resulted in a disproportionate development between the balance of trade and the balance of payments. Despite a negative trade balance since 1983, the overall balance of payments remained positive until the late 1980s. The balance of payments improved during the 1980s because of the windfall profits of North Sea oil (Keegan, 1984). The deep recession in the early 1980s, although severe for the UK, was cushioned by these profits, especially in the wake of the major rise in the price of oil in 1979. The effects of North Sea oil have been contradictory. On the one hand, North Sea oil profits helped to finance public expenditure and to improve the balance of payments, so supporting the exchange rate of the pound. At the same time, it intensified competitive pressure. The appreciation of the pound made it harder to export from, and easier to import into, the UK. On the other hand, the high exchange rate of the pound relative to the declining importance of manufacturing, reduced the cost for 'British'-

based multinationals transferring production abroad. Overseas assets could be acquired relatively cheaply. The stock of British direct investment abroad reached £110 billion at the end of 1986 (up from £80 billion in 1985), amounting to a postwar record of 28 per cent of GDP (*Financial Times*, 18.3.87). British takeovers in the US reached the level of $5.2 billion in 1985, up 33 per cent from 1984 (*Financial Times*, 20.2.87). The surge of UK takeovers in the US accounted for more than £12 billion in 1986, indicating reliance on acquisitions at the expense of productive investment in the UK (*Financial Times*, 5.1.87). During the 1980s, the strength of the pound, rather than implying sound economic conditions, put a gloss on the difficulties of imposing work profitably. Large balance of payments surpluses were not supported by a growth in productive capital formation. They expressed, rather, the decreasing strength of the link between money and exploitation. The return of large balance of payments deficits by 1989 highlighted this difficulty. The global role of the City, and therewith the divorce of money from productive growth, was not a sign of the strength, but an expression of the weakness of capitalist reproduction on a world scale.

In the UK, the abandonment of tight monetary policies in 1982, together with the deregulation of the City, led to a major reflation of the economy based on the growth in consumer spending and average wages rises outstripping productivity growth (Deakin, 1992; Keegan, 1989; Nolan, 1989). High interest rates and the control of the PSBR supported the exchange rate of the pound which, in turn, supported consumer spending through cheaper import prices. During the 1980s, 'domestic demand for manufactures had grown by 20 per cent but the UK output of manufactures by only 9 per cent' (Keegan, 1989, p. 160). Imports grew twice as fast as exports (ibid., p. 202), the effect of which was disguised by oil revenues. When these revenues started to fall in 1986, the dissociation between credit-sustained consumption and labour productivity made itself felt in balance of payments deficits and intense speculative pressure on the pound (see Ch. 4).

The rapid deterioration of the non-oil balance showed that the recovery of the 1980s had been sluggish. The damage caused by the squeeze on manufacturing in the early 1980s was so great that, even by 1987, the recovery was only to the levels of the 1970s (Keegan, 1989). How was Britain to pay her deficits when oil runs out? Although, during the 1980s, the pound devalued against some currencies, especially the German Mark, high interest rates, which encouraged money holders to invest in sterling, further undermined productive activity as the debt burden increased. At the same time, banks accumulated huge losses as debtors could not meet their obligations. It thus became clear that the economic 'base' of the world's leading banking centre was not able to support the exchange rate of the pound. The attempt to force employers, through the cost of credit and a high exchange rate, to increase productivity and to restrain wages failed. In other words, the miracle of the 1980s, that is the credit boom, came to a dramatic end. The credit boom of the 1980s and the role of the City in global financial markets was based on a dramatic accumulation of debt which was not supported by capital growth, i.e. the expansive exploitation of labour. The pound's forced exit from the ERM highlighted both the strength of the underlying problem of insufficient productivity growth and the power of global financial pressure responding to working-class resistance to intensification of work through speculative pressure on the pound.

Some commentators, such as Smith (1993), have argued that the recession of the 1990s was to a great extent a consequence of the government's decision to join the ERM at an overvalued exchange rate (see Ch. 4). Similar arguments have been offered by, for example, Thirlwall (1988) and Strange (1971) to explain the decline in British competitiveness during the postwar era. The global role of sterling supporting the dollar as world currency has been interpreted as a major cause of the decline of Britain's competitive position. For example, Susan Strange argued that the 'main cause of the British predicament has not been the British economy but rather the decline of sterling and the failure of British policy to adapt to that decline' (Strange, 1971, p. 318). Similarly, Thirlwall (1988) argued that the lack of competitiveness was, in part, a consequence of sterling's overvalued exchange rate between 1950 and 1967, especially against European and Japanese currencies. The adjustment of sterling's exchange rate through the devaluation of the pound in 1967 is said to have been too late as serious damage to Britain's real economy had already occurred (Alford, 1988).

The maintenance of the pound's exchange rate led, as argued for example by Hirsch (1965), to persistent balance of payments crises, giving rise to stop-and-go policies and cycles. In other words, policy makers, rather than following Keynesian forms of economic planning, were constantly either reflating the economy through a growth in the money supply or deflating the economy through a squeeze on credit. However, this view is one-sided and is too narrowly focused on Britain. The stop-and-go cycle is not a 'British' problem. All other national states face similar problems. In the British case, the stop-and-go cycle was decisive because of the weakness of relative productivity growth (Alford, 1988; Matthews, 1968).

Low wage levels in Britain do not, on their own, amount to a competitive advantage and might well reflect poor productivity performance. 'Britain's labour costs per hour were low but when these are translated into labour cost per unit of output the reverse is the case' (Alford, 1988, p. 40). Amongst other things, there was, in Alford's words, an insufficient intensity of capital use, giving rise to low throughput per worker. The near full employment of the postwar era strengthened trade union bargaining, reinforcing established custom and practice which led to and maintained low productivity growth.

The devaluation in 1967 accommodated comparatively high unit labour costs through a depreciation of the exchange rate. The benefits of devaluation were shortlived as poor economic performance persisted. In other words, the exchange rate of the pound, while constraining the competitive position of the UK, was not the cause of Britain's decline. Rather, 'the exchange rate difficulties are symptomatic of more fundamental problems' (Alford, 1988, p. 87), namely that of the underlying problem of imposing a real breakthrough in productivity growth upon Britain's labour force. As in the 1960s when Britain resisted devaluation, and when the UK joined the ERM in 1990, the political reason behind the maintenance of a high exchange rate can be interpreted as a means of asserting pressure on employers to confront their workforce in an attempt to lower unit labour costs. Just as in 1992, the devaluation of the pound in 1967 signalled the failure of this attempt. Devaluation bailed out manufacturing by accommodating relatively high unit labour costs through exchange rate depreciation. Government used the pound's position within the Bretton Woods fixed exchange-rate system as an 'automatic pilot'. This pilot failed to achieve the desired depoliticisation of economic policy making as soon as the conditions of the world boom of the postwar era deteriorated. This was emphasised by the industrial militancy and social unrest of the late 1960s, causing incomes policies and labour legislation to fail, and leading the Heath government to engineer the shortlived and inflationary Barber boom of the early 1970s. It also failed to address the problems caused by high unit labour costs. Samuel Brittan's comment at that time is indicative of the problems faced by the then British government. Government, he argues, is responsible for carrying out fiscal and monetary policy to curb inflation and for securing that resources, including labour power, are used in the most efficient way. As Brittan (1970, pp. 62-3) put it on the eve of the breakdown of the Bretton Woods system, 'if the Government lacks the political will or strength to do so, no other method of adjustment, whether devaluation, import controls, or any other [such as a fixed exchange rate] will succeed.' Floating rates are seen as giving a much better chance of avoiding the vicious cycle of debt and low productivity because the pound would depreciate and so, theoretically, make exports cheaper and depress imports. This is seen to provide government with a certain degree of flexibility which could be used to tackle the 'roots' of inflationary pressure, namely the inflationary gap between consumption and productive activity.

After Thatcher: Major problems and Labour's proposals

The economic problems the Major government inherited from the Thatcher government are comparable, if not more intense, with those faced by all governments since the end of the second world war. As Eatwell (1992, p. 333) puts it, the economic problems before the election in 1992 are 'more severe than any faced by an incoming government since 1945'. The deflationary periods between 1979 and 1983 and between 1989 and 1993 led to a dramatic destruction of industrial capacity. During the first deflationary period, 45 per cent of industrial employment was lost and, although the productivity of the remaining labour force increased during the 1980s, industrial production in 1994 was hardly higher than in 1979 (see Pollard, 1994, p. 278). According to Michie (1992, p. 6), 'UK output rose by 6% over 1979-1991 compared with the OECD average (excluding the UK) of 35% with the UK coming in *twentieth* out of 21 OECD countries'. The 1980s do not represent a decade of investment and production, but rather of credit-based consumption, fiscal redistribution and financial profligacy. The exploitation of North Sea oil resources has not been 'associated with an equivalent accumulation of productive assets' (Eatwell, 1992, p. 333). Nor has credit expansion launched a boom in productive investment based on improved productivity performance. Instead, the asset base of the economy continued to deteriorate, average wage rises forged ahead of productivity growth, and the growth of consumer spending increased import penetration. The 1980s, rather than representing a break with the past, amounted to a 'culmination of the past' (Michie, 1992, p. 6).

The Major government's economic policy during the recession of the 1990s has been analysed in chapters 4 and 5. But would a Labour government have made a difference? For the Conservative Party, the 1992 election was an election to lose. 'Winning saddled the Conservative Government with the responsibility for ratifying the Maastricht Treaty and meant that it was a Conservative Government which was forced to preside over the sterling devaluation in September 1992, the first time a devaluation in the twentieth century was unambiguously the responsibility of a Conservative Government' (Gamble, 1994a, p. 20). Unlike the situation in 1964 and 1974, it was not Labour but the Conservatives who had to preside over the economic mess undermining their electoral standing after 1992 and their internal unity and cohesion.[13]

Elections do not lead to fundamental changes in economic policy. On the contrary, changes in the global political economy lead to changes in emphasis in economic policy. In short, economic development does not coincide with election cycles. As Gamble and Walkland (1984, p. 29) put it, 'economic trends are secular and resistant to Party influence' as well as 'government changes'. The trajectory of the Major government confirms this pattern. The shift in economic policy did not come about as a consequence of the 1992 election but as a result of the pound's forced exit from the ERM in September 1992. As Gamble (1984, p. 80) shows, during the postwar period, the 'adoption of new techniques for controlling inflation have in practice been the work of Labour Chancellors' and none of the 'changes were the result of party competition'. This circumstance holds also for the change in government from Callaghan to Thatcher in 1979. The Conservative Party under Margaret Thatcher was 'hardly responsible for introducing a monetarist counterrevolution in stabilising policy' (ibid.) as the move to a policy of sound money had already been introduced under the Chancellorship of Healey in 1975. Continuity in economic policy has been marked and economic policy issues have in reality been non-controversial (Gamble and Walkland, 1984, pp. 34, 35). Further, as Richard Rose (1984) argues, the policy of deflation in the early 1980s did not achieve significant cuts in public expenditure. The most significant cuts 'were those which arose as a result of Dennis Healey's cash limit squeeze in 1976-78' (Rose, 1984, p. 160). Indeed, as Rose, and Gamble show, it was the Labour Party in government which has 'more often been the party of financial probity', whereas the Conservatives have more often than not been the party of 'financial profligacy' (Gamble,1984, p. 80; see also Rose, 1984, p. 123). Behind the often heated public exchanges between the Labour Party and the Conservative Party, there exists, nevertheless, a coalition behind closed doors over policy. This has not changed in the 1990s. As Shaw (1994, p. 107) indicates, the 'economic differences between the two major parties are narrower now than they have been for about 20 years'.

Following its third consecutive defeat at the 1987 General Election, the Labour Party embarked on a comprehensive overhaul of its policies in the form of its Policy Review. The Review can be interpreted as a response to three election defeats, to the policies being pursued by the Thatcher administrations, to changing economic, social and political conditions, and to perceived changes in the attitudes and expectations of the electorate. The Review also represented a rejection of many of the policies advocated by the left within the party and associated with the Alternative Economic Strategy of the 1970s (Aaronovitch, 1981; CSE, 1980) on the grounds that such policies would be unsuccessful in harnessing sufficient support at General Elections.

The process of the review involved a number of stages. In phase 1, the party assessed the changes which had taken place in the 1980s and the challenges of the 1990s. It published its *Democratic Socialist Aims and Values* document which presented a broad outline of policy, and established seven groups covering different aspects of policy. Phase 2 was the 1988 Labour Party Conference where the seven Policy Review Groups published interim reports and the party issued its second document *Social Justice and Economic Efficiency.* In phase 3 the Review groups explored the key issues and problems identified in their interim reports and invited party members to submit their views as part of the Labour Listens Campaign. Phase 4, in May 1989, saw the publication of the results of the review process in the document *Meet the Challenge, Make the Change.* After some disagreement over the recommendations on defence policy, all seven reports were accepted by the Brighton

Conference in 1989. In phase 5, the final stage, the document *Looking to the Future* in 1990 was published. This document, which contained chapters on Creating a Dynamic Economy, Bringing Quality to Life, Creating New Opportunities, Freedom and Fairness and Britain in the World, formed the foundation for the 1992 General Election manifesto.[14]

The immediate response of the Labour leader, Neil Kinnock, to electoral defeat in 1992 was to tender his resignation. Under the new leadership of John Smith, the party continued to support many of the policies contained within the Policy Review. However, one criticism of the Review was that its economic policies were too orientated to the supply-side of the economy at the expense of Keynesian style macroeconomic management, this time to be launched at a European level. A return towards the demand-side was noticeable in the period after the election, particularly following the election of Bill Clinton in the United States Presidential elections. As Corry (1994) states, the aim of economic policy was to be explicit about such objectives as economic growth, employment generation and equality, with John Smith arguing at the 1993 Party conference that all instruments of economic policy must be geared towards these ends. The sudden death of John Smith in 1994 led to a reorientation of the Party with Tony Blair as leader and John Prescott as his depute. Under Blair, Labour's post-election concern emphasises the attainment of low inflation and the improvement of the supply-side of the economy.

The main themes of the Policy Review can be summarised as follows. Nationalisation is to all intents and purposes abandoned; industrial policy is to be geared around the supply of skills, research, and the creation of a modern infrastructure; European integration is espoused enthusiastically and the EU is seen as an arena within which Labour's objectives can best be attained; and monetary and fiscal policy is tailored to the attainment of a stable exchange rate, stable interest rates, and low inflation (Eatwell, 1992, pp. 334-335). In other words, as Corry (1994, p. 51) puts it, 'there is not and cannot be a "left" Labour macroeconomic tool as opposed to a right-wing Labour or Conservative one. ... The key is to make sure that we are trying to hit socialist objectives, taking account of all the constraints faced at the time'. This view on Labour's Policy Review is shared by Raymond Plant (1989, p. 8) who argues that 'in practical terms, the Policy Review is in many ways an attempt to bring the official outlook of the party into line with what has been a dominant force of its political practices in the post-war world'. Corry's notion that socialist objectives have to be attained within the framework of constraints reformulates Dennis Healey's warning to the Labour Party conference in 1982: 'Now comrades there is a problem here. General elections do not change the laws of arithmetic' (cited in Rose, 1984, p. xxxii). All governments have, according to Christopher Huhne (1990, p. 110), to attempt to meet four broad objectives: the achievement of an external balance; the control of wage inflation by linking wage rates to productivity; the provision of a steady growth of living standards; and keeping unemployment low. The expectation is that a left of centre government would add to this list the objective of fair distribution, to tackle poverty while maintaining incentives to work (ibid.).[15]

Labour's Policy Reviews amount to an explicit endorsement of a market based economy, commending, as Shaw (1994, p. 86) states, 'the market as the best mechanism for allocating most goods and services'. However, this endorsement does not mark a departure from previous positions. Any denunciations of the market in the postwar era were rhetorical rather than real. Further, both the Conservative Party and the Labour Party, when assuming office, have rarely overturned either the legislation or policies of the previous government.[16] Labour's Policy Reviews do not promise that a future Labour government will be an exception to this rule. Privatised assets will not be returned to the public domain and trade union legislation will not be repealed as the party is committed to retaining most Conservative labour legislation (see Shaw, 1994). Further, the Labour Party is not inclined to cede the unions political influence as during the Social Contract of the 1970s. Rather, Labour promises to 'induce the unions to alter their bargaining strategy by pointing out the implications for national economic objectives and welfare spending of given levels of pay increases' (ibid., p. 96). The Labour leadership, like the Conservative Party under Major, proposes to maintain a tight rein on public spending, to contain inflation, and to impress upon employers and unions the requirement of lower unit labour costs. During the early 1990s, Labour hoped to achieve these goals by opting firmly for ERM membership. The Labour Party endorsed the view that ERM membership would 'depress inflationary expectations by denying employers the option of a competitive devaluation if they succumbed to pay claims too easily' (Shaw, 1994, p. 98). Were employers not able to depress

197

the growth of wages and lower unit labour costs, they would 'price themselves out of markets with the result - as Smith pointed out - that "there would be unemployment, wouldn't there?"' (ibid.). Since the exit of the pound from the ERM, it is not only the Conservative Party under Major which has lost its moral authority. The Labour Party has also lost one of its key economic policy proposals.

The election defeat in 1992 spared the Labour Party from taking political responsibility for economic policy during the deep and prolonged recession. As Gamble (1994a, p. 20) puts it, 'the 1992 election interrupted a familiar cycle in British politics where short periods of crisis-ridden Labour government during which the government struggles to stay afloat and is eventually overwhelmed, are interspersed with longer, more stable periods of Conservative rule'. The Major government is a 'victim' of its own success. Peter Jay is surely right when he points out that Major's towering achievement has been to preside over the fall of inflation from 10 per cent in 1990 to 2.5 per cent in March 1994 (Jay, 1994, pp. 200-1). This 'feat' has only been matched by the Callaghan government which presided over a fall in inflation 'from 22.3 per cent 1975Q1-1976Q1 to 8.7 per cent 1978Q2-1979Q2' (ibid., p. 201). Similarly, under the Major government 'manufacturing pay rises between April and June 1993' were the 'lowest for at least 16 years' (German, 1993, p. 17).[17]

The future will show whether the consequences of bringing down inflation will cost the Conservative Party the next election, leaving the Labour Party to reap the benefits and to govern during the upswing of the economy. Nevertheless, it should be clear from the argument advanced in this book, that the struggle between the Labour Party and the Conservative Party is, to a great extent, a ritual conflict around symbols, which disguises a consensus between the parties on key policy areas. Any party in government is subject to the constraints presented by global financial markets, class struggle and Britain's position in the world market. The means available to government to deal with these constraints are broadly similar, and fiscal and monetary policy does not change because of electoral results, but rather because of the development of the class antagonism between capital and labour at the level of the global political economy.

1 It is, of course, fundamental to our approach (as we indicated in chapter 2) that these 'constraints' are not to be seen as existing separately from each other, but rather as internally related issues. For more on this, see Clarke (1988) and Holloway (1995).

2 Calculated from *PRO CAB 129/105*, 'Industrial Relations', 16.5.61.

3 *PRO CAB 129/105*, 'Economic Growth and National Efficiency', 10.7.61.

4 *PRO CAB 129/105*, 'Economic Growth and National Efficiency', 10.7.61. See sections 72 and 73.

5 On 'responsible unionism', see Aris (1994).

6 On Taff Vale, see Clegg, Fox and Thompson (1964).

7 De-escalation or the N-1 strategy was a policy designed to give a lead to the private sector in wage settlements. Each successive major settlement in the public sector was to be 1 per cent less than the last. In 1972 the NUM submitted a claim for a 30 per cent wage increase to which the National Coal Board responded with an 8 per cent offer in line with N-1. In the wake of the ensuing strike, a court of inquiry recommended a 20 per cent settlement which was later agreed by both the NUM and the government. For details see Hawkins (1976) and Jones (1987, p. 85).

8 The first stage in the repeal was the Trade Union and Labour Relations Act 1974 which restored the presumption that collective agreements were not intended to be legally enforceable. The second stage was delayed until 1976 when the Trade Union and Labour Relations (Amendment) Act was passed.

9 This section draws on Burnham (1990).

10 *PRO T236/3243*, External Sterling Plan, February 1952. For further details, see Burnham (1993a) and Procter (1993).

11 *PRO T234/720*, 'What went Wrong?', July 1959.

12 For a recent overview of theories of British 'decline' see David Coates (1994).

13 On government inheriting from previous governments see Rose and Davidson (1994).

14 The Review met with support and criticism and debates over whether the policies represented a radical departure from the past. On this debate see Jones (1988); Shaw (1990); Sawyer (1988); Garner

(1988); Coates (1988) and Wilton (1990).

15 The theoretical guide to this view is Rawls (1971) *Theory of Social Justice* which reformulates New Rights ideas on the trickle down effect of the unfettered operation of the market in terms of a left-liberal theory of social justice.

16 On this see Rose (1984), Gamble and Walkland (1984) and Rose and Davidson (1994).

17 For an analysis of how the Callaghan government held back pay rises in the 1970s, see Panitch (1986).

Bibliography

Aaronovitch, S. (1981), *The Road from Thatcherism: The Alternative Economic Strategy*, Lawrence and Wishart, London.

Abse, L. (1989), *Margaret, Daughter of Beatrice*, Jonathan Cape, London.

ACAS (1980), *Industrial Relations Handbook*, HMSO, London.

Addison, P. (1977), *The Road to 1945*, Quartet Books, London.

Alcock, P. (1993), *Understanding Poverty*, Macmillan, London.

Alderman, R.K. and Carter, N. (1991), 'A Very Tory Coup: The Ousting of Mrs Thatcher', *Parliamentary Affairs*, vol. 44, no. 2.

Alesina, A. (1988), 'Macroeconomics and Politics', in Fischer (ed.) 1988.

Alford, B.W.E. (1988), *British Economic Performance 1945-1975*, Macmillan, London.

Anderson, M. and Fairley, J. (1983), 'The Politics of Industrial Training in the United Kingdom', *Journal of Public Policy*, vol. 3, part 2.

Anderson, P. (1987), 'The Figures of Descent', *New Left Review*, no. 161.

Aris, R. (1994), *Continuity and Change: The Role of Trade Unions in State Industrial Relations Policy in Britain, 1910-*

1921, PhD thesis, University of Warwick.

Armstrong, P. et al., (1984), *Capitalism since World War II*, Fontana, London.

Arrighi, G. (1994), *The Long Twentieth Century*, Verso, London.

Ascher, K. (1987), *The Politics of Privatisation*, Macmillan, London.

Atkinson, R. and Cope, S. (1994), 'Changing Styles of Governance Since 1979', in Savage et al. (eds.) 1994.

Atkinson, R. and Durden, P. (1994), 'Housing Policy Since 1979: Developments and Prospects', in Savage et al. (eds.) 1994.

Atkinson, R. and Savage, S. (1994), 'The Conservatives and Public Policy', in Savage et al. (eds.) 1994.

Bain, G. (ed.) (1983), *Industrial Relations in Britain*, Basil Blackwell, Oxford.

Bain, G. and Price, R. (1983), 'Union Growth: Dimensions, Determinants and Destiny', in Bain (ed.) 1983.

Batstone, E. (1988), *The Reform of Workplace Industrial Relations*, Clarendon, Oxford.

Benn, C. and Fairley, J. (1986), *Challenging the MSC on Jobs, Education and Training*, Pluto, London.

Bird, Derek (1990), 'Membership of Trade Unions in 1988', *Employment Gazette*, May.

Bird, D. (1990a), 'Industrial Stoppages in 1989', *Employment Gazette*, July.

Blackburn, R. (1971), 'The Heath Government', *New Left Review*, no. 70.

Block, F. (1977), *The Origins of International Economic Disorder*, University of California Press, London.

Bond, P. (1990), 'The New US Class Struggle: Financial Industry Power vs. Grassroots Populism', *Capital and Class*, no. 40.

Bonefeld, W. (1992), 'Social Constitution and the Form of the Capitalist State', in Bonefeld et al. (eds.) 1992.

Bonefeld, W. (1993), *The Recomposition of the British State during the 1980s*, Dartmouth, Aldershot.

Bonefeld, W. and Holloway, J. (eds.) (1991), *Post-Fordism and Social Form*, Macmillan, London.

Bonefeld, W. and Holloway, J. (eds.) (1995), *Global Capital, National State and the Politics of Money*, Macmillan, London.

Bonefeld, W. et al. (eds.) (1992), *Open Marxism*, vols. 1 and 2,

Pluto, London.

Bonefeld, W. et al. (eds.) (1995), *Open Marxism*, vol. 3, Pluto, London.

Bordo, M. and Eichengreen, B. (eds.) (1993), *A Retrospective on the Bretton Woods System*, University of Chicago Press, London.

Brett, A.E. (1983), *International Money and Capitalist Crisis*, Heineman, London.

Brittan, S. (1964), *The Treasury Under the Tories 1951-1964*, Pelican, London.

Brittan, S. (1970), *The Price of Economic Freedom*, Macmillan, London.

Brittan, S. (1976), 'The Economic Contradictions of Democracy', in King (ed.) 1976.

Brittan, S. (1977), *The Economic Consequences of Democracy*, Temple Smith, London.

Brittan, S. (1984), 'The Politics and Economics of Privatisation', *The Political Quarterly*, vol. 55, no. 2.

Brown, A. (1988), 'Labour Market Policy In Britain: A Critical View', New Waverley Papers, Politics series no. 1, University of Edinburgh, Edinburgh.

Brown, A. (1988a), 'The Case Against Wages Councils: The Evidence Versus The Ideology', in Davidson and White (eds.) 1988.

Brown, A. and Fairley, J. (eds.) (1989), *The Manpower Services Commission in Scotland*, Edinburgh University Press, Edinburgh.

Brown, A. and King, D. (1988), 'Economic Change and Labour Market Policy: Corporatist and Dualist Tendencies in Britain and Sweden', *West European Politics*, vol. 11, no. 3.

Brown, A., Breitenbach, E. and Myers, F. (1994), *Equality Issues in Scotland: A Research Review,* Research Discussion Series No.7, Equal Opportunities Commission, Manchester.

Brown, W. (1981), *The Changing Contours of British Industrial Relations*, Basil Blackwell, Oxford.

Browning, P. (1989), *The Treasury and Economic Policy 1964-1985*, Longman, London.

Brunt, R. (1987), 'Thatcher Uses Her Woman's Touch', *Marxism Today*, June.

Bukharin, N. (1972), *Imperialism and World Economy*, Merlin, London.

Bulpitt, J. (1986), 'The Discipline of the New Democracy: Mrs Thatcher's Domestic Statecraft', *Political Studies*, vol. 34, no. 1.

Burgess, S. and Edwards, G. (1988), 'The Six Plus One', *International Affairs*, no. 64.

Burnham, P. (1990), *The Political Economy of Postwar Reconstruction*, Macmillan, London.

Burnham, P. (1991), 'Neo-Gramscian Hegemony and the International Order', *Capital and Class*, no. 45.

Burnham, P. (1993), 'Marxism, Neorealism and International Relations', *Common Sense*, no. 14.

Burnham, P. (1993a), 'Operation Robot and the Form of Britain's Integration into the World Economy in the 1950s', paper presented to the British International Studies Association, University of Warwick.

Burnham, P. (1994), 'Open Marxism and Vulgar International Political Economy', *Review of International Political Economy*, vol. 1, no. 2.

Burrows, L. and Walentowicz, L. (1992), *Homes Cost Less than Homelessness*, Shelter, London.

Busch, A. (1994), 'The Crisis in the EMS', *Government and Opposition*, vol. 29, no. 1.

Busch, A. (1994a), 'Central Bank Independence - an Option for Britain?', in Kastendiek and Stinshoff (eds.) 1994.

Butler, D. and Butler, G. (1986), *British Political Facts 1900-1985*, Macmillan, London.

Buzan, B. (1991), *People, States and Fear*, Harvester, London.

Cairncross, A. (1985), *Years of Recovery*, Methuen, London.

Callinicos, A. (1992), 'Capitalism and the State System: A Reply to Nigel Harris', *International Socialism*, no. 54.

Campbell, B. (1991), 'After Thatcher: A Class of Her Own', *Marxism Today*, January.

Camps, M. (1964), *Britain and the European Community, 1955-63*, Oxford University Press, Oxford.

Cerny, P. (1990), *The Changing Architecture of Politics*, Sage, London.

Cerny, P. (1993), 'The Political Economy of International Finance', in Cerny (ed.) 1993.

Cerny, P. (ed.) (1993), *Finance and World Politics*, Edward Elgar, Aldershot.

Clarke, R. (1982), *Anglo-American Economic Collaboration in War and Peace 1942-49*, Oxford University Press, Oxford.

Clarke, S. (1978) 'Capital, Fractions of Capital and the State', *Capital and Class*, no. 5.

Clarke, S. (1982), *Marx, Marginalism and Modern Sociology*,

Macmillan, London.

Clarke, S. (1988), *Keynesianism, Monetarism and the Crisis of the State*, Edward Elgar, Aldershot.

Clarke, S. (1990), 'Crisis of Socialism or Crisis of the State?', *Capital and Class*, no. 42.

Clarke, S. (1991), 'Introduction' to Clarke (ed.), 1991.

Clarke, S. (ed.) (1991), *The State Debate*, Macmillan, London.

Clarke, S. (1991a), 'Overaccumulation, Class Struggle and Regulation', in Bonefeld/Holloway (eds.) 1991.

Clarke, S. (1992), 'The Global Accumulation of Capital and the Periodisation of the Capitalist State Form', in Bonefeld et al. (eds.) 1992.

Cleaver, H. (1989), 'Close the IMF, Abolish Debt and End Development: A Class Analysis of the International Debt Crisis', *Capital and Class*, no. 39.

Cleaver, H. (1995), 'The Subversion of Money-as-Command in the Current Crisis', in Bonefeld/Holloway (eds.) 1995.

Clegg, H, Fox, A. and Thompson, A. (1964), *A History of British Trade Unions since 1889: Vol 1, 1889-1910*, Clarendon, Oxford.

Cliff, T. and Gluckstein, D. (1988), *The Labour Party: a Marxist History*, Bookmarks, London.

Coakley, J. (1984), 'The Internationalisation of Bank Capital', *Capital and Class*, no. 23.

Coakley, J. (1988), 'International Dimension of the Stock Market Crash', *Capital and Class*, no. 34.

Coakley, J. and Harris L. (1983), *The City of Capital*, Blackwell, Oxford.

Coakley, J. and Harris L. (1992), 'Financial Globalisation and Deregulation', in Michie (ed.) 1992.

Coates, D. (1975), *The Labour Party and the Struggle for Socialism*, Cambridge University Press, Cambridge.

Coates, D. (1980), *Labour in Power*, Longman, London.

Coates, D. (1988), 'Gaitskell takes on Thatcher', *Interlink*, no. 10.

Coates, D. (1989), *The Crisis of Labour*, Philip Allan, London.

Coates, D. (1994), *The Question of UK Decline*, Harvester Wheatsheaf, Hemel Hempstead.

Coates, K. and Topham, T. (1986), *Trade Unions and Politics*, Basil Blackwell, Oxford.

Cole, K., Cameron, J. and Edwards, C. (1991), *Why Economists Disagree*, Longman, London.

Commission on Social Justice/Institute for Public Policy

Research (1994), *Social Justice: Strategies for National Renewal*, The Report of the Commission on Social Justice, Vintage, London.

Coopey, R., Fielding, S. and Tiratsoo, N. (eds.) (1993), *The Wilson Governments, 1964-1970*, Pinter, London.

Cope, S. and Atkinson R. (1994), 'The Structures of Governance in Britain', in Savage et al. (eds.) 1994.

Corry, D. (1994), 'Living with Capitalism: The Macro-economic Policy Alternatives', *Renewal*, vol. 2, no. 1.

Cox, G. (1994), *After the Safety Net: A Study of Pay Rates in Wages Council Sectors Post Abolition*, The Low Pay Network and The Campaign Against Poverty, Manchester.

Crafts, N. (1994), 'Industry', in Kavanagh/Seldon (eds.) 1994.

Crewe, I. (1990), 'The Policy Agenda: A New Thatcherite Consensus?', *Contemporary Record*, vol. 3, no. 3.

Cronin, J. (1991), *The Politics of State Expansion*, Routledge, London.

Crozier, M. et al. (1975), *The Crisis of Democracy*, New York University Press, New York.

CSE, (1980), *The Alternative Economic Strategy*, CSE Books, London.

CSO, (1994), *Economic Trends*, HMSO, London.

CSO, (1995), *Social Trends 25*, HMSO, London.

Davidson R. and White, P. (eds.) (1988), *Information and Government*, Edinburgh University Press, Edinburgh.

Davies, H. J. (1988), 'Local Government Under Siege', *Public Administration*, vol. 66, no. 1.

de Brunhoff, S. (1978), *The State, Capital and Economic Policy*, Pluto, London.

de Ste. Croix, G.E.M. (1983), *The Class Struggle in the Ancient Greek World*, Duckworth, London.

Deakin, S. (1992), 'Labour Law and Industrial Relations', in Michie (ed.) 1992.

Dennis, N. (1993), *Rising Crime and the Dismembered Family: How Conformist Intellectuals Have Campaigned Against Common Sense*, The Institute of Economic Affairs, London.

Dennis, N. and Erdos, G. (1993), *Families Without Fatherhood*, Institute of Economic Affairs, London.

Department of Employment (1985), *Employment - The Challenge for the Nation*, Cm.9474, HMSO, London.

Department of Employment (1991), *Education and Training for the 21st Century*, Cm.1536, HMSO, London.

Department of Employment (1991a), *Access and Opportunity: A*

Strategy for Education and Training, Cm.1530, HMSO, London.

Department of Employment (1992), *People Jobs and Opportunity*, Cm.1810, HMSO, London.

Department of Health (1989), *Working for Patients*, HMSO, London.

Department of Health (1991), *The Health of the Nation*, HMSO, London.

Department of the Environment (1986), *Paying for Local Government*, Cm.9714, HMSO, London.

Department of Trade and Industry (1994), *Competitiveness of UK Manufacturing Industry*, HMSO, London.

Dorey, P. (1991), 'Politics and the Trade Unions', *Politics Review*, vol. 1, no. 1.

Dow, J. (1964), *The Management of the British Economy*, Cambridge University Press, Cambridge.

Duncan, S. and Goodwin, M. (1988), *The Local State and Uneven Development*, Macmillan, London.

Dunleavy, P., Gamble, A., Holliday, I. and Peele, G. (eds.) (1993), *Developments in British Politics 4*, Macmillan, London.

Dunn, D. (1990), *Poll Tax: The Fiscal Fake*, Chatto and Windus, London.

Dunn, M. and Smith, S. (1994), 'Economic Policy under the Conservatives', in Savage et al. (eds.) 1994.

Eatwell, J. (1992), 'The Development of Labour Policy, 1979-92', in Michie (ed.) 1992.

Eichengreen, B. (1990), *Elusive Stability*, Cambridge University Press, Cambridge.

Elbaum, B. and Lazonick, W. (eds.) (1986), *The Decline of the British Economy*, Clarendon Press, Oxford.

Elger, T. (1994), 'Thatcherism and the Contemporary Transformation of Class Relations in Britain', unpublished paper, University of Warwick.

Elger, T. (1994a), 'Shop Stewards and Shopfloor Trade Unionism in Britain', unpublished paper, University of Warwick.

Evans, J. et al. (eds.) (1986), *Feminism and Political Theory*, Sage, London.

Evans, S., Ewing, K. and Nolan, P. (1992), 'Industrial Relations and the British Economy in the 1990s: Mrs Thatcher's Legacy', *Journal of Management Studies*, vol. 29, no. 5.

Evans, T. (1988), 'Dollar is Likely to Rise, Fall or Stay Steady',

Capital and Class, no. 34.
Fairbrother, P. (1994), *Politics and the State as Employer*, Mansell, London.
Fairley, J. (1995), 'The Changing Politics of Local Government in Scotland', *Scottish Affairs*, no. 10.
Farnham, D. and Lupton, C. (1994), 'Employment Relations and Training Policy', in Savage et al. (eds.) 1994.
Feinstein, C. (1972), *National Income, Expenditure and Output of the UK 1855-1965*, Cambridge University Press, Cambridge.
Fine, B. and Poletti, C. (1992), 'Industrial Prospects in the Light of Privatisation', in Michie (ed.) 1992.
Fine, B. and Harris, L. (1985), *The Peculiarities of the British Economy*, Lawrence and Wishart, London.
Finegold, D. and Soskice, D. (1988), 'The Failure of Training in Britain: Analysis and Prescription', *Oxford Review of Economic Policy*, vol. 4, no. 3.
Finn, D. (1987), *Training Without Jobs: New Deals and Broken Promises*, Macmillan, London.
Fischer, S. (ed.) (1988), *National Bureau of Economic Research Macroeconomics Annual 1988*, MIT, Cambridge.
Ford, J. (1988), *The Indebted Society: Credit and Default in the 1980s*, Routledge, London.
Ford, J. (1991), *Consuming Credit*, Child Poverty Action Group, London.
Friedman, B.M. (1989), *The Day of Reckoning*, Vintage, New York.
Gamble, A. (1984), 'Stabilization Policy and Adversary Politics', in Gamble/Walkland, 1984.
Gamble, A. (1986), *Britain in Decline*, 2nd edition, Macmillan, London.
Gamble, A. (1991), 'After Thatcher: Following the Leader', *Marxism Today*, January.
Gamble, A. (1994), *The Free Economy and the Strong State*, 2nd edition, Macmillan, London.
Gamble, A. (1994a), 'Conservatism: the Golden Age that Never Was', *Renewal*, vol. 2, no. 1.
Gamble, A. and Walkland, S. (1984), 'Theories of Adversary Politics', in Gamble/Walkland, 1984.
Gamble, A. and Walkland, S. (1984), *The British Party System and Economic Policy 1945-83: Studies in Adversary Politics*, Oxford University Press, Oxford.
Gamble, A. and Walton, R. (1976), *Capitalism and Crisis:*

Inflation and the State, Macmillan, London.

Garner, R. (1990), 'Labour's Policy Review: A Case of Historical Continuity?', *Politics*, vol. 10, no. 1.

Garrett, G. and Lange, P. (1991), 'Political Responses to Interdependence', *International Organisation*, vol. 45, no. 4.

George, S. (1988), *A Fate Worse than Debt*, Penguin, Harmondsworth.

George, S. (1992), *The Debt Boomerang*, Pluto, London.

George, S. (1991), *Britain and European Integration since 1945*, Basil Blackwell, Oxford.

German, L. (1993), 'Before the Flood', *International Socialism*, no. 61.

Glennerster, H. (1994), 'Health and Social Policy', in Kavanagh/Seldon (eds.) 1994.

Gilbert N., Burrows, R. and Pollert, A. (eds.) (1992), *Fordism and Flexibility*, Macmillan, London.

Glyn, A. (1989), 'The Macro-Anatomy of the Thatcher Years', in Green (ed.) 1989.

Glyn, A. (1992), 'The "Productivity Miracle", Profits and Investment', in Michie (ed.) 1992.

Glyn, A. and Sutcliffe, B. (1972), *British Capitalism, Workers and the Profit Squeeze*, Penguin, Harmondsworth.

Goldthorpe, J. (1978), 'The Current Inflation: Towards a Sociological Account' in Hirsch/Goldthorpe (eds.) 1978.

Goldthorpe, J. (1984), 'The End of Convergence: Corporatist and Dualist Tendencies in Modern Western Societies', in ibid. (ed.), *Order and Conflict in Contemporary Capitalism*, Oxford Univesity Press, Oxford.

Goodman, J. and Whittingham, T. (1969), *Shop Stewards in British Industry*, McGraw-Hill, London.

Gough, I. (1975), *The Political Economy of the Welfare State*, 1st edition, Macmillan, London.

Grahl, J. (1990), 'After ERM: Hard Times', *Marxism Today*, November.

Grant, W. (1993), *The Politics of Economic Policy*, Harvester Wheatsheaf, London.

Green, F. (ed.) (1989), *The Restructuring of British Industry*, Harvester Wheatsheaf, London.

Guttmann, R. (1989), 'Der Strukturwandel des amerkanischen Finanzkapitals', *Prokla*, no. 74.

Habermas, J. (1976), *Legitimation Crisis* , Heineman, London.

Hall, P. (1986), *Governing the Economy*, Blackwell, Oxford.

Hall, S. (1988), *The Hard Road to Renewal: Thatcherism and the Crisis of the Left*, Verso, London.

Hall, S. (1993), 'Thatcherism Today', *New Statesman*, 26.11.93.

Harman, C. (1993), 'Where is Capitalism Going?', *International Socialism*, no. 58.

Harris, K. (1988), *Thatcher*, Weidenfeld and Nicolson, London.

Harris, N. (1983), *Of Bread and Guns*, Penguin, Harmondsworth.

Hawkins, K. (1976), *British Industrial Relations 1945-75*, Barrie and Jenkins, London.

Heath, C. (1971), *A Guide to the Industrial Relations Act 1971*, Sweet and Maxwell, London.

Helleiner, E. (1993), 'When Finance was the Servant: International Capital Movements in the Bretton Woods Era', in Cerny (ed.) 1993.

Helleiner, E. (1994), *States and the Re-emergence of Global Finance, From Bretton Woods to the 1990s*, Cornell University Press, Ithaca.

Hill, M. (1994), 'Social Security Policy under the Conservatives', in Savage et al. (eds.) 1994.

Hirsch, F. (1965), *The Pound Sterling: A Polemic*, Gollancz, London.

Hirsch, F. and Goldthorpe, J. (eds.) (1978), *The Political Economy of Inflation*, Martin Robertson, London.

Hirschman, A. (1970), *Exit, Voice and Loyalty*, Harvard University Press, Cambridge, Mass.

Hirst, P. (1989), *After Thatcher*, Collins, London.

HM Treasury (1994), *Chancellor Publishes Minutes of Monetary Meetings*, HM Treasury, London.

Holloway, J. (1995), 'Global Capital and the National State', in Bonefeld/Holloway (eds.) 1995

Holloway, J. (1995a), 'The Abyss Opens: The Rise and Decline of Keynesianism', in Bonefeld/Holloway (eds.) 1995.

Holloway, J. and Picciotto, S. (eds.) (1978), *State and Capital*, Edward Arnold, London.

Holloway, J. and Picciotto S. (1991) 'Capital, Crisis and the State', in Clarke (ed.) 1991.

Holmes, M. (1985), *The First Thatcher Government 1979-83*, Wheatsheaf Books, Brighton.

Holmes, M. (1989), *Thatcherism: Scope and Limits 1983-87*, Macmillan, London.

Howson, S. (1993), *British Monetary Policy 1945-51*, Oxford University Press, Oxford.

Huhne, C. (1990), 'Economics to the Left of the Right', in

Pimlott et al. (eds.) 1990.

Huntington, S. (1975), 'The United States', in Crozie et al. 1975.

Hutton, W. (1993), 'Three Thirds Britain', Will Hutton interviewed by Mike Power, in Wilks (ed.) 1993.

Hutton, W. (1994), 'Bad Times for the Good Life', *Guardian Supplement*, 2nd August.

Hyman, R. (1989), *The Political Economy of Industrial Relations*, Macmillan, London.

Ingham, G. (1984), *Capitalism Divided*, Macmillan, London.

Innes, D. (1981), 'Capitalism and Gold', *Capital and Class*, no. 14.

Jay, P. (1994), 'The Economy 1990-94', in Kavanagh/Seldon (eds.) 1994.

Jessop, B. (1992), 'Towards the Schumpeterian Workfare State', Lancaster Regionalism Group Working Paper, University of Lancaster, Lancaster.

Jessop, B., Bonnett, K., Bromley, S. and Ling, T. (1988), *Thatcherism*, Polity Press and Basil Blackwell, Oxford.

Jones, G. and Kirby, M. (eds.) (1991), *Competition and the State,* Manchester University Press, Manchester.

Jones, R. (1987), *Wages and Employment Policy 1936-1985*, Unwin, London.

Jones T. (1989), 'Is Labour Abandoning its Socialist Roots?', *Contemporary Record*, vol. 3, no. 2.

Kastendiek, H. and Stinshoff, R. (eds.) (1994), *Changing Conceptions of Constitutional Government*, Universitätsverlag Dr. N. Brockmeyer, Bochum

Kastendiek, H., Rohe, K. and Volle, A. (eds.) (1994) *Länderbericht Großbritannien*, Bundeszentrale für politische Bildung, Bonn.

Kavanagh, D. (1990), *Thatcherism and British Politics*, 2nd edition, Oxford University Press, Oxford.

Kavanagh, D. (1994), 'A Major Agenda?', in Kavanagh/Seldon (eds.) 1994.

Kavanagh, D. and Morris, P. (1989), *Consensus Politics from Attlee to Thatcher*, Basil Blackwell, Oxford.

Kavanagh D. and Seldon, A. (eds.) (1989), *The Thatcher Effect: A Decade of Change*, Oxford University Press, Oxford.

Kavanagh D. and Seldon, A. (eds.) (1994), *The Major Effect*, Macmillan, London.

Kay, G. and Mott, J. (1982), *Political Order and the Law of Labour*, Macmillan, London.

Keegan, W. (1984), *Mrs. Thatcher's Economic Experiment*, Penguin, Harmondsworth.
Keegan, W. (1989), *Mr. Lawson's Gamble*, Hodder & Stoughton, London.
Keegan, W. (1993), *The Spectre of Capitalism*, Vintage, London.
Kelly, J. (1990), 'British Trade Unionism 1979-89: Change, Continuity and Contradictions', *Work Employment and Society*, Special Issue, May.
Kemp, P. (1992), 'Housing', in Marsh/Rhodes (eds.) 1992.
Kempson, E., Bryson, A. and Rowlingson, K. (1994), *Hard Times? How Poor Families Make Ends Meet*, Policy Study Institute, London.
Kendall, I. and Moon, G. (1994), 'Health Policy and the Conservatives', in Savage et al. (eds.) 1994.
Keohane, R. and Nye, J. (1977), *Power and Interdependence*, Littel, Brown and Company, Boston.
Keynes, J.M. (1981), *The Collected Writings of J M Keynes*, volume XIX, Macmillan, London.
Kidner, R. (1979), *Trade Union Law*, Stevens and Sons, London.
King, A. (1976), 'The Problem of Overload', in King (ed.) 1976.
King, A. (ed.) (1976), *Why is Britain Becoming Harder to Govern?*, BBC, London.
King, D.(1993), 'Government Beyond Whitehall', in Dunleavy et al. (eds.) 1993.
Krasner, S. (1994), 'IPE: Abiding Discord', *Review of International Political Economy*, vol. 1, no. 1.
Labour Party (1976), *The Labour Conference 1976*, Labour Party, London.
Land, A. et al. (1992), *The Development of the Welfare State*, HMSO, London.
Lawson, N. (1988), 'An Independent Central Bank', Minute to the Prime Minister, 25.11.88, published in Lawson, 1992.
Lawson, N. (1992), *The View From No.11*, Bantam Press, London.
Lehman, H.P. (1993), *Indebted Development*, St. Martin's Press, New York.
Letwin, S.R. (1992), *The Anatomy of Thatcherism*, Fontana, London.
Lewis, J. (1994), 'Community Care', in Kavanagh/Seldon (eds.) 1994.

Lewis, R. (1983), 'Collective Labour Law', in Bain (ed.) 1983.
Lister, R. (1994), 'The Family and Women', in Kavanagh/Seldon (eds.) 1994.
London (1980), London Edinburgh Weekend Return Group, *In and Against the State*, Pluto, London.
Longstreth, F. (1988), 'From Corporatism to Dualism? Thatcherism and the Climacteric of British Trade Unions in the 1980s', *Political Studies*, vol. 36, no. 3.
Lovenduski, J. and Randall, V. (1993), *Contemporary Feminist Politics*, Oxford University Press, Oxford.
Ludlam, S. (1992), 'The Gnomes of Washington: Four Myths of the 1976 IMF Crisis', *Political Studies*, vol. 30, no. 4.
Malabre, A.L. (1988), *Beyond our Means*, Vintage, New York.
Mandel, E. (1970), *Europe versus America?*, New Left Books, London.
Mandel, E. (1975), *Late Capitalism*, New Left Books, London.
Mandel, E. (1987), *Die Krise 1974-1986*, Konkret Literatur Verlag, Hamburg.
Mandel, E. (1988), 'Der Börsenkrach, Dreizehn Fragen', in Mandel/Wolf 1988.
Mandel, E. and Wolf, F. (1988), *Börsenkrach und Wirtschaftskrise*, Internationale Sozialistische Publikationen, Frankfurt.
Marazzi, C. (1995), 'Money in the World Crisis', in Bonefeld/Holloway (eds.) 1995.
Marquand, D. (1993), 'Seeking a Radical Party', David Marquand interviewed by Nina Fishman, in Wilks (ed.) 1993.
Marsh, D. (1991), 'British Industrial Relations Policy Transformed: The Thatcher Legacy', *Journal of Public Policy*, vol. 11, part 3.
Marsh, D. (1992), *The New Politics of British Trade Unionism*, Macmillan, London.
Marsh, D. and Rhodes, R.A.W. (eds.) (1992), *Implementing Thatcherite Policies: Audit of an Era*, Open University Press, Buckingham.
Marx, K. (1975), 'Contribution to the Critique of Hegel's Philosophy of Law', in Marx/Engels 1975, vol. 3.
Marx, K. (1975a), 'Critical Marginal Notes on the Article by a Prussian', in Marx/Engels 1975, vol. 3.
Marx, K. (1975b), 'Economic and Philosophical Manuscripts', in Marx/Engels 1975, vol. 3.
Marx, K. (1975c), 'On the Jewish Question', in Marx/Engels 1975, vol. 3.

Marx, K. (1976), *Capital*, vol. 1, Pelican, London.

Marx, K. (1978), *Capital*, vol. 2, Pelican, London.

Marx, K. (1986), 'The Grundrisse', in Marx/Engels 1975, vol. 28.

Marx, K. and Engels, F. (1975), 'The German Ideology', in Marx/Engels 1975, vol. 5.

Marx, K. and Engels, F. (1975), *Collected Works*, Lawrence and Wishart, London.

Matthews, R. (1968), 'Why Has Britain Had Full Employment Since the War?', *Economic Journal*, no. 78.

Mattick, P. (1980), *Economics, Politics and the Age of Inflation*, Merlin Press, London.

Maynard, G. (1988), *The Economy Under Mrs Thatcher*, Basil Blackwell, Oxford.

McCrone, D. (1991), '"Excessive and Unreasonable": The Politics of the Poll Tax in Scotland', *International Journal of Urban and Regional Research*, vol. 15 (13).

McCrone, D., Paterson, L. and Brown, A. (1993), 'Reforming Local Government in Scotland', *Local Government Studies*, vol. 19, no. 1.

McGlone, F. (1990), 'Away from the Dependency Culture?' in Savage/Robins (eds.) 1990.

McGrew, A. (1992), 'Conceptualising World Politics', in ibid. et al. (eds.), *Global Politics*, Polity, Cambridge.

McKie, D. (ed.) (1993), *The Guardian Political Almanac 1993/4*, Fourth Estate, London.

McKie, D. (1994), *The Guardian Political Almanac 1994/5*, Fourth Estate, London.

McRobbie, A. (1994), 'Folk Devils Fight Back', *New Left Review*, no. 203.

McVicar, M. and Robins, L. (1994), 'Education Policy: Market Forces or Market Failure?', in Savage/Robins (eds.) 1994.

Menger, C. (1963), *Problems of Economics and Sociology*, University of Illinois, Urbana.

Michie, J. (1992), 'Introduction', in Michie. (ed.) 1992.

Michie, J. (ed.) (1992), *The Economic Legacy, 1979-1992*, Academic Press, London.

Michie, J. and F. Wilkinson (1992), 'Inflation Policy and the Restructuring of the Labour Market', in Michie (ed.) 1992.

Miliband, R. et al. (eds.) (1987), *Socialist Register*, Merlin, London.

Millward, N., Stevens, M., Smart, D. and Hawes, W.R. (1992), *Workplace Industrial Relations in Transition*, Dartmouth,

Aldershot.

Milward, A. (1984), *The Reconstruction of Western Europe, 1945-51*, Methuen, London.

Milward, A. (1992), *The European Rescue of the Nation State*, Routledge, London.

Mizen, P. (1994), 'In and Against the Training State', *Capital and Class*, no. 53.

Mizen, P. (1995), *The State, Young People and Youth Training*, Mansell, London.

Monks, J. (1994), 'A Change of Mood is in the Air', in New Statesman and Society (1994), *Guide to Trade Unions an dthe Labour Movement*.

Morgenthau, H. (1978), *Politics Among Nations*, Knopf, New York.

Morris, T. (1994), 'Crime and Penal Policy', in Kavanagh/Seldon (eds.) 1994.

Mullard, M. (1987), *The Politics of Public Expenditure*, Croom Helm, London.

Murray, C. (1994), *Underclass: The Crisis Deepens*, The Institute of Economic Affairs, London.

Murray, P. (1988), *Marx's Theory of Scientific Knowledge*, Humanities Press, London.

Nash, M. and Savage, S. (1994), 'A Criminal Record? Law, Order and Conservative Policy', in Savage et al. (eds.) 1994.

Negri, A. (1988), 'Keynes and the Capitalist Theory of the State Post-1929', in ibid. (1988), *Revolution Retrieved*, Red Notes, London.

Nevin, E. (1990), *The Economics of Europe*, Macmillan, London.

NIESR (1990), National Institute of Economic and Social Research, *Economic Review*, NIESR, London.

Nolan, P. (1989), 'The Productivity Miracle', in Green (ed.) 1989.

O'Connor, J. (1973), *The Fiscal Crisis of the State*, St. Martin's Press, New York.

OECD (1994), *Economic Outlook*, OECD, Paris.

Offe, C. (1984), *Contradictions of the Welfare State*, Keane (ed.), Hutchingson, London.

Olle, W. and Schöller, W. (1982), 'Direct Investment and the Monopoly Thesis of Imperialism', *Capital and Class*, no. 16.

Ollman, B. (1993), *Dialectical Investigations*, Routledge, London.

Overbeek, H. (1990), *Global Capitalism and National Decline*,

Unwin, London.

Painter, R.W. and Puttick, K. (1993), *Employment Rights*, Pluto, London.

Panitch, L. (1976), *Social Democracy and Industrial Militancy*, Cambridge University Press, Cambridge.

Panitch, L. (1986), *Working Class Politics in Crisis*, Verso, London.

Peck, J. (1991), 'Letting the Market Decide (with Public Money): Training and Enterprise Councils and the Future of the Labour Market Programmes', *Critical Social Policy*, vol. 11, no. 1.

Perlman, F. (1973), 'Introduction', in Rubin 1973.

Pierson, C. (1993), 'Social Policy', in Dunleavy et al. (eds.) 1993.

Picciotto, S. (1984), 'The Battle at Talbot-Poissy', *Capital and Class*, no. 23.

Picciotto, S. (1991), 'The Internationalisation of Capital and the International State System', in Clarke (ed.) 1991.

Picciotto, S. (1991a), 'The Internationalisation of the State', *Capital and Class*, no. 43.

Picciotto, S. (1992), *International Business Taxation: A Study in the Internationalization of Business Regulation*, Weidenfeld & Nicolson, London.

Pilbeam, K. (1992), *International Finance*, Macmillan, London.

Pimlott, B., Wright, A. and Flower. T. (eds.) (1990), *The Alternative, Politics for a Change*, W H Allen, London.

Plant, R. (1989), 'Is Labour Abandoning Its Socialist Roots?', *Contemporary Record*, vol. 3, no. 2.

Pollard, S. (1994), 'Struktur- und Entwicklungsprobleme der britischen Wirtschaft', in Kastendiek et al. (eds.) 1994

Pollert, A. et al. (1991), *Farewell to Flexibility*, Basil Blackwell, Oxford.

Procter, S. (1993), 'Floating Convertibility: the Emergence of the Robot Plan, 1951-2', *Contemporary Record*, vol. 1, no. 7.

Radice, H. (1984), 'The National Economy: A Keynesian Myth?', *Capital and Class*, no. 22.

Radice, H. (ed.) (1975), *International Firms and Modern Imperialism*, Penguin, Harmondsworth.

Rawls, J. (1971), *A Theory of Justice*, Oxford University Press, Oxford.

Ray, G. (1987), 'Labour costs in manufacturing', *N.I.E.R.*, May.

Riddell, P. (1985), *The Thatcher Government*, Basil Blackwell, Oxford.

216

Riddell, P. (1989), *The Thatcher Decade*, Basil Blackwell, Oxford.

RIPE Editorial Board (1994), 'Forum for heterodox IPE', *Review of International Political Economy*, vol. 1, no. 1.

Robinson, A. (1986), 'The Economic Problems of the Transition', *Cambridge Journal of Economics*, vol. 10.

Rose, R. (1984), *Do Parties Make a Difference?*, 2nd edition, Macmillan, London.

Rose, R. and Davidson, P.L. (1994), *Inheritance in Public Policy*, Yale Univesity Press, London.

Rosewarne, S. (1993), 'The Transnationalisation of the State', paper presented to the CSE Annual Meeting.

Rowthorn, B. (1975), 'Imperialism in the 1970's - Unity or Rivalry', in Radice (ed.) 1975.

Rowthorn, B. (1992), 'Government Spending and Taxation in the Thatcher Era', in Michie (ed.) 1992.

Rubin, I. (1973), *Essays on Marx's Theory of Value*, Black Rose, Montreal.

Rukstad, M. (1989), *Macroeconomic Decision Making in the World Economy*, Dryen, London.

Sampson, A. (1983), *The Money Lenders*, Hodder and Stoughton, London.

Sandholtz, W. (1993), 'Choosing Union: Monetary Politics and Maastricht', *International Organization*, vol. 47, no. 1.

Savage, S. and Robins, L. (eds.) (1990), *Public Policy under Thatcher*, Macmillan, London.

Savage, S., Atkinson, R. and Robins, L. (eds.) (1994), *Public Policy in Britain*, Macmillan, London.

Sawyer, T. (1988), 'In Defence of the Policy Review', *New Socialist*, vol. 57, October/November.

Sbragia, A.M. (ed.) (1992), *Euro-Politics, Institutions and Policymaking in the 'New European Community'*, Brookings, Washington D.C.

Scott, P. (1994), 'Education Policy', in Kavanagh/Seldon (eds.) 1994.

Scottish Local Government Information Unit (1994), *Local Government etc. (Scotland)Act 1994 - A Guide*, SLGIU, Glasgow.

Seldon, A. (1994), 'The Conservative Party', in Kavanagh/Seldon (eds.) 1994.

Shaw, E. (1990), 'Labour's Re-think in Historical Perspective', *Contemporary Record*, vol. 3, no. 4.

Shaw, E. (1994), *The Labour Party Since 1979*, Routledge,

London.

Sinclair, P. (1994), 'Financial Sector', in Kavanagh/Seldon (eds.) 1994.

Smith, D. (1993), *From Boom to Bust*, Penguin, Harmondsworth.

Smith, P. and Morton, G. (1993), 'Union Exclusion and the Decollectivization of Industrial Relations in Contemporary Britain', *British Journal of Industrial Relations*, vol. 31, no. 1.

Smith, P. and Morton, G. (1994), 'Union Exclusion - Next Steps', *Industrial Relations Journal*, vol. 25, no. 1.

Soskice, D. (1984), 'Industrial Relations and the British Economy 1979-1983', *Industrial Relations*, University of California, vol. 23, no. 3.

Statler, J. (1979), 'British Foreign Policy to 1985', *International Affairs*, no. 55.

Stevens, J. (1991), 'The Politics of British Participation in European Monetary Union', *Quarterly Review*, National Westminster Bank, May.

Stewart, M. (1993), *Keynes in the 1990s, A Return to Economic Sanity*, Penguin, Harmondsworth.

Stoker, G. (1990), 'Government Beyond Whitehall', in Dunleavy et al. (eds.) 1990.

Stoker, G. (1991), *The Politics of Local Government*, 2nd edition, Macmillan, London.

Strange, S. (1971), *Sterling and British Policy*, Oxford University Press, Oxford.

Strange, S. (1986), *Casino Capitalism*, Basil Blackwell, Oxford.

Strange, S. (1994), *States and Markets*, 2nd edition, Pinter, London.

Taylor, R. (1994), 'Employment and Industrial Relations Policy', in Kavanagh/Seldon (eds.) 1994.

Ten Tuscher, T. (1986), 'Patriarchy, Capitalism and the New Right', in Evans et al. (eds.) 1986.

Tew, B. (1982), *The Evolution of the International Monetary System, 1945 -1981*, 2nd edition, Hutchinson, London.

Thirlwall, A.P. (1988), *Balance of Payments Theory and the U.K. Experience*, 2nd edition, Macmillan, London.

Thompson, G. (1986), *The Conservatives' Economic Policy*, Croom Helm, London.

Tiratsoo, N. (ed.) (1991), *The Attlee Years*, Pinter, London.

Tiratsoo, N. and Tomlinson, J. (1993), *Industrial Efficiency and State Intervention*, Routledge, London.

Tolliday, S. and Zeitlin, J. (1986), 'Shopfloor Bargaining,

Contract Unionism and Job Control', in ibid. (eds.), *The Automobile Industry and its Workers*, Polity, Cambridge.

Tomlinson, J. (1981), 'Why there was never a Keynesian Revolution', *Economy and Society*, vol. 1, no. 10.

Tomlinson, J. (1990), *Public Policy and the Economy since 1900*, Clarendon Press, Oxford.

Tomlinson, J, (1991), 'The Labour Government and the Trade Unions, 1945-51', in Tiratsoo, (ed.) 1991.

Tomlinson, J. (1991a), 'A Missed Opportunity?', in Jones/Kirby (eds.) 1991.

Tsoukalis, L. (1977), *The Politics and Economics of European Monetary Integration*, Unwin, London.

United Nations (1994), *Monthly Bulletin of Statistics*, UN, Geneva.

URPE (1978), The Union for Radical Political Economics, *U.S. Capitalism in Crisis*, URPE, New York.

van Ark, B. (1993), *International Comparisons of Output and Productivity*, University of Groningen, Groningen.

von Braunmühl, C. (1976), 'Die nationalstaatliche Organisiertheit der bürgerlichen Gesellschaft', *Gesellschaft*, vol. 8/9, Suhrkamp, Frankfurt.

von Braunmühl, C. (1978), 'On the Analysis of the Bourgeois Nation State Within the World Market Context', in Holloway/Picciotto (eds.) 1978.

Wachtel, H. (1990), *The Money Mandarins*, Pluto, London.

Walker, R. (1988), 'The Dynamics of Value, Price and Profit', *Capital and Class*, no. 35.

Walter, A. (1993), *World Power and World Money*, Harvester Wheatsheaf, London.

Waltz, K. (1979), *Theory of International Politics*, Addison Wesley, New York.

Weber, M. (1949), *The Methodology of the Social Sciences*, Free Press, New York.

Weber, M. (1968), *Economy and Society*, Bedminster, New York.

Webster, W. (1990), *Not a Man to Match Her*, The Women's Press, London.

Wickham-Jones, M. and Shell, D. (1991), 'What Went Wrong? The Fall of Mrs Thatcher', *Contemporary Record*, vol. 5, no. 2.

Wilber, K.C. and Jameson K.P. (1990), *Beyond Reaganomics, A Further Inquiry into the Poverty of Economics*, University of Notre Dame Press, Notre Dame, Indiana.

Wilding, P. (1992), 'The British Welfare State: Thatcherism's Enduring Legacy', *Policy and Politics,* vol. 20, no. 3.

Wilks, S. (1993), 'Economic Policy', in Dunleavy et al. (eds.) 1993.

Wilks, S. (ed.) (1993), *Talking about Tomorrow: A New Radical Politics*, Pluto, London.

Wilson, E. (1987), 'Thatcherism and Women: After Seven Years', in Miliband et al. (eds.) 1987.

Wilton, I. (1990), 'Labour Policy Review: Is It a Break With the Past?', *Contemporary Record*, vol. 4, no. 1.

Wolf, W. (1988), 'Casino-Kapitalismus oder die Dialektik von Boom, Crash, und Krise', in Mandel/Wolf 1988.

Woolley, J. (1992), 'Policy Credibility and European Monetary Institutions', in Sbragia (ed.) 1992.

Young, H. (1989), *One of Us*, Macmillan, London.

Young, K. (1994), 'Local Government', in Kavanagh/Seldon (eds.) 1994.

Index

balance of trade 41, 55, 74,
80-81, 90, 189
Baldwin, Stanley 103
Banham Commission 160-61
Bank for International
Settlements 67
Bank of England 82, 83, 86,
88, 89, 92, 105, 110,
179, 182, 184, 185
Bank of France 96
banks
capital adequacy ratios 64
central 12, 43, 45, 46, 53,
66, 70, 79, 109
*see also under names of
individual central banks*,
e.g. Bank of England
charges by 70
global debt crisis and 54
investment banks 189
lending by 60, 67-8, 107,
174
losses 42, 53, 60, 62, 64,
65, 68, 70, 84, 96
subsidies to offset 56-7,
67
Barber, Anthony 173, 192
Barber, Lionel 97
Basle Capital Adequacy
Accord 64
Belgium 94, 97, 102, 104
Benefits Agency 147
Benn, C. 127, 131
Big Bang (1986) 63, 188
Birch, Nigel 168-9
Bird, D. 119
Blackburn, R. 185
Black Wednesday 109
Blair, Tony 153, 196
Block, F. 103
Block Grant system 155-6
Board of Trade 172, 183
Bond, P. 67

Bonefeld, W. 7, 11, 14, 20,
31, 176
Bottomley, Virginia 140
Bradbury, John 103
Breitenbach, E. 128, 144
Bretton Woods Agreement 4,
19, 34, 38-42, 45, 46-7,
49, 51, 188-9, 192-3
Bridlington rules 121
*Britain's economic
renaissance* (Walters) 80
British Coal 90-91, 93, 134
see also coal industry
British Empire 187
Brittan, S. 50, 67, 69, 85,
168, 193
Brown, A. 115, 116, 119,
121, 124, 128, 131, 144
Brown, W. 176-7
Browning, P. 184
Brunt, R. 14
building societies 107
Bulpitt, J. 14, 15
Bundesbank 86, 88, 89, 96,
108
Burgess, S. 182
Burnham, P. 20, 28, 31, 181
Burrows, L. 144
Busch, A. 82, 108
Butler, D. 171
Butler, G. 171

Cairncross, A. 178
Callaghan, James 36-7, 49,
110, 174, 185, 194, 198
Campbell, B. 14
Camps, M. 183
capital
controls 19, 97
utilisation 192
see also financial capital;
investment
capital adequacy ratios 64

222

capitalist accumulation
  and class conflict 28-9, 30
  overaccumulation 29-30
capitalist state form,
  development of 23-6
*Caring for People,
  Community Care in the
  Next Decade and Beyond*
  (1989) 142
Carter, James Earl (Jimmy)
  53
CBI 82, 94, 100, 110, 122
central banks 12, 43, 45, 46,
  53, 66, 70, 79, 109
  *see also under names of
  individual central banks*,
  e.g. Bank of England
Cerny, P. 19, 32
check-off system 121
child benefit 146, 150-51
'childcare disregard' scheme
  126
Child Poverty Action Group
  (CPAG) 150
Child Support Act (1991)
  150, 151
Child Support Agency 147,
  150
Churchill, Winston Leonard
  Spencer 168
Citicorp 56
Citizen's Charter 113, 121,
  138, 160
City Challenge programmes
  159
City of London 63, 182, 184,
  185, 186, 187-9, 190,
  191
City Technology Colleges
  128
Civil Rights (Disabled
  Persons) Bill 148
Clarke, Kenneth 98, 100,
  110, 126, 129
Clarke, R. 179
Clarke, S. 3, 11, 14, 20, 25,
  26, 30, 37, 40, 47, 48,
  58, 61, 78, 123
class relations
  attempts to restructure 3,
  75, 77-9, 80-81, 90-91,
  99, 109-10, 117, 119,
  154, 192
  capitalist accumulation and
  28-9, 30
  financial policy and the
  working class 189-93
  and industrial relations 176
  and rise of the modern
  state 24-6
  social relations as 7-8, 10-
  11, 20-23, 30, 31, 74-5,
  77-9
Cleaver, H. 40, 42, 43, 51,
  54, 63
Cliff, T. 175
Clinton, William Jefferson
  196
closed shop 118, 173
Coakley, J. 60, 63, 186, 188,
  189
coal industry 63, 90-91, 93,
  134, 173, 174
Coates, D. 167, 170, 171,
  172, 174, 175, 176, 177
Coates, K. 37
collective bargaining 57, 61,
  116, 117, 121, 123, 135,
  167, 170-71
  two-tier system of 171-3
commodity markets 54, 182
Commonwealth 180, 181,
  182, 185
'Community Action' scheme
  127
community care scheme 141-

2

community charge *see* poll tax

company debt 40, 54, 59, 60, 62, 67-70, 83, 84, 105-6, 107

Conference of Socialist Economists (CSE) 20, 195

Conservative party
and European elections (1994) 99-100
and European Union 31-2, 94-5, 101-2
and law and order 151, 152
and local elections (1994) 99, 162
and local government reorganisation 160, 162
majority in 1992 election 85
role of ideology in 114

consumer expenditure 58-9, 60, 69, 190, 193, 194

contracting-out
health service 142
local government services 155, 158
prison service 152, 153
trade unions 116, 134

contracts of employment 133-4, 153

Contributions Agency 147

Cook, Robin 88

cooling off periods 173

Coopey, R. 170

Cope, S. 113-14, 138, 159, 160

Corry, D. 196, 197

council houses, sale of 144, 145

Council of Europe 181

Council on Prices,

Productivity and Incomes (CPPI) 169

council tax 127, 157-8

Crafts, N. 90

credit controls, deregulation of *see* financial markets, liberalisation of

credit expansion 34-5, 38, 39-48, 52, 54-5, 56, 60, 66-7, 80, 188, 190, 191-2, 193-4
curbs on 61-2, 76, 82, 115, 169, 188, 192

Crewe, I. 116

crime, reasons for 151
see also law and order

Criminal Justice and Public Order Bill 153

Cripps, Richard Stafford 167

Cronin, J. 167, 168, 170

currency convertibility 178, 182, 184

Davies, H.J. 158

Deakin, S. 106, 190

de Brunhoff, S. 11, 12, 13, 21

debt
company 40, 54, 59, 60, 62, 67-70, 83, 84, 105-6, 107
debtor countries 54, 55-7
debtor crisis (1982) 53-4, 64
ERM and 105-7, 191
monetarism and 52-70
personal 53, 60, 62, 65-6, 67, 69, 83, 84, 105-6, 107, 109-10, 114, 130, 145-6, 148-9
public 35, 43, 44-6, 47, 49, 52, 55, 57, 59, 65, 66, 74, 85, 87, 98, 107-8,

134, 190
subsidies for 56-7, 62
debtor countries 48, 54, 55-7
debtor crisis (1982) 53-4, 64
decolonisation 184
defence policy 195
see also military
deficit financing *see* credit
expansion
de Gaulle, Charles 184
Dehane, Jean-Luc 102
deindustrialisation 90, 177-8
Delors, Jacques 102, 186
see also Delors plan
Delors plan 81
*Democratic Socialist Aims
and Values* (Labour
Party) 195
Denmark 97
Dennis, N. 126
Department of Employment
115-16, 117, 120, 121,
123, 124, 131, 132, 136
Department of Health 139,
140
Department of Social
Security (DSS) 147
Department of the
Environment 156
Department of Trade and
Industry 102, 110, 130
depoliticisation of economic
policy 3-4, 9-10, 12, 21,
23, 26, 32, 35-6, 47, 49-
51, 78-9, 81, 82, 91-2,
103-11, 138-9, 142 192
deregulation of labour
market 47-8, 51, 52, 57,
61-2, 63, 114, 115, 116,
117, 133-4, 197
de Ste. Croix, G.E.M. 20
deutschmark 86, 87-8, 89,
94, 96, 97, 107, 108, 191

devaluation 48, 64-5, 105,
108, 169, 180, 184-5,
191, 192, 194
directors' earnings 124-5
disabled persons 59, 148
dollar 63, 66, 88, 108
balances with Bank of
England 182
devaluation (1985) 64-5
dollar-earning exports 179
and financial crash (1987)
66-7
parity to gold 38-9, 41-2,
45, 78
see also Eurodollar
markets
Donovan Commission 171-2
Dorey, P. 118
Duncan, S. 159
Durden, P. 143, 144, 145

Eatwell, J. 193, 196
Economic and Monetary
Union (EMU) 82, 97
see also Exchange Rate
Mechanism; European
Monetary System
Economic Development
Committees 170
economic growth 36, 37-8,
44, 46, 49, 58, 83, 86,
90, 98, 107, 109, 169,
170, 196, 197
economic theory
and economic policy 15,
76
Eden, (Robert) Anthony 183
Education Act (1993) 129
*Education and Training for
the 21st Century*
(Department of
Employment) (1991)
132

53, 64, 66-8
and incomes policies 176
and industrial recession
(1990s) 68-70
Major government and 75-
6
and market self-regulation
35-6, 47-8, 50-51, 52-3,
57, 61, 78, 120
and trade union exclusion
119, 120
and world boom (1980s)
55-67
monetary policy 11-13, 166,
193
as agent of restructuring
78-9
ERM and 79, 84, 86, 103,
105-6
EU and 13
increased independence of
Bank of England 92
and capitalist reproduction
20-21
of Labour government/
Party 194-5, 196
monetary targets 115
see also credit expansion;
monetarism
money supply *see* credit
expansion
Monks, J. 116, 122
Moon, G. 139, 140, 141
Morgenthau, H. 8, 9
Morris, P. 139
Morris, T. 151, 152, 153
mortgages
interest relief on 84, 98,
143, 145
negative equity trap 85,
107, 145
payment-arrears 107, 145-
6

Morton, G. 118, 120, 133
Mott, J. 25, 26
Muellbauer, John 89
Mullard, M. 54
multinational companies 13,
19, 43-4, 187, 188-90
Murray, C. 151-2
Myers, F. 128, 144

NAFTA *see* North American
Free Trade Area
(NAFTA)
Nash, M. 153-4
National Board for Prices
and Incomes 170, 171-2
national curriculum 128, 129
National Economic
Development Council
(NEDC) 121, 169-70
National Health Service 138,
139-42, 159, 160
National Health Service and
Community Care Act
(1990) 141
National Income
Commission 170
National Institute of
Economic and Social
Research (NIESR) 79
National Insurance
contributions 94, 98, 99,
126-7, 146
nationalisation 167, 196, 197
national vocational
qualifications 128
NEDC *see* National
Economic Development
Council (NEDC)
Netherlands 97, 102
Nevin, E. 180, 185
Next Steps 159
Niemeyer, Otto, 103
Nixon, Richard Milhous 41,

Social Contract 174-5, 197
Social Justice and Economic Efficiency (Labour Party) (1988) 195
Social Security Act (1986) 146
social security benefits 52, 61-2, 116, 125-6, 130, 146-9, 150-51, 154
  see also unemployment benefit; *and under names of individual benefits*, e.g. child benefit
Soskice, D. 188
Spain 97, 101, 103, 136
speculation, international 19, 34, 37, 39, 42-9 *passim*, 55-6, 58, 59, 66, 68, 69, 70, 80, 106, 107, 109, 184, 185, 190-91
state austerity policies 37, 48, 49-50, 51, 52-3, 59, 61, 62, 65, 70, 151
State Earnings Pension Scheme (SERPS) 147
Statler, J. 186
sterling 64, 76, 80, 81, 86, 88-9, 94, 97, 103-9, 166, 168, 174, 175, 178-86, 188, 189-93, 194, 196
  see also Exchange Rate Mechanism (ERM); gold standard
Stevens, J. 104
Stewart, M. 15
Stoker, G. 134, 155, 156, 158, 160, 162
Strange, S. 38, 39, 41, 43, 191
Strategy for Education and Training (Department of Employment) (1991)

132
stress related illnesses 122
strikes *see* industrial disputes
student loans 130
Suez crisis 184
Sutcliffe, B. 39
Sweden 93, 101, 103

Taff Vale 173
targeting of benefits 146-7
tariffs 183
taxation 19, 44-5, 49, 64
  air passenger 98
  allowances 98, 99
  average burden of 98-9, 127
  council tax 127, 157-8
  exemptions 56-7, 62
  on insurance premiums 98
  mortgage interest relief 84, 98, 143, 145
  poll tax 83, 84, 85, 105, 114, 130, 155-8, 162
  reductions in rate of 67, 76, 115, 116, 134
  relief on training 132
  value added tax (VAT) 85, 98, 99, 157-8
  see also fiscal crisis of the state
Taylor, R. 121, 122
teachers 128, 129
Technical and Vocational Education Initiative 128
Ten Tuscher, T. 14
Tew, B. 43
Thatcher, Margaret (Hilda) 1, 48, 53, 76, 78-83 *passim*, 115, 118-20, 122, 124, 125, 128-9, 130, 135, 137, 139, 143, 146, 151, 152, 155, 157, 175-6, 194

incentives for unemployed
to accept work 126-7,
146
inflation and 35, 36-7, 42,
45, 78, 85, 93, 104, 106,
107, 109-10, 124, 137,
169, 173
labour market deficiencies
and 115-16
in manufacturing 98
natural rate of 51, 57
productivity and 58
and trade unions 50, 61,
175, 176
UK figures 74, 83, 85, 87,
90, 92-3, 97-8, 106, 136,
175, 176, 193
white collar 136
youth 131-2
see also unemployment
benefit
unemployment benefit 52,
54, 58, 59, 61, 115, 125,
131, 146
Unemployment Unit index
136
United States
balance of payments 63,
64-5
balance of trade 41, 55
British takeovers in 190
budget deficit 55, 63, 64
corporate debt in 62
and debtor crisis (1982) 53,
54
devaluation of dollar
(1985) 64-5
see also dollar
and Europe 180-81, 183,
185
investment cuts in 58-9
labour costs in 102
personal debt in 62

Savings and Loans sector
62, 69
savings ratio 62
social security cuts in 59
'special relationship' with
Britain 166, 181
and world boom (1980s)
55-6, 63
see also under names of
Presidents of United
States, e.g. Nixon,
Richard Milhous
universities *see* further
education, reforms in
unmarried mothers, benefits
for 126, 149, 150
see also single parents
Urban Development
Corporations (UDCs)
159

value added tax (VAT) 85,
98, 99, 157-8
Vietnam war 41
Volcker, Paul 54
von Braunmühl, C. 8

wage costs *see* labour costs
wage differentials 124-5
wage drift 171
wage norms 170, 175
wage restraint 35, 40-41, 44,
45, 48, 49-50, 51, 77-8,
79, 80, 88, 93-4, 100,
110, 123, 167-8, 169-77,
191, 192
wage rigidities 103-4
Wages Councils 121, 124
Waigel, Theo 95
Walentowicz, L. 144
Walker, R. 67
Walkland, S. 6, 194
Walras, Leon 8

3 gop motels